T0204601

D1072148

The NOW Testament

Cycles A, B, and C

The NOW Testament
Cycles A, B, and C

Joseph M. Wadowicz

Ivy House
Publishing Group

www.ivyhousebooks.com

PUBLISHED BY IVY HOUSE PUBLISHING GROUP
5122 Bur Oak Circle, Raleigh, North Carolina 27612
United States of America
919-782-0281

ISBN 1-57197-456-3
Library of Congress Control Number: 2005932182

Copyright © 2006 Joseph M. Wadowicz

Printed in the United States of America

To My Best Friend:
The Wide, Wide World

Table of Contents
Cycle A

The Now Testament

Table of Contents
Cycle B

Table of Contents
Cycle C

The Now Testament

Foreword

When I was a boy, following a heavy summer shower, I often went puddle gazing. It amazed me that so much of the earth and sky could be captured in such small bodies of water. Later, I felt much the same way about Biblical stories—how, in so few words, they could illustrate so vividly God's loving ways and our own.

Similarly, I'm struck by the reflections of Monsignor Wadowicz. They are short and deceptively simple, yet each represents a small treasury of wisdom about what really matters in life. Some of this wisdom is reserved for church life; more, quite properly, is given for the life of the world.

I have not met Monsignor Wadowicz, but his reflections persuade me that he is a defender of the faithful rather than their prosecuting attorney. He views the church more as a community than as an organization and doctrinal controversies to him matter less than how Biblical truths change life, making us more fruitful in service, more patient in suffering and more loving one of another.

Monsignor Wadowicz is a true patriot. He knows that "my country right or wrong" is a little like saying "my grandmother drunk or sober"—it doesn't advance things very far. As a Christian, he is summoned to carry on a lover's quarrel with his country, a reflection of God's eternal lover's quarrel with the whole world. He recognizes that justice and peace are imperatives of the Gospel with real implications for Christian witness.

Preaching has been defined as "truth through personality." Clearly Monsignor Wadowicz is down-to-earth, unpretentious, humorous and poetic, a man with a critical eye and a forgiving heart. He certainly knows that the main purpose of preaching is to bring the message of the eternal Gospel to bear on our always-complex contemporary life.

I personally am grateful to Monsignor Wadowicz, an octogenarian obviously determined to die young as late as possible. My suggestion to readers of his refelctions is to ponder one each day. They are spiritual tonic for the soul.

—William Sloane Coffin

Acknowledgments

My personal gratitude to Father Joseph Nolan, editor of the *Good News* and theology teacher at Boston College, a source of continual illumination for more than a quarter century. His fingerprints are everywhere in these pages . . . To Father Thomas Bonacci, CP, whose animated biblical insights have been a stimulant these past two decades . . . To the late, beloved Father Bill O'Donnell whose brash, bold parish bulletin, "St. Joseph the Worker Church," (Berkeley, CA), has been a weekly delight for over a dozen years.

Heartfelt thanks to the much esteemed Reverend William Sloane Coffin, whom I've yet to meet, for his exhilarating willingness to compose the gracious Foreword.

Introduction

Church has not been God's best advertising agency. Religions try, but bite-sized thinking enhances division more than unity . . . Maybe if the world's belief systems formed a committee for friendly conversation, the Big Picture might have a chance.

Thanks to the discerning eye of Franciscan Father Emery Tang, who habitually captures the breathtaking beauty that surrounds us. The book jacket photo suggests the divine unconditional love story. It quietly portrays the blend of masculine virility with the tenderness of a mother. An apt picture of the Gospel's Good News message—the Creator's affection for creatures.

The thoughts in these pages are intended to welcome the religious illiterate, the church disenchanted, the spiritual nomad, as well as the atheist, the agnostic, and the confirmed worshipper. Life's straits are pretty much the same for all of the above.

The compact chapters are structured to offer condensed reflections on the Sunday readings used in Christian churches, throughout the three liturgical years—Cycles A, B, and C. Here is an attempted dialogue between timeless Gospel and the 21st century.

Vigor lives neither in the past nor in the future, but in the *NOW!* The vitality of the enduring scriptures is accessible to the timely mind, the today thinker. What the sacred writer had in mind when he wrote can only be guessed about and explored. Bible experts differ widely on this. What a text means to an individual personally has its own importance.

Cycle A

God's Country?

It's a curious experience to walk the ground that Jesus trod, to float on the sea he sailed on and to preach on the shore from which he preached. Palestine is a forbidding, harsh, stony terrain with the climate of California, the look of Utah and the size of Massachusetts. The roadsides periodically burst into beauty with an instant bounty of lush multi-colored bougainvillea.

One easily thinks of Jesus speaking to simple, superstitious people imprisoned by religious tradition and beleaguered by imperial Rome. It's a small wonder they thrilled to his eloquence and common sense. Even his tears over Jerusalem made sense. The historic tragedy of the place is endless: warfare, blood and violence. The forty years it took the Hebrews to get there is a couple-hour bus trip . . . maybe God did not want to go there! That Yahweh deeded that troubled real estate exclusively to the Jews is as reasonable as the Mormons claiming ownership of Utah, or the Moslems of India.

A durable constant in the Jewish tradition, however, is their regard for the Sabbath. To the devout Jew, hardworking and often oppressed, the Sabbath was a precious festival of relaxation, a weekly sanctuary of freedom from toil, a refreshment of spirit with the family. On this day, the poorest, most inconsequential individual could enjoy a simple communion with the Almighty. He was God's; God was his. Sabbath was a heavenly interlude to sanctify the week.

Advent is like that—a wake-up call to enjoy the thought of an affectionate God. Though, it's true, today's Gospel hard-line sounds more like a warning than an invitation, an echo of a Yuletide tune of dubious cheer: "You better watch out, you better not cry. You better be good. I'm telling you why . . ."

Why must God's coming strike dread? The Deity repents for the Deluge, then promises a rainbow in the Noah story. Reconciliation befits the heart of God more than retaliation.

So, deck the halls, decorate, bake, write the cards, and shop for those you care about. The magic time is here again. Have fun playing Santa!

1st Sunday of Advent
(Matthew 24: 37-44)

The Baptist: U-Turns Permitted

John was the hit of his day. He was six months older than his cousin Jesus, but quite different in personality. John sounds abrasive, confrontational—and who could blame him with his diet of locusts and wild honey?* His father, Zachary, was a priest, and as such, the son was entitled to be part of the priestly aristocracy. But John renounced this for the severity of the Judean desert and the rations of Bedouins.

His audience seemed to hunger for his message. They had not seen a prophet for four centuries. John certainly looked like one. He wore the same garb that the prophet Isaiah wore eight centuries before. The people wanted their holy men to be rabble-rousers, more wild than mild. This gave John certain integrity, credibility, so that when he pointed his finger, they paid attention.

His disciples were probably surprised when that finger pointed to a laid-back carpenter of Nazareth. Was this the one for whom the world waited? John said so! His job was to introduce the star and then step off the stage. John made no attempt to steal the show.

In his message, Jesus uses a word that his cousin featured: "repent." This word has the monotonous thump of a hysterical revival harangue. What did it mean to those who heard it at that time? The Hebrew word for "repent" is *teshuba,* from the root *shub,* meaning, "to turn." Thus,

---

* Locusts can be something other than grasshoppers. There are locust trees that yield fragrant, edible blossoms, which are delicious when dipped in batter and fried. There are even honey locust trees.

3

repent means to change course, to move in another direction. Our word "conversion" comes close. It implies a change of attitude and expansion of awareness.

Repenting doesn't mean going to confession; it is, rather, the interior light that makes one want to confess. It goes deeper. "Penitence" is from the Latin *penitus,* meaning "penetration." "I'm sorry" does not go as deep as "I do not like how I hurt you." Then, reconciliation can follow naturally.

Conversion is not a one-time thing. Like the marriage ceremony, it is only for openers. Each day is a renewed commitment. Conversion is a fresh way of thinking about oneself—a willingness to listen to oneself: what one likes, doesn't like, what works and what frustrates. It's a willingness to be gentle with one's feelings, as one attends to a hurting child. And with humor!

Conversion is taking care of oneself and wanting the best for oneself. This is not self-indulgence; it's self-preservation. Its primary obstacle is fear of the dark—the shadow side of oneself that one feels unable to handle. Exploring this is not a search-and-destroy mission. It's get-acquainted-with-yourself quality time—an attitude adjustment. Have a happy hour!

2nd Sunday of Advent
(Matthew 3: 1-12)

4

Rejoice! It's an Order

Americans are big on a good time. Eighty-five percent of salaries over one hundred thousand dollars go to entertainers and professional athletes. Americans are willing to pay dearly for whatever they enjoy.

In keeping with her founder's cheery attitude toward life and disdain for austerity showoffs, the Church suggests a festive mood in the center of her penitential season. Gaudette Sunday, this day, used to be called the Latin imperative, "rejoice."

The command to lighten up can be as efficacious as the dentist's behest to relax as the piercing drill whines in your face. Still, the mind can command feelings to defer to its bidding and the person is the more together for it. Emotions, like children, thrive on freedom as well as boundaries. The Church is wisely worried when religion is overly solemn. The laughing Christ sadly has not displaced the appeal of the lamenting Jesus. We associate gravity with importance. To look serious beats looking foolish.

Maybe that's why insecure people tend to be staid, even cheerless. They keep themselves inside and you outside. They are afraid to go public with their putative, painful inadequacy. Thus spontaneity and naturalness suffers. Stoicism can mask the fear to risk this.

It's possible that the Creator does not enjoy rigid, mirthless types any better than we do. It was a saint who declared, "A sad saint is a sad saint." To such irrefutable logic, the freethinking Voltaire is the assumed author of this bold insight: "I think God is a comedian playing to an audience afraid to laugh."

The Now Testament

Much of the 6 P.M. news is no laughing matter. So what have we to cheer about this rejoice Sunday? In the comic strip "Peanuts," Charlie Brown litanies the doleful list of the world's current woes.

Linus responds: "But the world is in better shape than it was six years ago."

Charlie Brown: "Are you kidding? Look at the head-lines. The world's a mess. How can you say that?"

Linus: "Because I'm in it now."

3rd Sunday of Advent
(Matthew 11: 2-11)

Follow That Dream

"Did you have a good time, dear?" queried mom as her youngster returned home from a nursery school Christmas party celebrating the birthday of Jesus. "Oh, yes!" cried the child. "We had ice cream, cake and clown hats, but Jesus never showed up." He doesn't show up for lots of people at Christmas time in our consumer culture!

The overture before Jesus's first appearance was a major hassle for Joseph. His betrothed teenager was pregnant, but not by her fiancé. What to do? Joseph was not about to take the rap for someone else's mistake.

A kind of heavenly telegram, an angelic message in a dream, resolves Joseph's dilemma. Dreams are desultory things. Freud claims them to be unfulfilled wishes. However weird or confusing, they tell us much about our secret selves. If Freud is correct, then Joseph's dream could mean that he wanted Mary, pregnant or not. He loved her enough to take her as she was and to care tenderly for the "fruit of her womb."

Usually we don't have angels to interact with us. We struggle quite alone with our difficult decisions. If we are lucky to have love in our lives, love is our angel.

Jesus did show up, and the world still hasn't gotten over it. Like the miracle of any birth, "Every child," someone said, "is an announcement from God that God is not finished with us yet." We are not called to understand children, but to care for them.

So Christmas is for kids from 2 to 102. It's reassuring to know that God trusts us enough to be us, and whatever the risk, to hang out with us. It's hard to imagine Jesus worrying about being snubbed at his own birthday party. He is not that insecure. From what the Gospels reveal, he seems to enjoy our enjoyment. So whether raucous, rowdy, or reverent, it's time to celebrate. The incomparable San Franciscan, the late Herb Caen, catches this Yule magic:

The miracle of Christmas is that it survives those who believe in it too loudly. It is the simple and childlike, after all, who keep this message alive . . . Christmas is in many ways annoying, exhausting, uplifting, dizzying, disappointing, exhilarating. But if we didn't have it, we'd have to invent something not half as good.

—from the *San Francisco Chronicle*

4th Sunday of Advent
(Matthew 1: 18-24)

All in the Family

Was the "holy family" ever dysfunctional? When the boy, Jesus, was missing for three days, Mary and Joseph probably argued about it. When, as an adult, he became a celebrity and his unconventional preaching upset the religious leadership, Mark 3: 20 records, "When his family heard about it, they set out to take charge of him because people were saying, 'He is gone mad.'"

Family can be a combat zone, a human mine field, an obstacle course, and a chronic disaster area. Family is where one's toes get stepped on along with one's ego: "Who said you could wear my sweater? Who left the milk carton in the refrigerator empty?" Still, statistics show that married people outlive single people by fifteen years. So, be nice to celibate people—their days are numbered!

Family is the school where growing up begins, where we learn to survive. Some, sadly, do not quite make it. What is good parenting if not good "husbanding" and "wifing?" And this surely takes never-ending negotiation. There is a big difference between a couple playing house and a couple buying one together. The inevitable storms that relating generates are only a better reason to go deeper together, to discuss what divides, and to hold when one wants to run. Pragmatic theologian Erma Bombeck defines marriage as, "The last best chance to grow up."

Whoever said the following said a mouthful: "There is no more ambitious enterprise or more precarious undertaking than raising a family. Because of growing, relationships are constantly shifting. Family is happiness and unbearable torment, sweetly comforting and fiercely infuriating. Yet family is what unites us more than what divides us. We never shake our self-centeredness. Family, at least, starts us on the road to mitigating it. The only way to save the 'I' in me is by reaching for the 'thou' in you . . . and say 'we.'"

The inimitable Andy Rooney of *60 Minutes* put it this way: "Our house is not an investment. Our house is a home. We live there. It's an anchor."

Andy notices the crayon marks on one of the bedrooms:

They've been there since the twins were four when they made them. It's nice to have a reminder now. Brian's marbles are still in the bottom drawer of the dresser. Sure, he's out of college, but what if he comes home and wants to play marbles again? When anyone asks me how much I think our house is worth, I just smile. They couldn't buy what that house means to me for all the money in both local banks.

The Sunday After Christmas
(Matthew 2: 13-15, 19-20)

10

God Goes Public

Maybe the Vatican should move to Jerusalem where three world religions owe their origins. Wouldn't it be edifying to see the major faiths celebrating each other's holy days: Hanukkah, Ramadan and Christmas, for instance? How about weekly dialogues, not so much on theological theories, but the human needs of each community?

This is what Epiphany is all about. God discloses to universal mankind. It is the theophany of Divinity's unity to His Technicolor creation. Epiphany broadcasts that God is not Hebrew, Protestant, Catholic or Moslem and not the private preserve of any religion. Nor is God contaminated for getting too close to creatures. Wherever people are, so is their God.

Epiphany is a churchly word, and it means to reveal, disclose and open up to. This could mean that God does not have to be looked for, He is not lost, but that God finds us. In fact, God never leaves us alone. The aggiornamento church of John XXIII has shown signs of being more comfortable in the world it is pledged to redeem. After all, its founder seems at home with the wayward. How did Jesus handle Levi, the chiseling tax collector, the crook Zacheus, the divorcee at Jacob's Well, the infidel centurion, the denying Peter, Dismas the thief, and the doubting Thomas? He was chastening at times and always courteous. It was the righteous religious that bugged him. It was these that got him killed.

Where does God find us if not in the stuff of our lives: our labor, our loves, our losses and our longings? He seems constantly to be peeking out at us from every human experience, every encounter and in the most unexpected places.

Thomas Merton, in his *Hidden Ground of Love,* puts it this way:

> *If we once began to recognize, humbly but truly, the real value of our own self, we would see that this value was the sign of God in our being, the signature of God upon our being . . . God seeks Himself in us, and the aridity and the sorrow of our heart is the sorrow of God who is not in us, who cannot find Himself in us because we do not dare to believe or trust the incredible truth that He could live in us, and live there out of choice, out of preference. But indeed, we exist solely for this, to be the place He has chosen for His presence, His manifestation in the world, His epiphany.*

Epiphany
(Matthew 2: 1-12)

Christ-ening

Mark Twain once whimsically observed that, "People find the texts in the Bible troublesome that they do not understand. I find troublesome the texts I do understand." Today's Gospel was troublesome to the first century Christians. After all, if baptism was for repentance and the forgiveness of sin, how come the sinless savior was going for it? But over even the objections of John the Baptist himself, Jesus insisted. For Jesus, being approachable pre-empted being above reproach. Identifying with sinners never presented a problem for him.

Maybe the Master wanted to emphasize a fresh aspect to this redeeming rite. According to the Gospel account of this Jordan incident, "After his baptism . . . a voice from Heaven said, 'This is my beloved Son and I am wonderfully pleased with Him.'"

Would not the current Christian baptism signify the same approval for the newly baptized? Namely that God wants us in His family?

Christening is a beautiful word for baptism. To christen is to "Christify." More than making one like himself, to "christen" means to make the Creator "wonderfully pleased"with this new child.

Only two Gospels record the birth of Jesus. All four report his baptism. The Feast of the Baptism of Jesus was celebrated long before his nativity in the early Church. It marked beginning his public proclamation of the Good News—that God is for us—that God is on our side.

The rite of baptism has had a checkered career in Church history. Initially, it was meant for adults who chose it after making a mature decision. Later, in the fourth century, Augustine picked up on Paul's theory that all mankind was separated from God by Adam's sin. The notion of Original Sin took hold and since baptism was seen as a blanket absolution, a kind of Divine presidential pardon, the rite began to shift from adults to infants. By the fifth century, the mood about baptism moved from it being about active conversion to being about passive pardon.

The rise of the charismatic movement since Vatican II has renewed religious curiosity about the baptism of the Spirit. This interior phenomenon implies a non-ritual, direct impact of the Holy Spirit on human life, such as when a new consciousness arises in a person, a sense that all one's petty follies, disappointments, vanities and losses, are part of God's plan for us. This awareness is an insight that our original baptism imprinted the great seal of God in our inmost soul and that the Spirit watches and waits for our waking from a drugged sleep.

The implications of Christening, Christification, can be intimidating were it not for the heartening image of a genial Jesus who understood what mattered in a human life. He probably would approve of this ancient Sumerian proverb, a proverb thousands of years older than he was: "Seek not eternal life, but love the child whose hand you hold and the woman whose embrace you enjoy."

The Baptism of Jesus
(Matthew 3: 13-17)

Silence of the Lamb

Routine can be an anesthetic and deadening. Habitual expressions tend to lose their meaning. At every mass, "Lamb of God, You take away the sin of the world" is invoked at least three times. The effect can be desensitizing. It was John the Baptist who first identified his cousin as the "Lamb of God." What did he have in mind?

As the son of a priest, John was familiar with temple ceremonial. He knew that every morning and evening, a lamb was sacrificed as atonement to God for the sins of the people. Even when starved by siege or war, this custom was faithfully fulfilled. To the Jewish mind, the ritual lamb was expiatory. It was a gesture to appease an offended deity. It was a definite improvement over human sacrifice. Still, it reflected a primitive form of worship.

Did John mean that Jesus was this Jewish sacrificial ritual lamb whose death would allay an annoyed God and thus absolve mankind? If so, this is still primitive thinking. It is hardly worthy for a god to demand innocent blood in place of the guilty.

So, what could "who takes away the sin of the world" mean? (Note the singular sin, not sins.) Could John have meant that the impact of Jesus is to show the world that sin is no obstacle to God? Can redemption mean that we are not saved from our sins but because of them? If this were not so, then our sins would be more powerful than God.

This is not to deny evil. We are up to our neck in it! We do it and it's done to us. So, what is this "taking away?" Might it be translated as "removal, gone, finished or nonexistent?" What better describes unconditional love than non-conditional forgiveness?

Unconditional love loves whether or not the beloved loves back, whether or not the beloved is even aware of the lover. Far fetched? Hardly! Parents take a healthy crack at this kind of loving. When your children rebel, reject your wisdom, or hurtle into heartbreaking decisions, can you still do less than care? It's just the way you are—their parent. To care for flesh and blood is not a choice for parents. The caring chooses them.

Jesus is not the only lamb ever innocently butchered. Human history is flooded with such blood. But it took the Lamb of God to show us that even the butchers rate God's unconditional love: "Father, forgive them . . ." In Romans 8: 38, Paul writes, "For I am convinced that nothing can separate us from His love."

Next time you say "Lamb of God who takes away the sin of the world" . . . you better believe it!

2nd Sunday of Ordinary Time
(John 1: 29-34)

16

Church: Now and Then

In a jocular mood, friends asked a popular priest, "What is the first thing you would do if elected Pope?" His prompt response generated loud laughter, "I would get married, then ordain her." Many a truth in jest! This whimsy capsules two current issues of dissent in today's Catholic Church.

Dissent is nothing new to a church that started with a baker's dozen and now records a membership of millions worldwide. The apostles argued among themselves. Paul took on Peter, the first pope (Galatians 2: 11). But the sense of fraternity was never threatened, any more than differences destroy a functional family. In fact, contrary opinions courteously and respectfully confronted enhance the vitality of a community.

There are scholars who claim that Jesus never intended to found a new church, especially since he lived and died a devout Jew. His apostles, all Hebrew, stayed faithful to temple ceremonials. The first-century Jews who converted to Christianity saw no discrepancy in maintaining fidelity to their Jewish ritual and belief in Christ. The Apostle Paul simply wanted to be the kind of Jew Jesus was. After the destruction of the Temple at Jerusalem by the Romans in A.D. 70, the rabbis in the Council of Jamnia decided to tighten up their ancient religion. They declared that Jewish Christians were no longer welcome at worship. What Jesus began in today's Gospel, two generations later had become the ex-communicated Christian sect. This spilled out in bad blood between orthodox Jews and the new separatists, which is unfortunately reflected in the caustic anti-Semitic tone in some of the Gospels.

As Christian numbers increased, so did governance. Hierarchical structure emerged. The bureaucracy of the Roman Empire was imitated in the Church. "Diocese" is a fourth century word meaning "province of the Roman Empire." In 315 B.C., Emperor Constantine made an illegal creed legal—in fact, made it the state religion. Membership flourished, if not by conviction, at least by political advantage.

The Church now copied the elegance of the royal court. Opulent vestments and majestic ceremonial dramatized her ritual. To counter this ostentation, austere desert hermits attracted attention, admiration and disciples. Monasticism flowered, and so did religious wrangling. The standard dissonance typical of all organized religion, then as today, produced its divisive impact: traditionalist versus progressive, conservative versus liberal, and high church versus low church. Splinter groups spawn. Reformers denounce entrenched authority. Heretics burn.

Jesus might not recognize today what he started any more than our founding fathers would recognize the America they began. Whatever its liturgy, whatever its dogma, whatever its diverse spirituality, church comes down to this: Christ has no one to love the world with but you and me. We are his body. We are the Church.

3rd Sunday of Ordinary Time
(Matthew 4: 12-23)

Be-Attitudes: Crisis Survival

Are the Beatitudes saying how lucky we are to suffer? So why reduce poverty, feed the starving and comfort the grieving? Persecute your best friends if it will bring them blessings! What can this Sermon on the Mount really mean?

Picture Jesus looking over the crowd and thinking to himself, "Look at 'em . . . clobbered by life, toughing it through, making it on scraps . . . Some are born good looking, others, double ugly. Some are naturally bright, others hopelessly dull. Some learn from their mistakes, others keep repeating them.

"How can I tell them that, no matter how bad a hand life deals them, God's favor will bless them for hanging in?"

So out comes this incredible reversal. The crises we shrink from—strain to avoid all our lives, but live through—will have God's promise of happy endings. Maybe Jesus is pointing out that in the mysterious mind of God, we misguided mortals, are looking for happiness in all the wrong places.

Beatitudes are not commandments. They are attitudes on how to face life when bad things happen to us. An emaciated, skin-and-bones holocaust victim still able to walk was asked by an American officer on camp liberation day if she could show him where the prisoners slept. She led him to the place. He stepped in front of her and held the door open for her. She was overwhelmed; "The officer held the door open for me!"

After years of inhuman brutality, this simple gentlemanly courtesy touched her to the quick. She could never again be deliberately unkind. Her suffering, his gesture and her awareness made her a Be-Attitude person.

As the annual Super Bowl hype competes for our attention, we can remind ourselves that none of us are *asked* to play in the precarious super bowl of life, yet we are all in the game. For some of us, it's still the first half; for others, it's the final quarter. But God has a game plan—The Beatitudes—guaranteed to make winners out of losers. God knows the score. He knows how the game ends. There simply are no losers when, after the tears, we are not bitter, but better.

4th Sunday of Ordinary Time
(Matthew 5: 1-12)

Salt-Light: Savor Flavor

The Beatitudes' gospel may elicit the debatable conclusion that suffering is the surest path to felicity. The Master's intent, on the other hand, was probably more to enhearten people with the idea that God can make good happen out of bad. "Redemption" is a word for this. Pain may be an inevitable life predicament, but it's not a priority. Still, over the centuries, the "Suffering Servant" has preempted the genial Jesus who apparently enjoyed parties, wine and people. Sad was seen as holier than glad. Harsh, anti-body asceticism drained out the flavor of wholesome spirituality. Religion became a downer.

The English poet Swinburne (1837–1909) laments in "Hymn to Proserpine:" "Thou has conquered, O pale Galilean, the world has grown gray from thy breath."

The Norwegian dramatist, Henrik Ibsen (1828–1906), has this complaint from Emperor Julian, the Emperor who was anxious to turn back the clock from Constantine's state Christianity, back to the old-time pagan gods: "Have you looked at these Christians closely? Hollow-eyed, flat-breasted all. The sun shines on them, but they do not see it. The earth offers its fullness, but they desire it not. All their desire is to renounce and to suffer, that they may come to die."

Oliver Wendell Holmes (1841–1935) considered entering the ministry, but was turned off by ministers: "They looked and acted so much like undertakers."

Robert Louis Stevenson (1850–1894) made this entry in his diary: "I have been to church today, and am not depressed!"

This is not the Jesus idea of religion. He emphasized joy too often. Stodgy preachers were also a bore to him. "Be salty," he urged. Neutral was too bland for him. "Lighten up! Enlighten!" he pressed: "You are the light of the world." No shrinking violets for him. He wanted followers who make a difference, who change what they touch, like salt and light. Shyness probably did not appeal to him because it was a defensive stance. Playing safe can be a subtly disguised egotism that is unwilling to risk judgment, or an anticipation of rejection. To be vulnerable is easier said than done, but it spells integrity—being on the outside what one is on the inside.

The sanctuary provided protection for pursued criminals in the Middle Ages. The Church can be a hideout for the faint-hearted today. Safe harbor is hardly demeaning, but Jesus expected his Good News promoters to be beyond shelter-seeking. So he labels them "salt" for seasoners and "light" for awakeners. Since he valued vitality and daring, he never poor-babied his chosen. "Fear not," he insisted time and time again. He knew that on the other side of fear the true self waited.

5th Sunday of Ordinary Time
(Matthew 5: 13-16)

Law and Order

For years, two partners enjoyed a thriving butcher business. Then one got religion and enthusiastically hassled the other to join up. The latter declined, reasoning thus: "Look, if I get religion, too, who's gonna weigh the meat?"

In some cultures, cheating is accepted standard practice. It is considered to be clever entrepreneurialism. Caveat emptor is its motto: "Let the buyer beware." This warning is hardly the basis for a trustworthy society, so laws are designed to dissuade cheating hearts.

But while legislation can punish, it cannot correct, even though our swelling prisons are euphemistically now called "houses of correction." Something else is needed. Law is not enough to promote the social order. Jesus had something to say about the problem in this Gospel.

He objected not only to murder, but also to the anger that provoked it. He deplored the willy-nilly divorce laws of his time. In that patriarchal society, males had all the legal privileges. Women had none. A husband could divorce his wife for spoiling the soup or criticizing her in-laws, no questions asked. Jesus also denounced swearing, not the crude epithets of the street, but frivolous oaths like "on my mother's grave," "my hand to God," et cetera, which trivialized the sacred. He caught the intent to trick, to con, that these extravagant gestures implied. "Talk straight," he urged. "Yes or no is enough, if you mean it. If you don't, a stack of Bibles will not be enough."

The radical surgery Jesus recommends, such as plucking out an eye, is typical apocalyptic language of the day, employed to make a point. It is to be taken as literally as when we exasperatingly say to a nuisance, "Do that again and I'll kill you!" The point he emphasizes is the decisive action demanded to rid oneself of whatever defiles one. For Jesus, laws simply do not go far enough. He lived in a religious culture that prided itself on rigid compliance with the revered Law of Moses. The minutest regulations were accorded absurd obeisance. Dressing a wound and setting a fracture was unlawful labor for the Sabbath. In a later age, affixing one's false teeth was ritually illegal. Jesus apparently scandalized the religious leadership by his casual disregard for ceremonial minutia. He saw life, to echo Auntie Mame, as a banquet to be enjoyed, not an ostentatious display of meaningless etiquette. His priority was the human being, not the law. The law was meant to promote and protect basic human needs. Laws that ignored this end he did not take seriously. He valued compassion over compliance. "I have come," he said, "so that you may have life, and that more abundantly." He did not say, "I have come to give you more religion." Churches need to be wary of the rules they impose since heedful consciences can be unnecessarily hurt. Orthodoxy can miss the mark. The pre-Vatican Church made hamburger a mortal sin on Fridays, but not lobster tail. How far such rules are from the common sense that was its founder's specialty! Christ taught that good pre-empted right. Stopping for a red light is the legal thing. Going through it to the hospital emergency room is the good thing. Supporting capital punishment is the legal thing; protesting it is the good thing. Law and order certainly beats anomie, but isn't it ironic that it's the law-and-order people who killed Christ?

6th Sunday of Ordinary Time
(Matthew 5: 17-37)

Temptation and the Right Stuff

The fact that Genesis presents two versions of creation suggests the metaphorical nature of the story. The "P," or "Priestly" version, deals with a royal and characteristically remote deity. There is no Adam and Eve in this one. The "J," or "Yahwist" version, reveals a more anthropomorphic God: companionable, vexable, but involved and rehabilitating. Adam and Eve are featured in this one.

This scripture was put together about six centuries before Christ with the intent of showing the harassed Diaspora Jews of the Babylonian exile a God more provident than the moody, indifferent gods of the ancient Middle East. It borrowed, nonetheless, from primitive Mesopotamian myths about the world's beginnings. These told of mystery trees of perilous power. The Genesis author employs this tree symbol to display the human freedom to choose good or evil.

The perennial problem of evil baffled the ancients as thoroughly as it does us moderns. They largely settled for a dualistic explanation; good gods battled bad gods. Whoever won had his way with us luckless mortals. The Hebrew writer, instead, establishes a single, supreme, beneficent God who trusts mankind enough to form it to the Creator's image and with the risky gift of free will. This trust naturally imposes liability on the trustee as well as the trustor—a more responsible position for both parties than the dualist concept provided. For when the forbidden becomes one's choice, God does not reject the transgressor, but simply allows the consequences of that choice. It is not about punishment, then, but simply about learning and accountability. Jesus brilliantly describes this mature reaction of the caring parent in his parable of the Prodigal Son.

Striking corollaries flow from this creation narrative:

1. The oneness of humanity with its environment. Adamah is the Hebrew word for clay. Eden can be located in the vicinity of present-day Kuwait. Nowhere is it called Paradise.

2. Here, Adam is alone with only God. God had decided that God is not enough. Animals are created. But pets are not enough for Adam.

3. So, a second human is created. Whether the second is an improvement over the first has been a subject of good-natured whimsy, but the equality of both is distinctly endorsed. Eve comes from the side of Adam, implying that her proper position is neither above, below, in front of, nor behind, but beside her man. Her dialogue, however, does appear more intelligent than his does.

4. The text does not identify Satan with the Serpent, which, to the ancient world, represented a god of fertility. The serpent is seen as crafty, in the likeness, perhaps, of seductive modern advertising designed to entice.

5. Eve likes what she sees and quite naturally wants to share what is pleasing to her with her significant other.

6. Eve's impulse to touch, taste and see could be interpreted as a blow for freedom. The choice to experience, to chance consequences, and to find out for

oneself is, admittedly, a crisis necessary for self-growth. The Prodigal's father understood this reality.

7. The text makes no mention of sin, of a fall, of temptation or of the woman as a temptress. God seems more annoyed at Adam's and Eve's defensiveness, their blame game, their egoistic insulation from the one asset singularly important to them—each other. They did not know that being honestly human is okay with God. Original Sin is simply not wanting to be who you are.

The story points out that mankind is not fallen, but unfinished, finite. Mistakes are par for the course. The Gospel symbolically highlights Jesus's own struggle with choices, if his right stuff is to come through. He dramatically communicates to us that goodness lies not in our escape from evil, but in our collision with it.

1st Sunday of Lent
(Genesis 2:3, Matthew 4: 1-11)

Transfiguration: A Religious Experience

"Surrealism" is defined by the dictionary as "literary and artistic movement that attempts to express the workings of the subconscious mind." Gospel authors appear to have mastered this device. In today's selection, two people, dead for ages, chat with Jesus, and God talks from a cloud. This account must have been important to the evangelists since it appears no less than five times in the New Testament. They were intent on stressing the Divine Presence in Jesus, his thorough Jewishness and the inevitable suffering that would dog him. The event described a religious experience for the favored apostles.

Such mystical phenomena are not uncommon. In the '60s, the University of Chicago authorized a scientific sociological study of the "religious experience."* Hundreds were screened and only the emotionally stable, healthy, balanced individuals were selected for testing. Non-churchgoers qualified as well. The results revealed that fully twenty-five percent of the United States' population admitted to authentic mystical experiences. There was a remarkable commonality in the details reported by each of the separately examined subjects. Each one described illumination, a sense of oceanic immensity, a feeling of oneness with the universe, a startling bitter-sweet, agony-ecstasy reaction and the conviction that creation was in good hands. Each of

---

* This study involved 1600 subjects and was sponsored by the Henry Luce Study Grant. Details of the study can be found in *Religious Experience: Psychology of the Abnormal* by Andrew Greeley.

them confessed that their individual problems and questions remained as before, but that it was now okay. They came away changed, transformed. They had connected with an unearthly goodness and found it impossible to talk about—even to their spouses. The event was ineffable and once was enough.

All these people had not the slightest doubt about the existence of God. This brush with divinity does not happen to everyone, but most of us have known good individuals who have impressed us, left us reverent, grateful, and at peace. People have the power to transfigure or to disfigure one another.

Life has a way of transforming us in its unspectacular way. In fact, it is so gradual that we hardly notice the movement from self-absorbed infancy, through testy adolescence, to attentive adulthood. We cannot help but recognize, however, that one factor stands out—no pain, no gain. Thus, the Gospel has Jesus, in the midst of his glittering incandescence, refer to his approaching suffering and death.

The 1999 movie nominated for several Oscars, *Saving Private Ryan,* deals vividly with this mysterious synthesis of misery and glory. Amid the harrowing scenes of the horror of war are sequences of selfless courage and moving nobility. Combat survivors are profoundly changed. The incredible closeness of comrades-in-arms enhances the preciousness of life. Violence can never again be valued as a viable policy. Private Ryan is transformed for life. He can never again be anything but real.

The adult fairy tale, *The Velveteen Rabbit,* by Margery Williams, deserves quoting here. A little boy's toys are chatting with each other and the Velveteen Rabbit is in earnest conversation with a worn, old Skin Horse:

> *"What is real?" asked the Rabbit one day when they were lying side by side near the nursery fend-*

er, before Nana came to tidy the room. *"Does it mean having things that buzz inside you and a stick-out handle?"*

"Real isn't how you are made, " said the Skin Horse. *"It's a thing that happens to you. When a child loves you for a long, long time, not just to play with, but really loves you, then you become real."*

"Does it hurt?" asked the Rabbit. *"Sometimes,"* said the Skin Horse, for he was always truthful. *"When you are real, you don't mind being hurt.*

"Does it happen all at once, like being wound up?" the Rabbit asked, *"or bit by bit?"*

"It doesn't happen all at once," said the Skin Horse. *"You become. It takes a long time. That's why it doesn't often happen to people who break easily, or have sharp edges, or who have to be carefully kept. Generally, by the time you are real, most of your hair has been rubbed off, and your eyes drop out, and you get loose in the joints and very shabby. But these things don't matter at all, because you are real, you can't be ugly, except to people who don't understand . . . But once you are real you can't become unreal again. It lasts for always."*

2nd Sunday of Lent
(Matthew 17: 11-9)

An Unlikely Missionary

This scene is worthy of a movie scenario. The setting: it's hot, it's high noon and Jesus rests beside Jacob's well. The disciples have gone shopping. A lone woman approaches. He ponders, "Odd time to be lugging a heavy water pot, here in the blaze of the noon-day sun. She must be avoiding her neighbors. A fringe person—a reject? Who could use the Good News more?"

Jesus asks her for a drink, and this ignores two rigid orthodox canons: 1) Never address a female stranger in public; and 2) Never have anything to do with a hated heretic, a Samaritan. But Jesus never permitted rules to have priority over people.

This lady had been around. She knew about men, how they operate. "He must be flirting," she suspects and responds with a sarcastic cold-shoulder reply to the effect: "Get lost, creep!" Jews were creeps to Samaritans. Jesus, however, is not put down. Confident people can only be put down by themselves.

The ensuing dialogue is not a little confusing. The subject is water, the Near East's scarcest, and therefore, most precious element. He piques her interest with a mystical reference to living water. She interprets this as flowing water, an attractive convenience, possibly eliminating the tedious daily to-the-well jaunt. Two-thirds of the planet is covered by water, yet only one-half have access to sweet, potable H_2O. Fresh water is Jesus's metaphor for the Spirit of God. Water aptly cleanses, refreshes, yet humbly conforms to the shape of the container that accepts it. It douses fire, rusts iron, wears away stone, yet it cushions a floating child.

When defeated by heat, water escapes into wispy vapor. Water speaks symbolically of the gentleness and might of God, the combination Jesus probably felt that all women deserved from men.

"This man is different," she observed to herself. "Maybe he's not on the make. He's a gentleman." She felt his regard. He recognized her thirst for more than one-night stands or a live-in lover. He saw more in her than she saw in herself. His respect awakened her respect for herself. Five failed marriages had left her a social outcast, the object of gossip. This made her irritable, suspicious, testy and ashamed. Maybe he sensed the abused child she might have been, damaged goods, and attracted only to men who would abuse her again and again. She may have felt no right to expect more. Low self-esteem could have kept her connecting with men like herself—losers.

Yet this second-hand, hurting, promiscuous woman was moved by Jesus's uncondescending concern for her. This shady, disreputable swinger became the first Christian missionary. The poet James Russell Lowell, in Sonnet IV, put the Christ-approach this way: "Be noble! And the nobleness that lies in other men, sleeping but never dead, will rise in majesty to meet thine own."

3rd Sunday of Lent
(John 4: 5-42)

34

Blindness: Religion's Possible Side Effect?

This lively, lengthy Gospel features a spunky blind man whom Jesus cured, and who was nervy enough to talk back to his religious leaders—the bishops of his day. This outspoken cheek probably appealed to the evangelist, since the narrative is tainted with notable hostility toward the Jews. When it was written, some three generations after Christ lived, Jews believing in him were no longer welcome to worship in the synagogues. This excommunication embittered the now-proscribed Jews and the New Testament blisters with anti-Semitism, thus sowing fateful seeds justifying mindless hate crimes over the centuries against hapless Hebrews.

Religious bigotry is nothing new, even in this educated age. The modern savagery in Northern Ireland, in Africa and in Yugoslavia matches the bloody brutality of the old Crusades. What makes human beings fight over religion? Why this contempt for those who believe another way? How can some be convinced that they know exactly what's on God's mind? Could this certitude provide a feeling of security or superiority?

The Pharisees have been the victims of bad press for twenty centuries. Pious hypocrisy is named for them, but they were very religious. Could this be a problem? It is when perfectionism gets in on the act. Pharisees were religious specialists, experts in applying the revered Law of Moses, which was regarded as the perfect reflection of the mind of God. Unwavering obedience to this code was the sure way of pleasing God. They taught that divine approval depended on a creature's total compliance. Thus, their religion centered around the structure of regulations and rituals rather than spontaneous compassion to human needs. The authority they enjoyed gave them a social prominence they liked, and they bristled at any challenge.

Jesus was raised in this exacting tradition. No doubt intimacy with his Father in prayer and his perception of the suffering around him enhanced his tenderness and balanced good sense. Sensitivity to people and their needs claimed priority over bureaucratic religious rules. So, he responded to the blind man, and on the Sabbath, when even treating an injury was forbidden activity. Making a mud pie with his spittle (thought to have remedial properties in those days) and applying it to the sightless eyes obviously broke the Sabbath. When it actually worked, the Pharisees were even more scandalized.

My seminary training back in the '30s and '40s taught me to be a good Pharisee. Priestly prerogatives seemed more sacred than service to constituents: Divorced . . . beware! Birth controllers . . . keep out! Spousal abuses . . . suffer your cross! I have been a Pharisee when, in my insecurity, I reverenced rules more than the ruled. I was not mature enough to understand the human predicament and that God wanted to show His mercy and support for others through me.

I trust more this God who forgives fools and Pharisees alike. I bless the grace that outgrows narrowness and insensitivity; certitude is now less important than the spirituality that makes me see better. I can even hear better, especially the heartening words of Jesus to the blind man, "Relax, here's mud in your eye!"

4th Sunday of Lent
(John 9: 1-41)

Lazarus: One More Time

"Where were You when we needed You?" Martha yelled at Jesus. "Your friend, our brother, is dead! Who will look after us now?" Did Jesus blow it? He dallied deliberately for two days. "He was . . . deeply troubled . . . He wept." A very human scene. Surreal time again . . . Jesus calls. Four days in his grave, Lazarus answers. Mummy-wrapped, he walks out of the tomb.

The English essayist C. S. Lewis (1898-1963) contends that Lazarus should be honored as the first Christian martyr since his first dying was only practice. He had to do it again. As a hospital chaplain, I have witnessed the miracle of Lazarus more than once. Through the magic of modern medicine and the deft endeavors of superbly trained staffs, stilled hearts have come to life again. Intriguing are the now-familiar tales of the resuscitated after they had been officially pronounced dead. Petty concerns no longer vex them, human relating becomes a priority, resentments seem frivolous and vendettas vanish. Death is no longer dreaded and is seen not as an ending, but a beginning.

I have known no more privileged moments than those spent with the terminally ill. To explore with them worries, fears, memories, and wistful fancies of "if I had it to do over," and the things that made them laugh. I fondly remember one brave patient in his middle years tragically stricken with a fatal pulmonary disease. I brought him the Eucharist one afternoon and afterward he mirthfully added, "Father, you have to read this letter. My brother is a priest in Joliet, Illinois and he had the eighth graders in his parish school write me—to cheer me up. Here's the winner. (I quote it exactly, word for word):

Joliet, Illinois
24 October 1969

Dear Mr. Lane,

I am an eighth grader. I attend Saint Mary Carmelite school (it is cheap and old) in a town about the size of Chicago. The population is about twenty thousand.

As I said, I am in eighth grade, with a complicated reader and a complicated math and two mean teachers and about twenty-three other eighth graders to cope with, and you think you got it bad.

Sincerely yours,
Michael Ardolino—(12)

This letter is one of my life's treasures. Mr. Lane was dead the following day.

Many of us have our own personal Lazarus marvels. It may have been a rescue from the slow death of narcissism, that deadening self-absorption that someone noticed and did not withdraw from, but stayed long enough to care. God breaks through in our lives when we least expect it. Even when we give up on Him, as Martha did on Jesus. Is God to be believed only when exclusively at our disposal?

I like Zorba the Greek's God: "God is just like me, only bigger and crazier."

Zorba sounds irreverent, but it is what a bold man of faith hears God say to him: "I am your resurrection and your life."

5th Sunday of Lent
(John 11: 1-45)

Winning and Losing

Are the above merely human categories? Is up one day and down the next all the same to God? The week we call Holy has something to say about this. Triumphant on Sunday, Jesus is dead on Friday. Similar extremes happened to Gandhi, Martin Luther King, the Kennedys and numberless other worthy history-makers. If this strange week sends a single clear message, it is that what is contradiction to us is not at variance with God.

As one hears the Passion read this day, one is struck by the restraint of the narrative. There is no amplification of any gory detail, but simply a terse, undramatic report of a slow, hideous Roman execution. How could this terrible black Friday get to be called good? One explanation is that the Evangelists did not see the crucifixion of Jesus as tragedy, but as glorification. Good Friday is not a day of obligation. Easter is. The day is called good because God turned what was bad on Friday into something good on Sunday. Evil and suffering are never the bottom line with God. God does wonders with them.

As Holy Week was seven days of paradox, so are the days of our lives. Good and evil are there in perpetual motion, durably interlocked in planetary rhythm. Roses have thorns, the sun makes the desert, blessings include curses, answers generate fresh anxieties, fame ends precious privacy, and compassion arises from personal suffering. The desirable and the undesirable are never far from each other. Such is the creation we live in. Plus and minus are in constant tandem. "Everything God has made," wrote

39

Emerson, "has a crack in it." Perfection has to wait for another world.

In this one, we are still in process. That is what growing means. Thus, crisis is our constant companion. The entire universe is a boundless arena of flux. Minutest particles endlessly connect, then separate, transforming matter into energy. Human beings are stardust, microcosms, made from the same stuff of the universe and just as indestructible. Even our inner disparities power us, as do the opposite poles of electricity. At least the very faults we deplore most in ourselves deliver us from smugness.

This verse, by an unknown author, describes the human dilemma:

Why did you make me, Lord
the way that I am,
which is just as I would not
wish to be?
Did you perhaps know what you
were about
and plan me thus for all
eternity?
If I had fashioned me,
I would have used a sterner stuff,
immune to pain of love
and deaf to tears;
unmoved by sentiment,
untouched by song.
But I, I am a fool; I feel too much.
At every little hurt,
I cringe and whine.
Did you intend that I
should win the cup by just
these handicaps of mine?"

What happened to Jesus happens to us. We feel betrayed when someone we trust lets us down. We've all been falsely accused at times, our intentions misinterpreted. Devastating illness has tortured us sometimes more than three hours. The scars of Christ are the wounds of the world: the homeless, the displaced, death squad victims, unwanted aliens, abused children, and humiliated women. The pageant of pathos staggers on. Why?

Why his Calvary? No outrage, no anger, no poor me. Here the terrifying power of evil and the indomitable force of love collide. Evil is not annihilated; it is assimilated. The power to forgive surmounts the power to offend.

Can it be that the mystery of the Cross untangles the mystery of God? Can it be that God is a synthesis of the finite and the infinite—that opposites meet here—that extremities come to blend in a Central Whole, evoking the acclaim, "Holy, Holy, Holy?" Is this not why Christ is nailed to this sign of contradiction, where the vertical joins the horizontal and evil is dissolved into good? Another name for this is "redemption."

Palm/Passion Sunday
(Matthew 26: 14-27, 66)

Rise and Shine

When last we tuned in, the bad guys were winning. The nuisance Jew was finally dead and buried. That was that!

Not so fast! The ending of one thing is usually the beginning of something else. For instance, matter gets atomized and energy gets born. Christ gets killed on Friday; Sunday he begins a universal existence, unrestricted by the boundaries of Palestine, unhampered by time or limitations of the body. No century will not claim him, no land will not know of him. Easter is Jesus out of control.

Easter announcement: "Fasten your seat belts—it's God's Mind-Blower time! Jesus is back, and the world will never be the same!" None of this can be proved, but has the world ever heard a story it most wants to believe: that pain is never the bottom line; that death is never the end?

Still, Easter's proof is all about us. The gorgeous Spring blooming from the tiny seed you buried in the base dirt . . . not a drop of water is lost in nature's cycle. Every element suffers change, is converted, renewed and used again. Could it be less for human beings—the very breath of the Creator?

A crusty, curmudgeon pastor repeated the same terse sermon every Easter. It went like this: "I don't know about you people, but I believe in the resurrection of the dead, because I see those who have been dead to going to church all year suddenly come to life on Easter Sunday."

I could never work up a critical lather about non-church attendance. People go to church for all sorts of reasons: the music, the ritual, the instruction, the peace and the lift. Others are totally bored with it. Worship is a charism, a gift; some have it, some don't. But there is more to religion than going to church or loyalty to a creed. Spirituality involves transformation—from an institution to personal relationship. It is more a sense of one's center from where God acts out His goodness within the person.

Jesus apparently did not criticize his disciples for their skepticism about his resurrection. He was patient with them, as I dare say, he is with our flawed faith. He gives them and us all the time we need. Growth is never rushed.

What happened to Jesus happens to us. When God zaps us, we, too, rise from our tombs of fear of life, of dread over our frailties, our bungling, and our lunacies. We are the risen Christ each time we calm a frightened child, understand a detractor who sees us as a threat, or confront an enemy, communicate, reconcile. Or when we decide that life will not beat us, as in the award winning movie, *Life is Beautiful.*

The Easter event is a cosmic symbol—a sign to reassure the faint-hearted that death and defeat are temporary in the natural sequence of existence. Death is simply not in God's vocabulary. True, our human parts wear out and our hearts will stop. But just as God exhaled us into existence, He will inhale us back to Himself. That's Resurrection.

Easter Sunday
(John 20: 1-9)

Thomas: "No Doubt"

The winsome letters of children to God blend wisdom with whimsy. For instance:

Dear God,

> *Why do people die: I don't want to die yet. I'm having too much fun now to die. I heard that your son died. I also heard you raised him from the dead . . . keep up the good work.*

Your friend,
Chuckie

Thomas heard the same report Chuckie heard, but the Thomas response sounded like "Oh, yeah, tell me another!" It's not hard to identify with this skepticism. Thomas is obviously not a sucker for hearsay. He seems to think for himself, to keep his own counsel. He apparently is a loner and not a people-pleaser.

When Jesus decided to head for Jerusalem and to his anticipated doom, Thomas, nicknamed the Twin, said to his fellow disciples, "Let's go, too, and die with him." (John 11: 16). However sincere at the time, this bravado failed to hold up when push came to shove. He cut and ran like the others.

Maybe Thomas was fed up with the way things turned out—the way he turned out. Maybe he was embarrassed at discovering this quality of specious pretense in himself. Embarrassment often leads to excuses. Thomas had excused himself from the group and thus missed Jesus's first appearance the week before. "I'm getting out of here," he may have decided; "I'm going to do what I do best—go fishing." It is typical to withdraw from company when we are annoyed with ourselves. We don't want others to see in us what we see in ourselves and do not like. So, we retreat, which is the precise opposite of what is needed. What is needed is contact—connection with people who know us, who level with us. We do not need further criticism, with which we have already abundantly indicted ourselves. We need courteous confrontation, such as Jesus engaged in with Thomas—no censure for his cynicism, just the firm brotherly welcome, "Touch me, Thomas."

However cynical, Thomas showed up again among his old associates. He did not share their exuberance, nor did he conceal his incredulity. There was nothing dubious about his point of view. Unequivocally he stated his conditions for belief. Jesus met them. Maybe that is why he made a return visit—for an honest agnostic's sake!

Doubts are not comfortable, but then sometimes neither are convictions. The former are often stepping-stones to the latter when the seeker genuinely wants to know. On the other hand, some make a career of doubting because making up one's mind means risking being wrong . . . a bitter pill for perfectionists! Others loathe a doubt because it means ambiguity, suspense and uncertainty—poison to the absolutists! Such a craving for certitude leaves one easy prey to bigots, zealots and fanatical dictators. Would to God that Hitler had had doubts!

Faith and doubt are usually in tandem. They need each other, as the muscle needs stress for its tone. Questions imply doubt and good teachers feast on them. Jesus never encouraged mindless conformity as a qualification for discipleship. Faith does not develop by denying doubt, but by confronting it as Thomas did. The encounter created a brand new conviction for him—not just that he believed in his Lord and his God, but that his Lord and his God believed in him.

2nd Sunday of Easter
(John 20: 19-31)

Emmaus: When Departing is Arriving

The climactic Emmaus story is our story. Like the two travelers, when the sky falls on us, we want to hit the road. Like them, we want to distance ourselves from the site of disaster. We need to escape.

Sometimes church is our escape. Sometimes nothing happens for us there. Even religion lets us down, but we need consolation as much as rest or nourishment. Where do we find it when work, play, trips or alcohol don't seem to keep their promises?

The Gospel has Jesus catching up to the travelers and they don't recognize him. Neither do we when that total stranger in the checkout line notices our troubled look and asks about it. Or that ominous, earringed teen resembling a refugee from the Klondike who stops to fix your flat. Goodness surprises us when we're not looking for it.

In the Emmaus event, the stranger dares to be impertinent enough to be pertinent: "What are you so concerned about?" he asks (Luke 24: 17). Then it begins—the healing, that is—when we open up to talk about what hurts. The stranger listens, seems annoyed at first and then launches into a scripture lesson. At times, no amount of religious theory can pierce the gloom. But the duo is impressed; they invite him to stay. He accepts. A revelation is in store.

One moral of this Gospel short story is that dialogue is a necessity of life. We were created social beings—relational. Silence may be golden when there is nothing to say, and solitude may tranquilize the febrile spirit, but dialogue is the catalyst for learning to be human. I need to think for myself, but not by myself. My ache may annoy me, embarrass me, so I keep it inside where it festers for lack of light and air. When I go public with this secret, I risk disapproval. But that is hardly terminal. Courage is the prescription. Loners can be losers until they open to let themselves out and others in. Inter-relating is a one-way exit from victimhood. When I disclose me, I discover me. Self knowledge is an important way of knowing God, whom we believe lives in our innermost selves.

Another implication from this Gospel is that God never leaves us alone. The English poet Francis Thompson (1859–1907) interpreted this insight in his majestic "Hound of Heaven": "I fled him down the nights and down the days; I fled him down the arches of the years . . . Yet was I sore adread lest, having him, I must have naught beside."

Escape can leave us empty until the unbidden and often hidden Christ catches up with us:

"All which I took from thee I did but take, not for thy harms, but just thou mightst seek it in my arms. All which thy child's mistake fancies as lost, I have stored for thee at home; rise, clasp my hand and come!"

3rd Sunday of Easter
(Luke 24: 13-35)

Quality Time

The shepherd job description occasions little call in this current culture. It is still Christendom's most persistently appealing image of Jesus, however. The world is populated with people who copy this likeness in their lives whenever they respond to the mordant moans of a straying sheep, an addict, an anonymous person in need of help, someone sexually confused, someone physically abused, an oldster who can't cope, or a person hopeless and terminally ill. They copy this likeness, too, simply in hugging a frightened child.

Caring parents know something about good shepherding. The late Erma Bombeck, whose blend of delightful whimsy and wise spirituality is so sorely missed, had this to say in a 1998 column:

> *Someday, when my children are old enough to understand, I'll tell them: I loved you enough to bug you about where you were going, with whom, and what time you would get home. I loved you enough to insist you buy a bike with your own money—which we could afford. I loved you enough to be silent and let you discover your friend was a creep. I loved you enough to make you return a Milky Way with a bite out of it to the drug store and confess 'I stole this' . . . But most of all, I loved you enough to say 'no' when you hated me for it. That was the hardest part of all.*

Mothers do not monopolize good shepherding. There are sensitive fathers like this one describing his thoughts as he views his newborn son for the first time:

> When you had three children, the novelty should have worn off, and yet my mind moved on tiptoe, oppressed with the wounds and indignity of what it meant to be born, to be repudiated into separateness by the mother flesh, on the road to becoming one of the world of three billion identities ... then to be brought to his mother for the first time and laid beside her warmth that was radiant without being thermostatically controlled. And how her gown would be opened and he would find a little consolation for the outrages that identity had brought him.

Husbands and wives good shepherd one another when they care. A 1987 PBS film called *There Were Times, Dear* dramatized this true story. A woman in her middle years must now cope with the progressive decline of the husband she has loved for thirty years, now slowly wasting away with Alzheimer's disease. He was once a handsome, strong protector; now she watches him become a dazed, drooling invalid who stares past her with vacant eyes. There is no safe distance from him. She bathes him, dresses him, frantically searches for him when he wanders off. She knows it will not get better. The story closes seven years later as she ties a bib around his neck and feeds him a piece of their wedding anniversary cake.

There are times when we need good shepherding. We may resent our need, even be ashamed of it. But when we reach out a hand to ask for help, may we touch the hand as good as the Good Shepherd himself!

4th Sunday of Easter
(John 10: 1-10)

Via, Veritas, Vita: Going My Way

"Then God said, 'Let us make a man—someone like ourselves'" (Genesis 1: 26). And man returned the favor.

This venerable but valid wisecrack on the creation story does point up the human inability to visualize the Creator except in familiar human images. A warrior monarch, a chastening judge, and a provident parent are some of the faces of God we've painted that say more about us than they do about the deity.

Like most children, I was quite at home with the idea of God. It was reassuring to know there was an authority superior to my parents. Francis Thompson picks up the poignancy of a child's musing when he writes:

Little Jesus, wast thou shy
once, and just as small as I?
And what did it feel like to be
out of heaven and just like me?

As a pre-schooler, I remember thinking that God was like the stray pet I brought home from the street and was allowed to keep. We liked each other. We thoroughly enjoyed being together, roughhousing together or just silently lying side by side. The animal was completely unselfish, never angry, with a limitless capacity to forgive any hurt, any neglect and grateful for a simple pat or a bone.

God, for me, was a loyal spaniel. Alas, going to church changed all that. The Baltimore Catechism and a few ter-

53

rorist nuns put God quite beyond reach. I recall, however, the fun it was, after learning to spell, to spell God backwards . . .

So, what is God really like? According to the sublime Gospel of John, the answer is unequivocally Jesus. He is the image, the revelation, the very snapshot of God in the flesh. Jesus defines himself as "The Way, The Truth, The Life"— words very familiar in Jewish religious life, since they apply to their revered Scriptures. Jesus is saying that he is now their living sacred book. How might we understand his self-interpretation today?

"The Way": Were you ever in a foreign country and lost? You stop a stranger and haltingly ask for directions to the station. He gallantly offers personally to show you the way and goes out of his way to guide. Could this be the intent of Jesus: "I'm walking beside you"?

"The Truth": Did you ever have a teacher who took the time to teach you how to teach yourself? Perhaps the art teacher who painted with you: "Try this tint, this stroke." Or the dance teacher who danced with you, or the piano teacher who dueted with you. All of them were helping you find your own truth, your own ability.

"The Life:" Did you ever meet someone and honestly say, "I have not lived until I met you!?" In this person, you encountered the real you. This Gospel makes God into mutuality with us, an intimacy through Jesus. He is human; so are we. He, then, is our brother. He is God's son. That makes us family. What Jesus does, we can do. He emphasized this: "In solemn truth I tell you, anyone believing in Me shall do the same miracles I have done, and even greater ones," (John 14: 12).

We, too, are "The Way, The Truth, The Life" whenever we care and serve as he did. That's what good parents are to their children.

Joseph M. Wadowicz

Achesay is a high school on an Apache Indian reservation in the White Mountains of Arizona. The setting is picturesque, but the reservation isn't: rampant unemployment, drugs, heart disease, and diabetes. In the fall of '98 the Falcons basketball team were stunned when they met their new coach, Kareem Abdul-Jabbar. He lived temporarily in those parts while he researched a book he was planning to write. Moved by the Indians' melancholy situation, he volunteered to coach. His salary for the year? One dollar. Himself a street kid who made it big—with a college degree and the pinnacle of athletic fame—he wanted to share his success. "I'm walking proof it can be done," he said.

To those muddled youngsters, Kareem became the symbol of "The Way, The Truth, The Life." And so do we when we go the extra mile, when we invest time with those who want to learn and when we care enough to be the best we can be.

5th Sunday of Easter
(John 14: 1-12)

55

Mother's Day: Grandmother's Too

"If you love me, you will keep my commandments" could be less an injunction than an observation. Something akin to the premise that when one falls in love, the whole wide world becomes easier to love. This is the transcending theme of the Good News: that mankind is clearly loved. To verify this, God invented mothers.

Mother's Day in the United States had its beginnings in Philadelphia in 1907 at the urging of Anna Jarvis. It took seven more years for Anna to convince Congress to officially proclaim a national day. Why it took so long for American male legislators to honor motherhood is somewhat surprising, since men generally praise the Creator for sparing them the pangs of pregnancy and the birth process. Again, in Erma Bombeck's words, "No man could stand being pregnant. The first time a man lost his breakfast three solid months in a row, he would make plans to have a nocturnal headache for the rest of his married life."

Parent Magazine some years ago made this comment:

> *American society has the collective need to idealize motherhood. If we didn't sell motherhood, no one would apply for the job:*
>
> Housekeeper, 140 hours per week, no retirement benefits, no sick leave, no private room, no Sundays off. Must be good with kids, animals and hamburgers. Must share bath.

The job has become more complicated these days, what with drugs, guns, gangs, rock music, video games and the need for additional income. Mothers must stretch themselves between kitchen and career, between parenting and profession.

Wondrous as the gift of motherhood must be, to behold your heart outside you, that lump in your throat with legs, mothers are no more than human. They cannot magically bring to motherhood more than they are as women. They cannot all be supermoms any more than all their offspring can be superstars. Mothers have the same limited supply of wisdom, patience and heroism as the rest of us.

Children are bottomless pits of need. Mothers can only try to meet them when their own needs are met. So they need good men, sensitive men, attentive men, not afraid to do "women's work": laundry, cooking, shopping, housecleaning and parenting. Without a whole man, she cannot be a whole mother (any more than he, without a whole woman, can be a whole father). A woman genuinely loved by her man has the best chance of not spoiling or distorting a child. Again, good parenting comes down to good "husbanding" and "wifing."

What parent, at one time or another, has not felt a failure at parenting? The frightening spate of school killings by teenagers has the nation wondering, "Where are the parents of these killers?"

"Do we really know our kids?" inquired *Newsweek* magazine, 10 May 1999. "Even honor roll kids say they feel increasingly alone and alienated, unable to connect with parents, teachers, even classmates . . . when parents abdicate, young people come up with their own rules."

A sixteen-year-old stated, "I'm proud of the fact that my mother deals with me. Even though I push her away, she is still there. Don't be afraid of us, but please notice us."

Despite mistakes in mothering, lucky ones get a second chance when they become grandmothers. Here's an endorsement from an appreciative seven-year-old grand-child:

> *Grandmas can't swim. They don't spank, either, and they stop my mother when she does. Mothers scold better and more. Mothers are married and grandmas are not. Grandma loves me all the time. She treats me like a person already grown up. Grandma told me once that Mom was caught by the principal for writing in her book 'in case of fire, throw this in first.' Since I heard that, I have never loved my mom more.*

Fourth graders were asked why mothers should be honored this day. One said, "For laughing at daddy's jokes." Another said, "For not running over my bicycle when she backs out of the garage."

Mother Erma Bombeck offers this fitting finale. Asked if she would change anything if she could do it over, she replied:

> *I would have sat on the lawn with my children and not worried about grass stains. Instead of wishing away nine months of pregnancy, I'd have cherished every moment. I would have realized that the wonder growing inside me was my only chance in life to assist God in a miracle. When my child kissed me impetuously, I would never have said, 'Later, now get washed up for dinner.'*
>
> *There would be more* I love you's . . . *more I'm* sorry's. *I would seize every minute . . . live it . . . and never give it back.*

Bless you, mothers, for blessing us!

6th Sunday of Easter
(John 14: 15-21)

Ascension: The Only Way to Fly

Remember Heaven's Gate, that eerie group suicide discovered in a swanky mansion in Rancho Santa Fe, California? The group was little known until Holy Week, 1997, when thirty-nine neatly clad bodies, their flight bags packed, imbibed a lethal potion in order to be lifted to "the kingdom level above the human." The human level was obviously disappointing enough for them to form a fellowship for flight from it. They included a successful realtor, a medical technician, an auto salesman, a bus driver and a paralegal. They were mothers and fathers, grandparents and young pursuers of a "dream." They simply walked away from families and friends and joined a cult founded by a former choir director and an ex-nurse. They said their goodbyes on videotape and were headed for the "mother ship" awaiting them on the other side of the Hale-Bopp comet.

What could cause intelligent, technologically sophisticated individuals skilled in computer design and programming to fall so gullibly for such lunatic fiction? Their abdication of personal autonomy extended even to their "Last Supper" when they gathered at a local chain restaurant. All of them ordered the same meal: chicken pot pie.

Fatuous conformity was not in Jesus's plan for his disciples. "Following" was an invitation to imitate his independence, not surrender to servile acquiescence. He welcomed questions, doubts, dissents and even denials. But his disciples had grown accustomed to his charisma. Dependency had set in. If they were to outgrow this, if they

61

were to build "the kingdom" here, not up there, then Jesus had to leave. It was time for them to make their own way with the mystical promise of his presence.

The Heaven's Gaters apparently lacked this vision. For Jesus, the happier level of existence did not happen from passive, wishful, "pie in the sky" thinking, or an illusory space ship, but from the active struggle with the hard stuff of life. Some of us stumble into this "promised land" when we decide to make a bold move, a step that often surprises us . . . like the courageous decision to quit a dull but lucrative job; to walk away from a dead-end relationship; to renounce what seemed a hopeless addiction. Ask any recovering alcoholic who has embraced the heroic Twelve-Step Program what it feels like to be free. They are no longer exhausted but find the fresh energy, the new connection with inner resources they never thought were there!

This is what Jesus wanted for his nervous disciples, but it could not happen until he cut out. His Ascension was the start of their adventure toward self-reliant selfhood, but it began with feeling powerless. They confronted their helplessness with prayer and things started to turn around.

The feast of Ascension suggests that life is a perennial mixture of good and bad. The beautiful and the ugly are partners on our planet. Tornadoes devastate and generate compassionate communities. Ability arises from disability. Watch the Special Olympics. It is suffering that creates compassion. We never know our right stuff until down for the count. Only the failed can relish the sweet smell of success. Life is a tender trap.

How sad the Heaven's Gaters staked their lives on a fairy-tale spacecraft when relief was just a prayer away.

7th Sunday of Easter
(Matthew 28: 16-20)

The Dancing God

Pentecost is one religious festival Christians share with their Jewish brethren. The word means "fifty," and commemorates fifty days since Easter for Christians and fifty days since the second day of Passover for Jews. Jews call it the Festival of Weeks, or *Shevuoth,* and it commemorates the anniversary of the covenant between God and Israel on Mount Sinai. Synagogues are decorated with greens on Shevuoth as the first fruits of the harvest were offered at the great Temple in Jerusalem. It was a happy holiday somewhat akin to our Thanksgiving Day and the evangelist Luke appears to want to identify the birthday of the Christian church with this Jewish festivity.

Of the three most important Christian feast days, Christmas, Easter and Pentecost, the last runs a weak third. Families do not gather for a Pentecost dinner or a Pentecost egg hunt. Yet, awesome were the events of that day. Luke has the Spirit of God happening like an earthquake, a hurricane and a firestorm. The impact so enthused the hidden, timid disciples that when they hit the street revealing their internal upheaval, the public concluded, "They must be drunk and it's only 9 A.M." (Acts 2: 11, 15).

Pentecost emphasizes that not only is the Spirit of God alive and well, but also boisterous, exuberant and tempestuous. It seems a shame that the churches have succeeded in taming God. Divinity has been domesticated to resemble a sedate, well-mannered funeral director. The very word "enthusiasm" is from the Greek, meaning "in God."

Back in American colonial days of 1630, a dynamic religious liberal, Anne Hutchinson (1591-1643), was exiled from the Massachusetts Bay Colony for believing "an unpredictable God of amazing grace." That Anne could get excited about an exciting God was too much for her accuser, a Puritan preacher, Thomas Hooker (1586-1647). Had he published a parish bulletin, how would the apparently humorless Hooker handle this typo gaff as it actually appeared in a church announcement?

At the evening service tonight, the sermon topic will be: "What is Hell? Come early and listen to our choir practice."

If joy is the infallible sign of the presence of God, humor can be a signal of God's nearness. If holiness has to do with the discovery of the truth about us, humor sees the laughable incongruities of our human condition. Humility accepts them with a smile and allows God to have the wild, extravagant gusto that God can have.

This bold exuberance is captured by a young woman then in her twenties, Nancy McCready, who pictures God in a form that may shatter one's sense of the sacred: a smart-stepping frolicker. She employs the antiquated Holy Ghost for the current Holy Spirit in her "Poem for Pentacost":

Start with my toes, you old Ghost.
Spirit the sole of my shoes
and teach me a Pentecostal boogaloo.
Sprain my ankles with dancing
Sandal around my feet to roam with me in the rain and feel
at home in my footprints . . .
Lift me, how! We'd better quit now,
Too all dizzy down giggly.
Stop—you're tickling me
(my funny bone's fickle for you)
Stop—I'll drop. I'm dying. I'm flying.
For I love you so—you old Ghost!

Pentecost
(John 20: 19-23, Act 2: 1-11)

That's the Life

What is God really like? Ask a child. They probably come as close as anybody. A puzzled eight-year-old corresponds with the deity:

Dear God,
Are you really invisible or is that just a trick?
Lucy

A tad more confident queries:
Dear God,
I am an American. What are you?
Robert

Confidence itself pens:
Dear God,
If you watch in church on Sunday I will show you my new shoes.
Mickey

The evolving conscience confesses:
Dear God,
I am doing the best I can.
Frank

(From *Children's Letters to God,* compiled by Hample and Marshall, Worlman Publishers.)

Children are comfortable with the notion of God. It may be consoling to them that there is an authority superior to their parents.

Life gets more complicated as we develop. The simplicities of childhood dissolve into the rarer air of ideas. Imponderables are pondered and that's how theories are born. Is God one of these—an abstraction? The Russian novelist Dostoevsky (1821-1881) addresses this question: "He who desires to see the living God face to face should not seek him in the empty firmament of the mind, but in human love."

This is the message of "Trinity." The Father reveals Himself to the Son. The Son relates this to the Spirit. The Spirit "renews the face of the earth." This is God's life: action. God is a verb.

The offspring imitates parental action because the child is of the nature of the parent. Can the creature do what the Creator does because the human is created according to the image of the Maker? Precisely, however defectively! I encounter you. I disclose me to you. You reveal you to me. We relate. Awareness expands. Humanness grows. Narcissism diminishes. Love is learned.

An early church Latin father, Tertullian (A.D. 155-220), was the first to use the term "Trinity." In another one hundred years, Christians were killing each other in the streets of Constantinople over the Trinitarian dispute of whether the Holy Spirit proceeded from the Father and Son, or just from the Father. It's monstrous how doctrinal disparity mediates such murderous mayhem! Still, Trinity is an extraordinary religious development. It reflects a personally involved God. The implication affirms that it is no more a sin for humans to be like God (holiness) than for God to be like us (incarnation). God is a social being like we are.

Another Trinitarian intimation is that God likes good company as much as we do. (It is hard to top Father, Son and Holy Spirit.) True, we are born alone and die alone, but in between, aloneness is not a recommended life policy. The

Creator surmised as much for Adam (Genesis 2: 18). Short of the capital penalty, solitary confinement is still the harshest punishment. We need each other to become human. Could it be that God needs us in order to better know His Divinity?

Someone said that when we talk about God, we say more about ourselves than we do about God. The judgmental God comes from a domineering, punitive mind. The saving God comes from a heart that has been lucky in love. Whatever hand life has dealt us—whatever mystery we may be to ourselves—the Trinity says each time we bless ourselves, "You belong to us, we made you, we love you—and don't forget it!"

In the name of the Father, and of the Son and of the Holy Spirit. Amen.

Trinity Sunday
(John 3: 16-18)

The Urge to Merge

The Latin sounds better to me than the English and it seems good enough for Texas! The Church, however, bluntly says it: "Body and Blood of Christ." Now that's a mouthful! Which is exactly what the Church intended: a Jesus to be ingested, digested and assimilated.

John's sixth chapter relentlessly and explicitly hammers home the preposterous proposal to feast on the body and blood of Jesus if eternal life is to be gained. It is one way of expressing the intimacy Jesus obviously craves with human beings . . . the day previous he had miraculously fed the five thousand. They wanted more and flocked to Capernaum for a refill. He takes this occasion to emphasize that there is more to life than a free lunch. Here is his divinity, his manhood, and his total humanity meant to nurture mankind to life's spiritual fullness.

It is possible that among his audience were those familiar with ancient pagan sacrificial practices. The Mystery Rites of Mithras, of Isis and of Hermes entreated the god honored to enter inside the worshipers, to become part of their existence and to transform them. They would not be inclined to interpret the words of Jesus in any cannibalistic sense as some apparently did. The writer of the Gospel is affirming that there is more here than Mithras, Isis and Hermes.

Being a souvenir or a memorial was not enough for Jesus. He wanted to be more than just a memory. He wanted to identify with his followers in all the events of their everyday lives. How could this involvement be better described than by making himself a staple sustenance: bread to nourish, wine to refresh? Enter the Eucharist, the real presence and an actuality only God could effect.

As a priest for more than half a century, I am awed at the miraculous power I have personally witnessed administering this sacrament. Most memorable are my experiences as a service chaplain.

There was the humiliated aircraft carrier fighter pilot. Abruptly bereft of his nerve, ashamed of his sudden fear to fly the mission, he knocked on my door one early morning before a scheduled dawn strike. We talked. "Would you like Holy Communion?" I asked. "Yes," he responded. He confessed. Rigged in flight gear, cartridge bandoleer and sidearm .45, he knelt and received the Eucharist. After a few quiet moments, he arose, erect, clear-eyed, no trace of tension. "I can go now," he said firmly. "It's okay." He was not troubled again nor would he ever feel alone.

A submarine on patrol for a straight, non-stop nine months joined our Task Group. Our carrier's skipper signaled welcome and genially offered whatever support was needed. Such goodies as movies and ice cream were suggested. "Thanks," the sub responded. "We have just a single request. If you have a Catholic chaplain, we would like Mass." Forthwith a copter—blithely styled "The Holy Helo"—lowered me to the narrow, pitching catwalk of the surfaced submarine. Awash with waves, agitated by the rotating overhead blades of the "whirlybird," my Mass kit stayed watertight, but I was water soaked to the skin. Led to the messing area—the only accommodating space in tight quarters, I prepared for Mass over the galley sink. "Mind drying out my drenched flight suit?" I asked. Mass was said in my underwear. I have never celebrated a holier one.

Joseph M. Wadowicz

Then there were the Marines. The heading to the following unpublished, personal recollection: "A Chaplain—Before a Field Mass."

There they sit, bone tired, grimed, sweaty, unshaven, always armed and unassumingly alert. In this still moment, they idle, free from the dull burden of gun and gear—grateful for the chance to pause. There they lounge against a propped elbow, silent, brooding—a range of race and rank joined by the calamity of war. Alone with the outrage of bloodshed, they are brothers at the ammo-casing altar of worship.

They grin as we wisecrack while we "rig for church." Eyes will lighten as they softly respond with the Mass prayers. They thirst for words that say God's presence—some kind of meaning for their apocalypse. A tear glistens . . . loneliness? Loss of a buddy? Thankfulfulness for safety so far? Who knows or dares to guess?

My throat clutches . . . it's awesome being here representing the Prince of Rebels among these young rebels . . . their language may be profane, their stories ribald, their gestures obscene, their thoughts shocking, but for the moment, their anger and errancy are at parade rest. They have come to hear him who came to call not saints, but sinners . . . may they hear well, before they duel again with the horseman of death. God help them—and me.

In this era of consolidating corporations and bewildering bank absorptions, Corpus Christi celebrates the Creator's coalescence with creation, the friendly merger with fragile humanity. It affirms that we become what we feed on: His hands, His tongue and His heart. He has none other than ours. It means making Eucharist whatever is meaningful to us: our children, our spouse and every human being.

The words of consecration are pronounced not just over the host and the chalice, but over the assembly as well. Eucharist, then, is not something we do, but something we are—His presence in our world. As it is reverently received, an important awareness is, not merely who we are, but Whose!

Corpus Christi
(John 6: 54-58)

Go, Rather, to the Lost Sheep

Fresh out of college, first day on the job, the new elementary school counselor watched the children playing soccer. At the far end of the field she spied a little girl standing by herself. Eager to be helpful, the counselor walked up to the youngster inquiring, "Are you okay?" "Yes," responded the child. A bit later, the kids still charging about the field, the counselor noticed that the solitary little girl had not moved. Concerned, she approached the little loner and asked, "Can I be your friend?" The child eyed the adult suspiciously and then replied, "All right." "But why are you standing there all alone?" queried the counselor. "Because," answered the girl exasperatingly, "I'm the goalie."

What the counselor lacked in athletic savvy she made up for in sensitivity and in the willingness to be compassionate. Precisely the qualities Jesus expected from his chosen Apostles—responsiveness to people who are hurting.

Note the type of staff Jesus handpicked. They were mostly working stiffs and there probably was not a scholar in the bunch. Nor were they especially religious. None of the twelve were from the priestly caste. Matthew was a Quisling—a tax collector for the Roman occupiers, a sellout. Simon the zealot was a terrorist, instantaneously ready to give his life for Israel's freedom and to slip a shiv into the likes of the tariff trafficker. But Jesus got them to get along together. He apparently wanted ordinary men familiar with the hard struggle of making a living and raising a family. His heart and his sympathy were focused on the suffering.

Another Gospel item to note: the apostles are commissioned to attend primarily to the religious rejects—those not welcome to worship in the synagogues, the disreputable, the morally peripheral, the fringe folk . . . "Go, rather, to the lost sheep . . ."

I do not remember this pastoral focus in my seminary "daze" of the 30s and 40s. Advocacy of the errant was regarded as an apostolate for more unconventional clergy, like the factory "working priests" of France or those providing night ministry to streetwalkers in American cities. These callings seemed almost alien to the formal function of the parish church bent on "saving the saved"—the regular Mass-goer. When I was commissioned as a Navy chaplain, sincere colleagues would ask me, "When are you coming back to the real priesthood?"

We had studied assiduously. Rigorous theology explored the "revealed" nature of God. But after four postgraduate years, the "Great Unknown" remained so, at least for me. The more accessible subject, human nature, received scant attention. But that was a different era. The expanding insights of modern psychology were largely suspect in theological circles of those days. Still, the heavily academic exposure allowed me to feel equipped to teach salvation to the world. At ordination, I was ready. I had the answers. My elite education gave me an illusion of intellectual grandeur. I occupied the moral high ground. I knew what was right, what was wrong; who was in, who was out. Worst of all, an insufferable certitude attended this attitude.

Mercifully, grace and life experience made a dent eventually. Certainty has flown; anxiety follows, then faith decides to hang in. I don't have to know now, God does. That's enough. Mystery, contradiction and paradox are unforeseen educators; people become the living books to study. The compassion Jesus demanded of his auxiliaries is acquired much like everyone else's, from personal suffering. The demons I am expected to deal with must first be my own.

"Go, rather, to the lost . . ." Jesus commanded. Who could better appreciate his "good news?" Who, more than these, need the assurance that even prodigals are his elect? "For He gives His sunlight to both the evil and the good, and sends rain on the just and the unjust, too" (Matthew 5: 25). Salvation is given not because we deserve it, but because we need it. We are saved not because we are good, but because God is!

11th Sunday of Ordinary Time
(Matthew 9: 36-10, 10: 8)

Father's Day: Me, Too!

"What did you get for Father's Day?" one-liner Henny Youngman was asked. "The bills for Mother's Day," he answered. Second banana is okay with most fathers. They don't much mind being left out. Mothering seems to come easier for females than fathering does for males. Maybe it's because women tend to listen; men, to lecture. A man would never invent this holiday.

Work takes dads out of the home, so their absence is not as keenly felt as when Mom is missing due to her paying job. After hearing her night prayers, the four-year-old questioned her mother, "If Santa brings our toys, if the Stork brings baby brother and if God gives us our daily bread, what's daddy doing around here?"

A first-time penitent offered this version of the old confessional prologue, "Bless my father, for he has sinned." In his letter to God, a more benign six-year-old wrote:

Dear God,
    My pop is mean. Please get him not to be, but *don't hurt him.*
Arnold

I remember my father. As an immigrant, he never attended an American school and was never confident of his English. His words were few, but always gentle. I recall not the least pain from him. He worked long hours waiting tables, which he loved and was very good at. He never demanded perfection from me. (I don't know where I picked up this madness.) I would have liked more conversation with him—discussion about a book we were reading together, why he went to church, who God was to him, and what his first date was like.

Adlai Stevenson observed, "Paternity is a career imposed on you without inquiry into your fitness." An inventor, Anthony Monde, remarked, "Most fathers want their children to have what they never had—like top grades in school." Harpo Marx admitted, "I was the same kind of father as I was a harpist . . . I played by ear."

Observing the travails of my three married sisters, I concluded that celibacy was a snap compared to matrimony. I often wondered what kind of father I would make. The test presented itself in 1980. Retired from the service, I headed for southern California to look after my widowed mother, then in her mid-eighties. I wanted to find my own place first. "Why not baby-sit our house?" suggested dear friends in that area. "We'll be gone for three weeks, but the kids go with the house." There were two: a boy, age ten, and a girl, age thirteen. I liked them. I had baptized them as infants. I assumed my unaccustomed charge with buoyant ardor . . . in three days, I wanted to kill myself. In three days, the kids wished I had. I can't remember more unremitting anxiety: "Where are they? How are they? Why don't they phone?"

When the parents returned and normalcy again was restored, I streaked back to "the foot of the cross," blessing the Almighty for their survival and my own. So, let my earnest voice join the chorus of national congratulations to all fathers. In *Write That Down for Me, Daddy,* Harry Wayne Addison illustrates the selfless quality of a father's heart that will save "the choice piece of meat for the kids, or take the other egg because it wasn't fried just right, or wear the same old suit so she can have a formal, or sit in a cold car in the school yard until 3 A.M. waiting for the bus to bring them back from a ball game."

Here's another bull's eye from Erma Bombeck: "How unusual is it to be the only man in a room full of women at a school play at 3 P.M.? And yet once you have had a father as a part of your life, you will never be the same again. They bring to it another view of yourself that you cannot see through a mother's eyes. A bloody nose doesn't seem as tragic, screwing up seems ordinary, mistakes not as earth-shaking. Maybe fatherhood has nothing to do with a biological function. Maybe it's a generic term for someone who enriches, makes a difference to lives he touches and would be sorely missed had he never been."

So on this Father's Day, I am grateful for noticing all the things I missed in my father, and for noticing the rich experience and education of fatherhood that being a priest has denied me. All these observations point up what it takes to be a good father, which is what I dearly want to be to all who honor me when they call me "Father."

12th Sunday of Ordinary Time
(Matthew 10: 26-33)

Going for the Gold

Hardly a pain free ambition! Olympians train daily and gruelingly for years before they compete. In this desultory Gospel excerpt—sayings of Jesus strung together—he sounds like an exacting coach demanding 110 percent performance. Jesus wants winners on his team. Yet losing, he advises, is a way of winning.

Champions know what they need to lose: excess weight, indulgent habits. But what's this about denying one's family? How can devotion to them diminish homage to him? Can he be saying that there is a way of loving family that is not good for family? Possessive parents are positive that they love their children. A doting mother insists that she loves the son she is spoiling. A scrupulous father is convinced he cares when he over-controls his daughter.

A reprise from marvelous Erma Bombeck, her life over at sixty-nine, continues to share her light and Jesus's gospel of "tough love" in her 1978 book, *If Life Is A Bowl Of Cherries, What Am I Doing In The Pits?*:

> *Someday when my children are old enough to understand the logic that motivates a mother, I'll tell them:*
>
> *I loved you enough to let you see anger, disappointment, disgust and tears in my eyes.*
>
> *I loved you enough not to make excuses for your lack of respect or your bad manners.*
>
> *I loved you enough to let you stumble, fall, hurt, and fail.*

The Now Testament

I loved you enough to accept you for what you are,
not what I wanted you to be.

Family is a built-in self-denial system, a sure cure for inherent narcissism. Not to worry, then, whether you love family more than Jesus. How one loves deserves more attention than whom. The Gospel's telling line is "Who brings himself to naught for my sake discovers who he is." This could hardly involve conscientious self-contempt. Any put-down of a human being is hardly a tribute to its Creator.

It is the self-seeking that Jesus admonishes. Self-absorption is the mark of infancy. Growing takes breaking past the familiar, the safe and the secure. Winners risk this and losers do not.

The winner: "I'm not okay but that's okay."
The loser: "I'm not okay, but neither are you."

The winner: "I could be wrong, but welcome the right answers."
The loser: "I must never be wrong."

The winner: "My imperfections are a fact of life—I accept, but disapprove."
The loser: "My imperfections are accidents—they are not really me."

The winner: "I was wrong, it's my fault."
The loser: "I was wrong, it's your fault."

The winner: "I want to be who I want to be."
The loser: "I want to be who you want me to be."

The winner: "There is good and bad in me. I admit both."
The loser: "There is good and bad in me. I must hide the bad."

The winner: "It's up to me to find out what's right."
The loser: "It's up to you to tell me."

The winner: "When I'm wrong and admit it, I feel right."

The loser: "When I'm wrong and admit it, I still feel wrong."

The winner: "I accept your applause and applaud you also as a winner."

The loser: "I want your applause, but don't believe it when I get it."

We human beings are both winners and losers. We all get our turn at winning some and losing some.

Was it Chesterton who said, "Whatever is worth doing at all is worth doing badly"? Winners can live with losing. Losers can't stand losing, so they reject the risk and make the win impossible. When going for the gold, even the loser is a winner.

13th Sunday of Ordinary Time
(Matthew 10: 37-42)

It's Your Birthday, USA!

The learned St. Augustine (A.D. 354-430) was reputedly so conversant with ancient Greek philosophy that he could quote yards of Socrates and lots of Aristotle by heart. Yet he admitted that he knew of no words more beautiful, more touching than those in this day's Gospel:

"Come to me, all you that are weary and are carrying heavy burdens and I will give you rest. Take my yoke upon you and learn from me for I am gentle and humble in heart. And you will find rest for your souls. For my yoke is easy and my burden is light."

I cannot encounter these blessed words without hearing their eloquent echo in the moving lines of the young Jewish American poet, Emma Lazarus (1849-1887) inscribed on the base of the Statue of Liberty in the New York harbor:

"Give me your tired, your poor, your huddled masses yearning to breathe free. The wretched refuse of your teeming shores. Send these, the homeless, the tempest-tossed, to me. I lift my lamp beside the Golden Door."

For my immigrant parents, the first sight of this freedom colossus was a never-to-be-forgotten religious experience. My mother, age fifteen, and my father, age nineteen, arrived separately and alone in 1910, brimming with new hope. They met in New York City and were married in 1914. Uneducated, doomed to peasant poverty in their native Hungary, they now had the thrilling opportunity to work, to learn, to make a living, to buy a house and to send their kids to college. These were undreamed-of possibilities until they landed on Ellis Island. On each national holiday, they reverently unfurled the Stars and Stripes as they would a sacred icon. Another pinnacle awaited them when they became naturalized citizens.

Steadfastly they gleaned from our elementary school primers the basic facts of American history required of candidates for citizenship. The Fourth of July celebrates this nation's birth. On this day in 1776, the Declaration of Independence was signed, starting a republic that has become the longest living original government among the current world powers. To love one's country may well be like loving one's spouse. Neither is perfect, and it is folly to ignore respective defects. The simplistic slogan "Love It or Leave It" hardly invites the loyalty that working at problems demands. We have much to work on.

Trees are dying from the poisoned air we breathe daily. Fish cannot live in the polluted waters. Global warming and nuclear proliferation insist we pay attention. And this is just the environment! Then there is the political corruption: Watergate, Irangate, Monicagate and unconscionable campaign spending. One hundred million dollars were squandered on the last presidential election. Candidates are literally bought and paid for.

A thriving economy is cheered. Yet among the first-world countries, we stand alone without a national health protection plan. Twelve thousand people are killed annually by handguns, yet legislators still argue endlessly about gun control laws. In Orange County, California alone, an automobile is stolen every twelve minutes. We lead the world in cars, televisions and computers—also in crime, violence and drug addiction. Our prisons bulge with two million inmates. We have high schools graduates who can't read beyond third grade level. Intended to supplement financially our schools, the lottery pays a winner fifty million dollars as libraries are closed and teachers cut back.

Patriotism cannot mean unquestioned agreement with all governmental decisions. In 1991, the *Los Angeles Times* invited me to do a guest column on this subject. It was headed "A Patriot? One Not Afraid to Challenge Injustice." I close with this quote from the article:

> *This nation is founded on protest. The founding fathers were treasonable rebels. Their sense of honor did not include mindless conformity to the reigning sovereign. They respected a value higher than a narrow, unquestioning submission to a legitimate authority. The Declaration of Independence eloquently affirms their ethic. This precious document clearly defines that our allegiance is owed not to a government, a leader, the military, or the flag, but to humanity, mankind, us!*

God bless America and His whole wide world!

14th Sunday of Ordinary Time
(Matthew 11: 25-30)

Ecology Theology: Seed

The audience was hostile. He was too liberal for them—too laid back. He did not take their exacting religion seriously enough. Like grim musicians mechanically focused on the notes of the score, they missed enjoyment of the music they were playing. I imagine Jesus would have appreciated at least polite jazz, where the instrumentalist joins competence with freedom, technique with improvisation. Their God was a flinty hangin' judge who brooked no exception from the law. Maybe Jesus tried to tease them with a less uptight image of his Father. So he told them the humorous story of the near-sighted sower with the bad aim. At least it might give farmers a chuckle.

The parable was his teaching tool, just as every gifted instructor uses vivid illustrations to clarify abstract ideas. The parable was a kind of verbal cartoon meant to caricature distinctive characteristics familiar to the listeners. In this one, Jesus wanted to highlight the outrageous extravagance of God: prolific with His grace, and indifferent to where it is squandered. He wanted to point out that salvation was such a fabulous harvest—far beyond a creature's wildest dreams or paltry efforts—that even futile human lifestyles could not obstruct it. Twenty-five percent of the seeded area was enough for God to produce a rich yield.

We are all a varied assortment of absorption. I am a mixed terrain of footpath, rock garden, thorn bush and fertile soil. I am the footpath when I am too busy to smell the roses—or when people walk on me and I am too timid to make waves, or to fight city hall, because I will lose anyway. So, I opt for passive victim or settle for people pleasing.

Then there is the stony side—stubborn, opinionated, law-and-order conservative who believes nothing should be done for the first time. This is the shallow, superficial me that avoids thinking things through, but goes for slick slogans and quick fixes: "Fly now, pay later," or "Make that a double, Bartender."

The thorny side likes to argue. It looks for things to be angry about. It's the judgmental blame-gamer, snug and smug only at life's complaint counter. When unconscious of these parts of me, nothing grows there.

But then there is the "good ground," the receptive, willing-to-look-at-the-rough-edges side of me. It's the attitude open to the feelings that this incompleteness elicits, and the part of me that listens to what others see in me. This is my fertile soil, the humus that takes what nature gives—wind, sun, rain; the baked earth, the frost of life and the blooms.

The parable suggests that an imperfect world is no impediment to God's plan for it. None of our obstructionist pavement, rocks or thorns can finally hinder the efficiency of His grace. The jagged shards of our unfinished personalities are grist for His mill. With God, nothing gets wasted. If only the twenty-five percent of us is good ground, this is more than enough for God to guarantee a harvest thirty, sixty and one hundred times times more than His original investment.

15th Sunday of Ordinary Time
(Matthew 13: 1-23)

Ecology Theology II: Weed

If there is one bedeviling fact of life this side of eternity, it is the relentless reality that "the right stuff" is never found in a pure state. Life on this troubled planet is a vexing network of triumph and tragedy, sense and nonsense, harmony and blue notes, manicured lawn and crab grass. Something is always out of joint.

Human history is a record of the good, the bad and their coexistence together. Bacteria outnumber us and provide our immunity; fresh air spawns tornadoes; technical marvels please as well as pollute. Mankind has never been more literate, more widely educated and more cultured, yet the century ends as one of the bloodiest in all civilized annals.

How come?

One reasonable conclusion is human beings are not finished yet; we are still in process, as is our universe. We've only just begun. We are imperfect. It's the way we were made, so it must be okay with the Creator. That's why Jesus told this parable about the weeds and the wheat living together.

"Shall we pull out the weeds?" the laborers asked. A surprising response from the landowner: "No. If you pull up the weeds, you might uproot the wheat along with them. Let them grow together until harvest." Patience is recommended. I don't remember this lenience when growing up. There was just no room for mistakes and consequent punishment did not seem to make matters any better.

God appears to handle the problem another way: Live with it! Divine logic makes more sense. To oppose an evil head-on is like hammering a nail—the harder it's hit, the deeper it goes. Or, drive out the demon and the angel goes, too. In this world, good and bad are never far apart. They are hooked on each other, like upstairs/downstairs, inside/outside. The problem of evil is no more easily explained than is the wonder of good.

With God, nothing gets wasted. The weeds that are eventually separated fuel the oven that bakes the bread. The leftover piece of dough ferments, a form of putrefaction, which leavens the fresh dough into a tasty loaf. Unleavened, the bread is flat, brittle and tasteless. Similarly, the remarkable twelve-step programs are successful because our faults tend to unify us more than our virtues.

The parable teaches that God is no less forbearing than the good parent watching its little one struggle to walk—creeping, rising, failing, and colliding. Crawling is imperfect compared to walking tall, but it's a necessary step in that direction, thus making the imperfection part of the perfection. The playwright knows that unless he injects a villain, the audience will walk out after the second act. The introduction of evil creates the drama, the tension. How can virtue triumph if not challenged? Demons faced are terrorists disarmed because they are threats without power.

Maybe that's why God created us half-baked . . . because He likes a good story. Since each one of us is the combination of "wheat and weeds," we are each exciting bestsellers. So relax! If you must be serious about yourself, try something really difficult: give up working on yourself. Cut out trying to improve. Just try to be gentle with your faults, like God is. The perfection of love is to love the imperfect.

16th Sunday of Ordinary Time
(Matthew 13: 24-43)

Ecology Theology III: Heed

Who sits in your favorite chair, orders your favorite dish, tunes to the station with your favorite music? What/ who is the most important reality in your life? Who else— you, of course! Unless you are your own best friend, your most attentive provider, you are of little use to yourself or anyone else. Self-affirmation is not self-indulgence when heeding yourself includes feeding me.

Each of us is a uniquely significant thread in the world's skein. In fact, each of us is a hidden treasure, a pearl of great price, and a dragnet catch packed with the useful and the useless. Each of us is worth discovering and investing in. The English physician Sir Thomas Browne (1605-1682) wrote, "We carry within us the wonders we seek without us."

The search can be life-long, but lucky ones stumble onto this precious trove even without looking for it. Life shows me to me, if I care to notice. When the real me, not the imagined or ideal me, invites my focus, a perilous adventure is launched, full of unexpected twists and turns, but eminently worth the candle.

I fancy that to know oneself is as important as seeking to know God. To Augustine, the enterprise was mutual. The mystics explain that one gets to know oneself in order to forget oneself. Thus do others get our clearer attention. The process is a reliable map to buried treasure.

I get to know the real me better when I disclose me to you: what I think, what I feel, and what I fear. This works better than a solitary, subjective introspection. This candid human sharing is a holy pilgrimage to the center of myself, where God lives. The prophet Isaiah confers divine dignity upon the listening other, "God lives in whose sight I stand." The following verse captures the sanctity inherent in genuine relating:

> *I sought my soul, my soul I could not see.*
> *I sought my God and my God eluded me.*
> *I sought my neighbor and I found all three.*

Self-revelation is not an easy issue for those who have not experienced a proper welcome to this world. Children deprived of the regard and affection essential to their forming years can never trust themselves or others, later on, in a close adult encounter. Spontaneity and intimacy are fugitives to beware of; self-worth is a fiction to them. Still, their truest selves stand on the other side of this fear.

In the parables, the finder had to decide whether to window shop or to buy. The decision was the chancy step from spectator to participant. It was time to invest—to shoot the works!

What each of us has to go on is the legacy of both parents. We are the best and the worst of our mothers and fathers. The dragnet of the third parable describes the situation—a mixture of useful and useless stuff. But going for it means transcending what was, for what is not yet. It means giving a proper burial to the past, so its ghosts no longer haunt . . . in this holy ground is where buried treasure is most likely to be found.

To paraphrase playwright Arthur Miller from *After the Fall:*

> *Sooner or later we need "to take our lives into our arms." This means giving to myself what I want from you. When I expect from you, what I cannot give myself—understanding, acceptance—I am doomed to*

disappointment. To do unto yourself what you would have others do unto you is down payment on the "pearl of great price."

Whatever our misshapen childhood, our misspent past, Paradise Lost needs to be revisited and reconciled with before the bounty is to be claimed. Thus unfettered, one is freer to live life more lightly, to connect with everything, but to belong to oneself. Surprise, surprise! Your treasure was not-under your nose, but behind it . . . God does not make junk.

17th Sunday of Ordinary Time
(Matthew 13: 52)

Fast Food

Miracles are meant to get our attention. They are not necessarily suspensions of the laws of nature, but they are unusual phenomenons that signal the mysterious hand of God. Jesus feeding thousands with the morsels of a box lunch appears no less than six times in the New Testament. All four evangelists mention it. The connection to the Eucharist is readily noticed.

This Gospel can have another focus, namely, Jesus's response to his personal grief. The crafty Herod wantonly executed his favorite cousin, John. A heartless killing is crueler when it is senseless as well. The news must have stung Jesus. Would he be next? Better get out of town! He needed time to mourn and to be alone: ". . . He withdrew in a boat to a deserted place by himself."

Grieving turns us in on ourselves. Aching loss is our consuming feeling. This anguish should not be anesthetized if life's slow rain is to fill the empty cup. Mourning must not be rushed or aggravated by hollow cheerleading. Grief seeks solitude where relentless tears will not be seen.

But unexpected emergencies sometimes intrude on this self-absorption. It happened to Jesus. The crowd refused to leave him alone—they were hungering to hear him, to be healed by him. His heart went out to them. "Moved with pity," he attended to them without annoyance or complaint.

When pushed past self-pity and devoid of any sense of inner resources, we know what it feels like to be "running on empty." To reach deep down and animate any latent scrap of energy, however meager the offering . . . well, miracles can happen. This could be one interpretation for the meaning of the "Loaves and Fishes" marvel. God can use our "little" when given with good heart, and make a lot from it. This is not an uncommon miracle in our consumer society. In Sacramento, California, an organization for the homeless is called "Loaves and Fishes." Two ex-United Farm Workers organizers, who from nothing raise money to feed 800 people daily, house 130 recovering addicts in local apartments, offer childcare for low-income working mothers and provide a medical clinic, founded it. Again, "The Loaves and the Fishes"!

In Orange County, California, SOS—Share Our Selves—of Costa Mesa serves the needy, no questions asked. Twelve hundred patients are seen every month in their superb, fully equipped medical and dental clinics. Groceries for families are daily supplied. Indigent children get new shoes and clothes as they start the school year so they can look like all the other kids. This flourishing miracle of mercy began by little else than an ordinary housewife with a wide heart—a "Loaves and Fishes" reprise.

In our Grief Support Group a few years ago, a young widow of a slain policeman with three children described the paralyzing depths of her depression. Her mourning-induced immobility ended when her five-year-old son plaintively tugged on her skirt saying, "I lost my daddy, too. I need you now." Her heart came alive again. Loving replaced lamenting.

What compassion can Jesus still "have for the multitude" if not ours? John Jackson, of the *Indianapolis Star,* was the newspaper's photographer on assignment in 1987 to cover the devastating earthquake of Ecuador. In this catastrophe, he witnessed a simple scene of compassion that deeply moved him. In his words:

Joseph M. Wadowicz

The line was long but moving briskly. And in that line at the very end stood a young girl, about twelve years of age. She waited patiently as those at the front of the line received a little rice, some canned goods or a little fruit. Slowly but surely she was getting closer to the front of that line, closer to the food. From time to time she would glance across the street. She did not notice the growing concern on the faces of those distributing the food. The food was running out. Their anxiety began to show, but she did not notice. Her attention seemed always to focus on the three figures under the trees across the street.

At long last, she stepped forward to get her food. But the only thing left was a lonely banana. The workers were almost afraid to tell her that that was all that was left. She did not seem to mind to get that solitary banana. Quietly she took the precious gift and ran across the street where the three small children waited—perhaps her sisters and a brother. Very deliberately she peeled the banana and very carefully divided the banana into three equal parts. Placing the precious food into the eager hands of those three younger ones—'One for you, one for you, one for you.' She then sat down and licked the inside of the banana peel.

In that moment, I swear I saw the face of God.

*18th Sunday of Ordinary Time
(Matthew 14: 13-21)*

99

Water Walk

Any Gospel mention of Simon Peter invariably gets my attention. I can quite imagine what Jesus saw in him. Sure, he was impetuous, rash, fickle, and when push came to shove, unreliable. He seemed to resist new ideas and persisted in questioning. But he was never dull. There was boldness to him, an eagerness to take a dare.

He probably could not believe what his eyes were beholding—Jesus treading the sea toward their storm-tossed craft in the middle of the night. Amazed, he wanted in on that action . . . (like the first time I witnessed a bungee-jump—"Wow! I'd like to try that!"). Impulsively Peter enthused, "Bid me to come to you on the water!" "Come," said the Lord, "if you dare."

Peter dared. Suddenly, reality and the storm struck together. Peter, the Rock, sank like one. Was this abrupt precipitancy foolhardy on his part? Is it reckless for an ardent jogger to attempt the marathon only to finish last?

Who of us has not experimented with Peter's willingness to take a chance on an uncertain enterprise? As when you agreed to take your sister's three teenagers for the summer . . . or when you offered a home to your alcoholic brother-in-law . . . or volunteered to take the elderly shopping. Your heart was in the right place, you meant well, but you just couldn't cut it.

How foolish is going out on a limb to try something new and different only to wind up over our heads? How else can we find out about ourselves except through crisis? The Chinese word for this concept comprises two characters: danger and opportunity. Those who risk these know something about self worth. To a winner, the outcome is not as important as the challenge. Faith does not need to know the results. Nor is Faith an automatic lever one pulls to get out of trouble.

This Sunday's readings stress changes in both Elijah's and Peter's understandings of themselves. The swaggering prophet had just mass-murdered 450 defeated priests of Baal by slitting their throats (I Kings 18: 22, 40). Now on the lam from the infuriated pagan Queen Jezebel, he is shaken and in fear for his life. God shares a secret with him during his Mount Horeb hideout. In the ferocious hurricane, earthquake and firestorm, God is not to be found, but in a tiny stage whisper (1 Kings 19: 11-13). This is often missed because God's medium is a still, small voice. Elijah recognizes that his zealous violence is not of God. About to drown, Peter discovers that showing off does not pay off.

We all dread helplessness, yet it can be God's opportunity. A certain woman has no particular religious belief, but she does have MS, multiple sclerosis. Consequent unsteadiness has made her hyper-wary, lest she stumble. This deliberate alertness has made her more attentive to others. She finds herself focusing intently on their conversation and feels more connected, more energized. "I'm not grateful for this damn MS, " she admits, "but I am grateful for it making me more human."

Trouble can make us whiners or winners. Both probably have their turn with us. When flattened by life's rampage, it is normal to be afraid and even to rant "Where is God in all this . . . where?" As Peter found out—right in the eye of the storm. He's holding out His hand!

19th Sunday of Ordinary Time
(Matthew 14: 22-23)

Homecoming

Mary's bodily ascension into heaven is a traditional belief signified by the word *assumption*. It is an awkward, Latiny word with many meanings. Among them: implication, premise, opinion and an unproved guess. Then there is also the snooty term *apotheosis,* clumsier still, meaning "elevation to divine status." *Ascension* was already taken. *Translation* is a closer fit, but connotes literary activity. So, *assumption* will have to do.

It is a bold dogma for this skeptical age. Beyond proclaiming an afterlife, it affirms the mystical unity of the soul with its life-long companion, the body, in that supernatural existence. How this is possible is not for us to know this side of eternity. Far out as this may sound to the agnostic ear, attending the funeral of a loved one may assist credulity. Would a provident Creator permit this longing to see again a lost love only to frustrate it?

When Pope Pius XII declared the assumption to be an official doctrine of the Church in 1950, a surprise reaction came forth from the renowned Swiss psychologist, Carl Gustav Jung (1875-1961). He hailed this pronouncement as "the most important religious event in four hundred years." How could a Protestant minister's son and erstwhile colleague of Freud make such a public claim? Though he endorsed no particular faith, he profoundly valued religious spirituality as an essential ingredient in mental health. Jung saw this homage to Mary as a special recognition of women's dignity and their modern struggle for independence and equality. To him, the Church was attesting to the impartiality of God's mind: women are as important as men.

The centuries have not reflected this conviction. To Plato (422-348 B.C.), a disciple of Socrates, "A woman is only a lesser man." *(Republic,* Book V). In Jesus's day, both Roman and Jewish law courts refused women as admissible witnesses. Tertullian (A.D. 160-230), a north African hardliner Latin Church father, leveled this zinger: "Woman! You are the gateway of the devil. You persuaded him (Adam) when the devil dared not attack directly. Because of you, the Son of God had to die." Roman emperor Claudius (214-270) was considered eccentric because he liked women. A thousand years of Christianity produced little change in gynephobic logic. The premier Catholic theologian, Thomas Aquinas, (1225-1274), in his celebrated *Summa Theologica* wrote: "As regards the individual nature, woman is defective and misbegotten" *(*Part 1, 9:92). If the fertilized ovum developed into a female, to Thomas this was conception gone wrong.

A medieval custom observed 15 August through 15 September was Our Lady's Thirty Days. It was considered a time of extraordinary blessings: wild beasts would not attack; poisonous plants could not harm; crops grown then stayed fresher longer. This charming superstition at least celebrated the wholesome influence of a good woman. Contented husbands know about this.

The holy-card Mary of crowns and jewels and silks is hardly the gospel Mary. The regal icon pious generations have made of her was once a pregnant, unmarried teenager, a displaced alien, a distraught parent. Ahead of her time, she resembled an independent feminist. She argued with an angel, ignored the strict convention of confinement for pregnant women and took off to visit her cousin, Elizabeth. Her Magnificat is scarcely the language of a shy maiden. She knew her worth.

This feast day is not meant to extract more devotion to Mary. She is presented as a prototype of discipleship. Her vocation is ours. In her nine months, as she did the humdrum chores of a housewife, she was fashioning His (Christ's) body to give to the world. If where we are means that Jesus is there, too, then we are every bit as important as his mother. It need not come as any surprise that the same beyond-imagining glory awaits us all.

20th Sunday of Ordinary Time (the Assumption of Mary)
(Luke 1: 39-56)

Peter: Rock and Role

George Bernard Shaw is said to have quipped, "The Church was founded with a pun." If this is so, then Simon is once again playing straight man to the word play of Jesus. It's conceivable that the Lord was poking fun at the impulsive fisherman by calling him "Rock," much as when Joe Garagiola is called "Curly," or PeeWee Herman, "Tarzan." Simon Peter's inconstancy was no surprise to Jesus. In fact, he predicted it.

Nonetheless, Peter's insight into Jesus's identity wins him the position of key man in the new church. Peter was its first CEO. Jesus follows this up with the forecast that messiahship will involve more gore than glory, which upsets Peter. Could the novelty of power have gone to his head? He presumes to advise the Master on how to be the messiah. "This must never happen," he urges grandiosely and is soundly rebuked. One moment he is a confirmed senior partner, the next, a "Satan" for his folly. The "Rock" is now an obstacle to stumble over. Later, he panics enough to deny his messiah three times.

The Gospel appears to take pains to reveal the fallibility of Peter I. But his gaffs are niggling compared to the lapses of some of his successors. There were among them, saints and there were sinners. For many, papacy and pomposity were partners. One pontiff, Leo X, single-handedly fractured Christendom when he excommunicated Martin Luther in 1521. A grave mismanagement of authority! A Borgia became the notorious Alexander VI the year Columbus discovered America. At age seven, he was tonsured a cleric; at age eight, appointed abbot of a monastery;

at age thirteen, a cardinal. At age thirty-seven he was elected pope, four days before ordination. He sired six children. The world power the Church has become would have been inconceivable to first century Christians. It grew sturdy enough to protect Rome, and possibly civilization, from the marauding Huns, Attila (in A.D. 453) and Genseric (in 477). It has survived every empire, every dynasty, because its existence does not depend on the likes of a Peter, a Leo, an Alexander or a John Paul II.

The Church is believable not because of Apostolic succession, or Petrine primacy, or its majestic pageantry. It merits mankind's homage when it is Christ's presence in the world—as it happened to Peter one early morning on a Galilean beach. An unforeseen kindness came his way—all the more meaningful because unexpected. Wrapped up in his guilt-ridden self, humiliated for his cowardice, release came from the Master he had disowned.

It came with no reproach, no nagging, no "How could you?", but just the bottom-line challenge of any serious relationship: "Do you love me?" (The only healing prescription for the wound of spousal infidelity.) Peter's three affirmations expiated his three denials. He was never the same again. He could now dare to live and love once more. Jesus had given Peter back to himself—a self that now understood what authority was for—for empowering, not for retaliating or for controlling.

The Church is not a community of the saved, but of the saving. We are the presence of Christ in our world not because we are innocent or sinless, but because we are willing to forgive one another, to write off getting even, to grant another chance.

But belief in the all-loving, all- forgiving God is hard to reconcile with many believers' concept of Hell. The current occupant of Peter's chair addressed this issue as reported in the Catholic press (CNS) 6 August 1999, by Cincy Wooden:

Vatican City: *"Eternal damnation is never the initiative of God; it is the self-imposed punishment of those who choose to refuse God's love and mercy,"* Pope John Paul II said. *"Damnation or Hell is the 'tragic situation' of eternal separation from God,"* he said. *"Damnation cannot be attributed to an initiative of God because in His merciful love, He cannot want anything but the salvation of the beings He created.*

The Pope said people must be very careful in interpreting the biblical descriptions of Hell, which are symbolic and metaphorical. "The 'inextinguishable fire' indicates the complete frustration and vacuity of life without God," he said.

"Rather than being overly anxious and worried about the possibility of damnation," the Pope said, *"people should focus on trusting in Jesus, who defeated death and guaranteed access to Heaven."*

21st Sunday of Ordinary Time
(Matthew 16: 13-20)

Life: Lost and Found

Why this stinging chewing-out of Peter, minutes after Jesus's ringing endorsement of him? No one else in the Gospel gets called "Satan" . . . a scathing label for the first pope! Isn't it natural to talk someone you care about out of walking into a trap of perceived peril? When someone close to you is fearfully facing grave surgery and confides "I don't expect to come out of it . . ." Well, isn't it normal to counter with, "Don't talk like that!" and be fervently convinced that the worrier's apprehensions are somehow canceled by this urging? But in reality, "Don't be afraid; it's going to be all right," is not as reassuring as, "It pains me to hear your pain. You are worried. Can you tell me about it?"

A supportive person accepts being a victim with the victim. The shallow cheerleader is more the executioner, because to dismiss the wound is to discard the wounded. Pain denied is pain doubled; pain shared is pain halved.

Peter had become hooked on Jesus. He had never known such a straight-talking, remarkable friend. He hated to lose him. Just like ourselves, we who even get angry at the one we need for getting sick or for going on vacation. As with Peter, our reaction is natural, but hardly helpful, because the focus is on self, not on the other. Jesus needed support, not soft-soap.

He probably read the handwriting on the wall. His candid, common-sense critique on matters religious won him popularity with the people, but not with the religious leadership. He may have been worried and he needed to talk about it. With who better than his trusted companions?

111

Maybe he decided, "I can't turn a blind eye to the misery and hypocrisy all about me . . . I can't ignore self-righteous officials who elevate minuscule ritual over human compassion. I've got to speak out about what is important to me, whatever the consequences, no matter whose toes get stepped on . . . my days are numbered." Jesus did not let Peter get away with his hollow solace.

What follows is a healthy dialogue on useful and useless lifestyles. Cloistered lives can miss the adventure and growth that challenging ordeals often provide. However appealing, safety rarely tests one's mettle.

Terry Anderson reports his harrowing Iranian hostage travail in his autobiographical *Den of the Lions*. He tersely describes what happened to him from 1985 to 1992: the chaining; the miserable, meager food; the vermin; the blackness; the heat; the cold; the toothaches; bathroom only once a day; the longing and anguish over family. For almost seven years, he survived on prayer. From it all, he emerged a man transformed—less arrogant and self-centered, more patient, sensitive, and grateful. Terry had to lose his old life to find his new self.

Few in this century have made the non-violent impact of Martin Luther King. He chose to lose the comparative protection of a conventional ministry to find bravery not only for himself, but also for millions of his fellow African-Americans. Before he was killed, he confessed, "I am at the end of my powers; I have nothing left. I've come to the point that I can't face it alone." What he lost for himself, he found for others.

To get our attention, God often uses some rough tactics. God is a specialist at tough love. A gritty coach knows championships are not won softly. So, he demands 110 percent from those who wish to make his team. God seems to want us to be champions in the game of life. Champions at life are those who love it and love all living things.

Michel Quoist catches this struggle in his percipient little volume *Prayers*, page 116:

> *Lord, why did you tell me to love all men, my brothers? I have tried, but I have come back to you, frightened . . . Lord, I was so peaceful at home, I was so comfortably settled . . . You have forced me to open my door. As soon as I started to open the door, I saw them . . . they come bending under heavy loads—loads of injustice, of resentment and hate, of suffering and sin . . . ah, Lord! I have lost everything; I don't belong to myself any longer, there's no more room for me at home."*
>
> *"Don't worry," God says. "You have gained all. While men come in to you, I, your father, I, your God, slipped in among them.*

*22nd Sunday of Ordinary Time
(Matthew 16: 21-27)*

Resent or Relate: A Choice

The Labor Day weekend nationally signals farewell to summer and "hello" to BTSS—"Back to School Syndrome." It's grind time again and the Gospel seems to match the mood. It prescribes the earnest measures for the treatment of grief-givers. They include: 1) Private confrontations, 2) Witnesses *and* 3) The community. And if none of the above take, finally, 4) Excommunication. It all sounds more judicial than it does Jesus.

For Jesus to advise treating the intractable "as you would a gentile or a tax collector,"—that is, with traditional Jewish disdain—is simply not like him. He never discarded anyone. He made one tax collector his apostle. Gentiles were never excluded from his courtesy. The words the Matthew author ascribes to Jesus are the tested formula orthodox rabbis recommended for resolving disputes. Its most urgent part is the first step: direct, personal, private, polite confrontation.

This Gospel makes the point that life's principal priority is relationship. Human beings learn to be human by human relating. When relationships founder, grievances need airing. Facing an offender candidly, considerately, is one way to restore a damaged alliance. There are obstacles to this, however, like the fear of hurting feelings. But to opt for silence is to hurt the aggrieved even more, because indifference sets in. Then there's the evasive logic: "What good will it do? No one will change. Why bother? Who am I to find fault?" Passive-aggressives have a hard time with confronting: "Be nice. Don't make waves. Forget it." And the annoyance gets buried alive, only to haunt and decay the association. Some prefer alienation to reconciliation, if the relationship is not valued.

Healthy bonds flourish on frankness. With a trusted friend, disapproval is never terminal. But what if you can't wait to tell the "so-and-so" off? There is nothing like anger to feel justifiably self-righteous! Anger is a perfectly respectable emotion when it is named, claimed and aimed by its owner. Such as, "I am furious and I don't like it. I need to talk to you. Your friendship matters to me." This responsible self-revelation is not an accusation and thus generally avoids defensive recriminations.

Confronting means you give a darn. It is a bridge to unity and it rejects apartness. It believes the confrontee's strength can handle the negative feelings. The confronter refuses the brooding and the grudges that poison. He chooses to relate rather than resent. Innocence is not the monopoly of the child; it is the lifelong attribute of the honest person.

History is a resonant witness to the power of courageous confrontation. In this century alone, the intrepid non-violent protests of Martin Luther King sounded the nation's wake-up call to a sounder racial equality. The astonishing reversal of apartheid in South Africa can thank the brave, relentless, persistent dissent of Nelson Mandela. The ensuing Christ-like policy of nonretributive amnesty for perpetrators of anti-racial cruelty who publicly admit their crimes has brought about an unexpected, remarkable social tranquillity.

Getting along with one another includes not getting along. Reconciliation includes honest confrontation. There is no getting along with human beings unless there is truth between them. None of us are sole possessors of the truth; we are pursuers of it. The Gospel recommends that it can be more readily found when people communicate.

23rd Sunday of Ordinary Time
(Matthew 18: 15-20)

116

Forgive: Not So Fast!

John F. Kennedy is said to have said, "Forgive your enemies, but don't forget their names." I doubt if Jesus would object to this street-wise version of forgiveness that he features in today's Gospel. In that time, the Rabbis recommended a traditional limit of three pardons per wrong doer. Peter may have been pleased with himself for extending the clemency quota times two plus one, to equal seven. Jesus rejected any numerical limitation.

One problem about forgiveness is that it is seen as a duty. It is more a disposition. Martin Luther King claimed that "Forgiveness is not an occasional act, it is an attitude." Forgiveness, therefore, cannot be willed or commanded anymore than a good heart can be a subject of decree. It is a way of being human. All of Jesus's teaching, stories and encounters emphasize being human over being religious. The religious specialists killed him.

The child learns good-heartedness from good-hearted people, such as parents who are not possessive, nor permissive, nor excessively punitive, but open to the child: the child's thoughts, feelings and experiences. To a child thus blessed, benevolence comes as easily as breathing and playing. So, the forgiving heart is conscious more of having received forgiveness than giving it.

Since forgiveness cannot be successfully commanded or willed, the more one obliges self to forgive, the deeper goes the resentment. The will to forgive needs to be replaced by the willingness to be open. Open to all the hurt and hate and wish for vengeance that is seething inside. Forgiveness takes time. It should not be rushed.

A trigger-happy forgiver, who can't wait to be the grand appeaser, generally promotes more problems he or she is in such a hurry to pardon. Perennial martyrdom thrives on perpetual victimhood. The hurt and the hate are necessarily felt steps before sound healing has a chance.

A man lost his life savings, as well as his wife, to a trusted friend. Active in an Alcoholics Anonymous program, he bitterly complained, "I just can't forgive the S.O.B." His sponsor suggested, "If you can't forgive him, pray for the S.O.B." He gave it a go . . . "I gave up trying to forgive and prayed for him, 'Lord, give him what he deserves, but what You think, not what I think.' One day the resentment disappeared. It no longer bothered me. I gave up controlling and let God handle it."

All good prayer involves surrender of control. It helped the aggrieved out of the stagnant mire of self-pity. Letting go of the past freed him for a fresher future. He felt more connected to the human race. Prayer reduced the toxic resentment that fosters a self-image of being trapped in the clutches of the offender. The blame-game snaps the trap even tighter, because it blinds the offendee from exploring his or her part in the offense. Jesse Jackson caught this insight: "When you pray for your enemy, look inside yourself and examine what you may have done to make him your enemy."

Healthy forgiving is not forgetting. Nothing that hurts should be ignored. There are things to be learned from injury. Nor is forgiving excusing. People need to be accountable for their choices and for the consequences that result. When Pope John Paul II visited the prison to forgive his would-be assassin, the Pontiff did not commute the prisoner's sentence. Crime and sin differ. The former is punishable, the latter forgivable.

The forgiving heart finds the open hand more comfortable than the clenched fist. It tires of holding the offender hostage. To forgive is a lightsome, liberating chore. Years after Auschwitz, a survivor happened to meet a fellow survivor:

"Have you forgotten the Nazis?"
"Yes."
"I haven't. I'm consumed with hatred for them."
"They still have you in prison."

Christendom this week joins with their Jewish brothers and sisters as they reverence their High Holy Days. A Rabbi, having reviewed his sins for the past year and while praying for forgiveness, addressed the Almighty, "But You, God, did some mean things to me as well. I'll make a deal–I'll forgive You if You forgive me."

Was it Robert Frost who bravely cited this familiarity with the Deity? (If memory serves): "Dear God, forgive the many little tricks I've played on Thee, and I'll forgive the great big one You played on me."

24th Sunday of Ordinary Time
(Matthew 18: 21-35)

119

Labor versus Management

The outrageous parable in this Gospel features an obviously unfair labor practice. Jesus is suggesting that God's time clock does not record overtime, part time or comp time. Full time workers or single hour stragglers, they all get the same wage. What labor union would tolerate this or hire Jesus as a Labor/Management negotiator? Would the gospel estate owner find anyone to work for him the next day given his unorthodox employment policy? Probably the one-hour workers would be inclined to show up. I doubt if the dawn-to-dusk toilers would.

What is Jesus trying to say in this astonishing story? Upsetting the labor market was no doubt not his intent as much as it was to upset his hearers' idea of God. He joins the prophet Isaiah in this day's first reading (Isaiah 55: 8): "For My thoughts are not your thoughts, nor are your ways My ways, says the Lord." God's thinking is simply upside-down from ours.

This should be no surprise to God or to us. We are limited; God is not. God is sufficient unto Himself; we have unending needs. That is why God is better at unconditional loving than we are.

So, this story is not about a wage dispute. It is a mind-bending illustration revealing the wide heart of God for eleventh-hour beneficiaries of the Good News. The canonization of the thief, Dismas, crucified at his right, from the lips of the Savior himself, is vivid proof that heaven can be stolen in the last minute: "This day you will be with Me in paradise," (Luke 23: 43). Deathbed conversions find unexpected equality with long lifetimes of faith. Unfair? How fair is the worry of being unemployed all day? How fair is a living wage for a needing family compared to the meager pittance for only one hour's labor?

The parable affirms again that elitism has no place in God's kingdom. The moral majority can expect no VIP recognition. The failed and the faithful are equally welcome. The contemporary French dramatist Jean Anouilh highlights this theme in a marvelous one-act play about the Last Judgement—I paraphrase the text: The multitudes of mankind are buzzing outside the pearly gates: "Who's in? Who's out?" A rumor spreads: "Everyone is getting in." The righteous protest: "Not fair! Jeffrey Dahmer gets free admission with Mother Teresa. Shameful!" Thus, the "first" become "last."

God apparently refuses to limit His prodigal mercy to our penny-pinching bookkeeping. He must know that much of human life is the mysterious matter of getting "the breaks." Some get more than others. The splendid Gallic insight says it all: *tout comprendre, tout pardonner,* meaning "To understand all is to forgive all." Saints may have enjoyed "breaks" sinners never had. The word "grace" comes to mind. Ultimately, the score will even out.

It's a sad reality, but humans tend to see each other as competitors. Someone else's success is seen as another's loss. God, instead, sees creatures as His cooperators—partners in the creation project. Wise parents know it takes time for the child to learn about life. They watch and wait. The parable confirms God's patience with this human process. The words of the vine grower are more a promise than a reproof.

Petty minds have trouble accepting the excesses of the Creator's affection for His creatures, saints and sinners alike. In our myopic view, we believe that reward and punishment is the only way to run the world. The Good News stresses that human beings are doomed to the grace of God. There is no exit from it unless one insists, and freely rejects it.

So, thank God for not being able to figure God out! Thank God for God's blessed unfairness! We can look forward not to God's judgment, but to His, "Hello, come on in to my big surprise party!"

25th Sunday of Ordinary Time
(Matthew 20: 16)

Promises, Promises

Parents may readily identify with this parable about the yea and nay brothers. The yea-sayer gave lip service, but did not deliver. The nay-sayer just gave lip, at least for openers, but then reflects and corrects. A child's flat-out "No" to a parent's behest is rankling, to say the least, but rewarding when the defiance is deplored and the job gets done. Exasperating, however, is the, "Yes, certainly, right away, sir" ploy with no intention to execute. The spouse who hears, "Yes, dear, whatever you say," knows the frustration of not being taken seriously.

The *yes-sir* son is operative in the passive-aggressive personality. This type avoids show-downs for fear of losing. Charm, therefore, is cultivated. Diplomacy is esteemed over directness. Sarcasm may be a mild concession to hidden interior irritation, and the witty may even exploit humor as a concealed weapon. But, by all means, be polite! . . . The second son was this. He called his father "sir" and probably congratulated himself for successfully humoring the old gent.

Frankness characterizes the *no* son. He can be arrogant and insensitive, but having thought it over, he reverses his decision. Abrasive behavior should warrant a return to the scene of the crime for a playback with the offended party. Artless straight talk that airs honest feelings can make even the falling-out an occasion for closer bonding.

The *no-sir* son's refusal may be seen as a callous obsession with his own selfish needs. The "No" to his father could well be a "Yes" to himself—a rite of passage from puerile obeisance to developing self-autonomy. In fact, this respect he gives himself is eventually projected beyond himself. Acknowledging his need enhances awareness of the other's need. He had to rebel openly before obeying freely. The Gospel story ratifies his power struggle with authority in order to gain inner direction.

His brother takes a less strenuous path . . . namely to agree outwardly, play the game, and talk the talk. Walking the walk is not for sophisticates. He does not seem spiteful, just spineless; not malicious, but shallow . . . both boys have their respective ways, at different times, in every human life story. It should come as no surprise that benevolence depends upon enlightened self-interest.

The parable suggests again that the Good Shepherd does not prefer mindless sheep to comprise his flock. He obviously accepts their right to get lost and rejoices when they are recovered. He seems quite at home with conflict. He differed openly with the swaggering, presumptuous Simon Peter. He was attentive to non-conformist doubting Thomas and withstood narrow-minded religious officials to their faces. What seemed a tragic ending on the cross became the beginning of a new, universal, vitalizing spirituality.

Personal autonomy and external authority are locked in uneasy tension within the human psyche. There is no growth without this struggle. May this advice be useful: think for yourself but not by yourself. Consult! Trust the lights that flicker in the mind, as well as the mistakes that seem inevitable. A reprise of Chesterton: "If anything is worth doing at all, it's worth doing badly."

26th Sunday of Ordinary Time
(Matthew 21: 28-32)

Grapes of Wroth

"Bloody murder" shrieks this parable as the tenant farmers massacre the rent collectors. The Scriptures reek of violence because they reflect human perversion. One scholar remarked that the Bible is more the word of God about man than about God. Human beings invariably tend to annihilate the enemy, even more so than their animal kin. While big beasts devour lesser ones and big fish swallow little fish, full bellies seek quiescence. Not so the human lust for blood. When aroused, this restless inhumane distortion is not easily sated.

Reports of mass murders are no biblical anomaly. In Exodus 32: 28, Moses has three thousand Israelites slaughtered for worshipping the golden calf. In Numbers 25, twenty-four thousand more are slain for worshipping Baal. The prophet Elijah slits the throats of 450 vanquished Baal priests (1 Kings 18: 40). For centuries this day's parable has justified the cruel Christian persecution of Jews. In the first Crusade, crusaders en route to rescue Jerusalem from the grip of the "infidels" detoured to butcher ten thousand Jews in France and Germany. All with the blessing of Pope Urban II (1086).

Why this human horror? What makes educated, civilized people spend big bucks to support a brutal prizefight? Why does violence fascinate us? Can it be because we are still in process—an unfinished product? Is the mark of murderer Cain a curse on our species? Will we ever emerge from the cave?

Behavioral experts explain the impulse to violence as a reaction to weakness. Brutality feels stronger than impotence. The cornered mouse takes on the cat. So beware of contending with an enemy that has nothing to lose. Violent people are unhappy people. Depression and insecurity make one anxious. Anxiety creates hostility. Anger is the other face of fear.

Why do ultra-conservatives irritate me? Probably because of the unrecognized structure-hungry part of me that I roundly resent. Unconsciously, I fear it taking over again. So, while this repudiated need for repressive governance is not reconciled in me, I deplore people who are hooked on it. If I do not make peace with the unseen enemy in me, I fight the one I see in you.

The bloody excesses of the Bible and the cruel burnings, tortures and imprisonment of dissenters in Church history are the mark of an insecure authority that does not trust itself, but only its power to control. Thank God the Church has outgrown this ferocity and sees itself more the collaborator in the human enterprise than its enforcing legislator. The flaming wroth of an outraged God of the Old Testament can now be understood as the extravagant apocalyptic metaphor of a God that gives a darn about what human beings do.

Thank God mankind is learning to face an enemy with imagination: to walk in its shoes, to hear an opposite viewpoint with courtesy. Thank God we can admit that what we loathe in others is what we loathe in ourselves. This disconcerting fact of life needs to be looked at squarely, but ever so gently. Better sour grapes than grapes of wroth.

27th Sunday of Ordinary Time
(Matthew 21: 33-43)

A Matter of Manners

For me as a child in the 1920s, going to church was not much fun. Samuel Longhorne Clemens (1835-1910), familiarly, Mark Twain, felt similarly. In his own words, "People cannot stand much church. They draw the line at Sunday, once a week and they do not look forward to it. But consider what heaven holds: a church that lasts forever. And they long for it, and they think they are going to be happy and enjoy it."

An endless choir meeting in a drafty cathedral was not Jesus's idea of heaven. Nor was it that of the prophet Isaiah in this day's first reading (Isaiah 25: 6-10). Both saw God's Kingdom as a sumptuous party to which all mankind is invited. Most of us are party animals. Any excuse will do to celebrate: painting the house, burning the mortgage, finding a job, retiring from one, a bon voyage or a homecoming. Frolicking with friends is a singular delight of life. Why not eternal life?

Nevertheless, the Gospel parable strikes a strange note to the modern ear. How can the invited homeless, the habitués of alleys and by-ways, be expected to be in black tie for the big bash? It was an Eastern custom of that time for royalty and the rich to provide appropriate attire for guests to harmonize with the decor of the banquet chamber. To accept the invitation and reject the dress code was to insult the host.

The "guest without the wedding garment" chose to be an outsider, which is where he wound up. Maybe he wanted to stand out, to be noticed for his non-conformity, but it was insensitive to those about him. It's like wearing a

T-shirt at a formal nuptial. He symbolizes anomie, which the dictionary defines as "A collapse of social structure governing a given society: a state of alienation; personal disorganization resulting in anti-social behavior; lawlessness." Without standards, society is doomed to chaos.

It is natural to resist cookie-cutter uniformity. Non-conformists come in two sizes: free souls and cranks. The free souls are sensitive to people. Being inner-directed makes them more accommodating, adjusting and cooperative; more flexibly easy. The cranks, who think their non-compliance represents independence, are less secure and are therefore defensive, indifferent to feelings, rigid, stubborn and looking for a fight.

Like the street people in the parable, who were unexpectedly invited to the fancy banquet, we too, were invited to the banquet of life without our choice. But once in it, the Gospel suggests standards to help us have a good time, just as there are directives for the smooth functioning of our automobiles. The resistant rugged individualist can ignore these and put maple syrup in the gas tank.

Our natures function best in a community where politeness is prized and practiced. But none of us are born with consideration for others. We have to be taught. Infantile narcissism needs to be outgrown if the mature adult is to experience the rich gratification of caring for and about human beings. The English author Hilaire Belloc (1870-1953) credits this quality: "Of courtesy it is much less, than courage of heart or holiness, but in my walks, it seems to me, the grace of God is courtesy."

28th Sunday of Ordinary Time
(Matthew 22: 1-14)

Caesar Si, God Si

"Read my lips—no taxes to Caesar." Had Jesus said that, he would have fallen into the same trap former president George Bush did. This day's Gospel sounds something like those campaign debates, though less tiresome. As the debaters tried to entrap each other in words, so did his antagonists try to stick it to Jesus.

The Gospel is not about taxes; it's about two distinct jurisdictions. They often have their differences. Caesar represents the state and the Church represents God. Church and state quarrel with one another just as husband and wife do. But a committed marriage thrives on differences when they are squarely dealt with—not ignored, denied or penalized . . . I rarely learn much from one who agrees with me.

God and Caesar clash on many issues like abortion, immigration, armament, pacifists and capital punishment, to name a few. Both need to speak their minds freely even when accord is never achieved. Jesus does not appear to have a dispute with Caesar. His response implies that governance has its own rights. But Tiberias, the Roman emperor in the Lord's time, solved the church/state wrangle by making himself both; Caesar as well as God. Thus making atheists, according to Roman law, out of worshippers of any other than Caesar. As were accused the early Christians who refused to incense Caesar's image.

So, here's the problem; namely, when the state assumes a divine claim, it rejects any accountability to a higher court. Governments make this spurious claim when they condemn their dissenters. France, for instance, faced this dilemma during the Nazi occupation. What was a citizen to do: collaborate, resist or compromise? The French reaction included all three options, with scant guidance from the advice, "Render to Caesar what is Caesar's and to God what is God's." Jesus's brilliant reply was not specific about what was Caesar's and what was God's. He let his hearers work out their priorities. Some French succumbed to Caesar, some bravely withstood him; some just dragged their feet. Cardinal Faulhaber of Munich wore a Star of David on his cassock publicly to protest Hitler's inhumanity to the Jews.

There are ways to defy tyranny. Clearly, the most humane way is non-violently. Thousands marched peaceably in Selma in 1965 to protest racial segregation. Things got turned around after that. Now hotheads bomb abortion clinics and compound the problem, as do our current profusion of international terrorists, who defy not only Caesar, but also God Almighty!

Violence in behalf of the noblest cause can never resemble the cool, sensible balance recommended by Jesus. All human beings are God's, including misguided Caesars. The oppressed need protectors; the oppressors need protesters—like the martyred Archbishop Romero of El Salvadore. Caesar deserves his people's "Si" only when he affirms their "No."

29th Sunday of Ordinary Time
(Matthew 22: 15-21)

All You Need Is . . .

Is there a more used, abused and misused four-letter word in the English language than "love?" People love their cat, their car and their computer. At least these can be seen to be enjoyed. But how does one love the invisible, the indefinable, a mystery? Yet the primary commandment mandates exactly this: to love God with everything you've got—heart, mind and soul.

Moses thought 613 commandments were necessary for the Israelites: 365 negative, 248 positive. And these were expected to be committed to memory. David reduced these imperatives to eleven, Isaiah to six, Micah to three. Jesus whittled the lot to one Great Commandment: a three-pronged precept—love God, neighbor and self. Thus giving to human creatures the importance of the very Creator. Every person becomes God in disguise.

Though human beings have an instinct for it, love needs to be learned. We are born narcissistic, the center of the universe, insisting on our priorities over everyone else's needs. Outgrowing this infantilism is life's relentless objective. That is why "love" is a commandment; it's good for us. And we are not that good at it until we get the knack of it . . . like practicing the piano, or dutiful exercise and a healthy diet. It takes deliberate choice and time and heart. In Mitch Albom's bestseller, *Tuesdays With Morrie,* Morrie seems to have the hang of it: "Love is when you are as concerned about someone else's situation as you are about your own."

Some may find loving God, who is good, easier than loving people, who are not so good. But the Great Commandment allows no exceptions—even enemies are included. Which boils down to the reality that we love God only as much as we love our worst enemy. Does that mean loving Adolph Hitler, Charles Manson, Jeffrey Dahmer, the embezzler or your life's savings, or the molester of your child? Must we love all the boors, bullies, bounders and battle-axes who barge, batter and blunder into our lives? That's the mandate! But it does not command that we like them.

The Gospel uses a Greek word for this love—agape. It means the unselfish regard for another. It implies respect, benevolence, wishing the other the good it needs rather than merits. The doctrine of Redemption expresses this quality of love. We are redeemed not because we deserve it, but because we need it. It is mostly like the way we want to be loved: not for our looks, brains, money or talent, but for ourselves, as we are, warts and all.

We generally learn how to care when we are cared for. Deprived of this necessary nurturance, an emotional cripple may emerge. This could be the explanation for the inhumane deviates of human history. The Great Commandment, therefore, is no inter-office memo prescribing preferred behavior. It directly identifies what really connects us to one another. It is a genuine kick to listen to the uniqueness of the one with whom we are speaking: to allow that one to be the person God made—imperfect, unfinished, in process. This lump of protoplasm that all of us are is an eternal substance, redeemed and desired by God.

Caring about human beings is not a chore or a challenge, it's our human fulfillment—the actualization of our species. This love does not seek to be loved; it rejoices when it has the chance to love. Here is a true love story, as told by Dr. Robert Tuttle, Jr.:

He is sitting at his desk in his second grade classroom. Suddenly, he is aware of a puddle between his feet and the front of his pants are wet. He cannot imagine how this happened. The poor little guy is so embarrassed he wants to die. It never happened before; he doesn't know how it happened. When the guys find out, he'll never hear the end of it; the girls in the class will never speak to him again.

"Please, dear God," he prays, "I'm in big trouble, I need help now!"

He looks up from his prayer and a classmate named Susie is carrying a goldfish bowl filled with water. Suddenly she loses her grip of the bowl and dumps the water right into the boy's lap. The boy pretends to be angry, but he is praying, "Thank you, Jesus! Thank you, Jesus!" Now, instead of being the object of ridicule, the boy is the recipient of sympathy. The teacher rushes him downstairs and gives him gym shorts to put on while his pants dry out. All the children are on their hands and knees cleaning up the mess.

But now Susie becomes the center of scorn. She tries to help, but they tell her to get away. "You klutz! What a dumb thing to do!" So it goes for the rest of the day. He is surrounded by sympathy while poor Susie is shunned.

After school the two are waiting for the bus. Susie is standing off by herself. He goes up to her and whispers, "You did that on purpose, didn't you?" Susie whispers back, "I wet my pants once, too."

30th Sunday of Ordinary Time
(Matthew 22: 34-40)

Human/Holy

This has to be a disconcerting Gospel to us titled clergy: your Holiness, your Eminence, your Excellency and your Reverence! The Church excuses itself for exploiting these pretentious designations by explaining that it is honoring the office, the position, more than the person occupying it. Jesus's criticism was directed toward the ostentation that status could beget, rather than its nomenclature. After all, Jesus was called "Rabbi," "Master," "Lord," and even added that it was befitting (John 13: 13). Titles are helpful when they define an occupational specialty, like Officer, Doctor and Your Honor. Jesus admonishes against pretensions lest authority misuse its rank in behalf of pushy, pompous self-seeking.

There are few addictions more intoxicating than power. Pursuers of it often mask an inner insecurity that they imagine a top job will miraculously dispel. Tyrants personify this fantasy and stop at nothing in order to maintain their illusion of superiority; such ambition can be an occupational hazard for the clergy. The allure of prestige and preferential privilege can easily obscure the eagerness to minister. That is why Jesus insists that the key word for religious leadership is service. That is why he washed his disciples' feet. "The greatest among you must be your servant."

What precisely is service to the faithful? Is it teaching church doctrine, administering sacraments, or presiding at liturgy? The lights went on for me as a military chaplain. The men needed more than all the above. Theology and formal ritual were not enough to help them experience the presence of God in their bewildering chaos. They wanted a chaplain who could bring the touch of God into their foxholes. They wanted a priest who could feel the fear they feared and could talk about it. They wanted a human being that longed for the safety they longed for, the homes they longed for, and that could link it all to the Gospel. They needed a spiritual guide through their doubts without reproach, without censure. They could relate to a Padre as vulnerable as they were, but whose humanity left them with a hint of the God they tried to pray to. Going public with gut feelings, my searching mind and insights that mattered to me, helped make my message more personal and believable.

True, the troops awarded me no black belt for sanctity or bravery; I owned neither, but one endorsement I dearly valued above all others, namely, authenticity. They rated me "real" . . . to be real meant being down to earth. Being down to earth meant being in touch with me—another way of being in touch with them. Preaching to them, I spoke mainly to me. They listened and heard what seemed custom-built words for them. We shared the same world, the same humanity and the same hunger for meaning.

When Jesus said, "You have but one teacher . . . one Father in heaven . . . one Master," it is a way of saying that allegiance was owed no authority other than one's honest conscience. So, I gave up trying to be a saint: being human was much harder. I have yet to find a holier enterprise than being what God made me–human!

31st Sunday of Ordinary Time
(Matthew 25: 1-12)

What Kind of Fool Am I?

"At least this time the groom was late," whispered the wife to her husband, after hearing the Gospel about the wise and foolish bridesmaids. Wedding celebrations can be elaborate, extravagant affairs in most cultures, not to mention exhausting to the gladsome bride and groom. The honeymoon must indeed be a welcome recess from the hearty partying. But remote honeymoons were not the norm in Jesus's day. The couple stayed at home—generally a parent's—and were royally feted for a solid week by rollicking well-wishers. The bride and groom were even addressed as "Prince" and "Princess" and probably had the time of their lives, as did the celebrants. It was a social event not to be missed.

To be selected a bridesmaid was a singular honor for a young girl. Lighted lamps were a legal ordinance for all wayfarers in the dark of night and a positive must for those chosen to gaily escort the groom to his bride. But, boys will be boys, and the bachelor party may have gone longer than expected. The groom, thus delayed, suddenly surprised the napping maidens and their burned out lamps. Five were prepared for this and five were not. The parable describes the first as sensible and the others as airheads.

Why so? Maybe the Gospel is highlighting its endorsement of tough love. The foolish maidens seemed to be the mañana types. They were improvident and careless. The wise maidens were not about to reward this by bailing them out with their own extra resources.

Another possible point . . . the oil may be seen symbolically as the energy and enthusiasm that lights our spirits. This cannot be transferred. It can be observed and imitated, but it is the exclusive property of the individual. Each must generate one's own individuality.

Both wise and foolish most of us are, at one time or another. One moment I can be sage, and the next an idiot. I can read Homer in the original, but can make no sense of my bank statement. An English poet, Edward Young (1683-1765) had this observation in his meditative "Night Thoughts":

> *At thirty a man suspects himself a fool;*
> *Knows it at forty and reforms his plan;*
> *At fifty chides his infamous delay,*
> *Pushes his prudent purpose to resolve;*
> *In all the magnanimity of thought*
> *Resolves and re-resolves,*
> *Then dies the same.*

I am foolish . . .

- When I think being busy is being useful.
- When I think thinking is more important than feeling and deny each equal time.
- When I believe I learn more from books than from people—living books.
- When I believe I understand whatever I can define, label or even explain.
- When I do not plan and provide quality time in each day to pray and to play.
- When I search for a guru instead of consulting my experience.
- When I give away my authority to anyone who can hire or fire me or who is smarter.

- When I believe the glib speaker because he or she is saying what I want to hear—like smooth-talking political candidates.
- When I am solemn and think I am serious; when I am stubborn and think I am resolute.
- When I am afraid to give up something to find out if I really need it.
- When I cop out to shyness because of your assertiveness.
- When I seek approval from you that I deny myself.
- When I think my high ideals make me an ideal person;   when I reach for perfection without recognizing and accepting my imperfections.
- When I forget that evil cannot be destroyed, only transformed; when I fail to use my brokenness in my ministry.
- When I condemn myself for being wrong, weak, scared, angry and human.
- When I lose my taste for surprise and do not laugh at myself uproariously at least once a day.

I am wise when I am good to my fool. Dr. Theodore Rubin put it this way in his *Thoughts From a Psychoanalyst's Notebook:*

> *I must learn to love the fool in me—the one who feels too much, who talks too much, takes too many chances, wins sometimes and loses often, lacks self control, loves and hates, hurts and gets hurt, promises and breaks promises, laughs and cries. It alone protects me against the utterly self-controlled masterful tyrant whom I also harbor*

*and who would rob me of humanity, aliveness,
humility and dignity but for my fool.*

*32nd Sunday of Ordinary Time
(Matthew 26: 1-13)*

The Whine of Life

The parable of the "Talents" and the three recipients sounds like a Wells Fargo commercial. For cautious, non-entrepreneurial, conscientious, fiscal ultra-conservatives, the bank is the place . . . The story is talking big money, however. *Talanton* is a Greek work for an enormous monetary unit of silver, at least the equivalent of a lifetime's earnings. The tale has a distinct Dow Jones flavor to it and Jesus does not use it for a lesson in Economics 101—he is not talking about high finance; he is talking about two winners and a wimp.

The winners gambled (invested sounds less pejorative) with their boss's money and lucked out. The wimp played it safe and got clobbered. What is Jesus saying in this story? Could he be endorsing the lottery, Vegas high rollers, and penny-ante poker? Or is he saying something about this gamble called life?

Some of us find gambling exciting. It's a kick to win. But this is impossible without the risk of losing . . . we win some; we lose some—that's life! Obviously, the parable is not putting down winning in the stock market, it is emphasizing what it takes to play the chancy hand life deals us.

A courageous example of the winning spirit is the contemporary British physics genius, Dr. Stephen Hawking. He is totally paralyzed from head to toe. His voice is barely audible. Nothing of his body works except his mind. Stricken with a rare motor neuron disease while studying for his doctorate at Oxford University, he was overwhelmed but never defeated. He continues to make enormous scientific contributions and writes books.

The parable could also be aimed at smug true believers that wrap themselves in the security blanket of conventional religion and avoid the launching pad of dynamic spirituality. Perceptive Pope John XXIII addressed misguided religious complacence: "We are not on earth to guard a museum, but to cultivate a flourishing garden of life." This takes live wires—industrious, resourceful, inventive initiators not afraid of change and willing to take a chance on doing something for the first time. Mr. One Talent was light on these enterprising attributes and was probably surprised to discover that playing it safe was not the way to make up for these deficiencies. It was easier to whimper to his employer, "I knew you were a hard man." His whine was right about that.

Fear can make wimps of us all, whenever we allow inertia priority over action, timidity over temerity. Here's my personal chagrin list . . .

I am a wimp:
- Whenever I cop out.
- When I settle for peace at any price and do not stand up to your put-down.
- When I do not confront because I expect to lose.
- When I take the popular side, the politically correct side, though I believe it's the wrong side.
- When I hint at what I want and do not ask for it up front.
- When I soft-soap, flatter you, so you will like me.
- When I blame you for my goof.
- When I prefer to be confused rather than make a hard choice.
- When I am defensive instead of decisive.

- When I choose to be a criticizing spectator rather than a participating player in the game of life just because life is unfair.
- When I mistake solemn for serious.
- When I cover my embarrassment with a nervous laugh, or force a guffaw at the boss's joke that isn't funny.
- When I say yes and mean no, or say no when I mean yes.
- When I condescend, patronize or bully you; when I allow you to condescend, patronize or bully me.
- When I bury feelings of emptiness, helplessness and annoyance to make you think I am in control.
- When I make excuses instead of efforts.

33rd Sunday of Ordinary Time
(Matthew 25: 14-30)

Your Majesties!

Pontius Pilate thought it a good joke on the condemned Jews to make a condemned criminal their king. Maybe even Jesus could appreciate the joke, since he never took kingship that seriously, at least not for himself. I savor the fancy of the puzzled governor asking, "Are you a king?" and the possible needling reply of Jesus, "Isn't everybody!" At least, this is the message of his gospel—the regal significance of all human beings.

But then crucifixion was no laughing matter. Even the families of the crucified were in disgrace. Victims of this hideous execution were regarded by pious Jews as accursed by God. Jesus experienced this malediction when he lamented abandonment by his Father . . . and so he died, an outlaw, a political prank, on an upright deathbed—a total failure. So be it, he resolved. The matter was out of his hands. He left it all in his Father's. And from this frightful catastrophe emerged an unforeseen, unimagined royalty that extended to the most rejected, the weakest, and the neediest of human beings.

From his cross, Jesus showed the world what aristocracy meant—not the lineage by blood or succession or usurpation, but the nobility of a compassionate heart. Kingliness is readily identified as munificent benefactors to the needy, but for Jesus, especially the needy are given the importance and dignity of his own royal self. And who of us have not needed a square meal, a refreshing drink, a comforting hand when sick, or a kind courtesy when imprisoned in an addiction? This is honor bestowed on us royals by other nobilities. We take our turns at giving and taking, but all of us, givers and takers, share equal sovereignty with him. Which makes any deliberate harm to another human being a sacrilege, any killing a deicide. People are Christ incognito.

Good Fridays continue to proliferate on our comely planet. Hundreds of skulls protest the killing fields of Cambodia. Entire tribes of Native Americans have disappeared in the wake of the United States' heartless march to its manifest destiny.

To this bleak history, the relentless validation persists: "As often as you have done this to the least of my brothers and sisters, you have done it to me."

The cross has ever been a symbol of contradiction. Vertical and horizontal meet at the center where good and evil collide and where evil is transformed—just as black Friday turned into luminous Easter Sunday. Our human natures naturally shrink from our crosses—custom-built to suit our dimensions. But there is no escaping them and to embrace them takes bravery beyond most of us.

Somehow they are endured. We discover a surprising, reassuring stamina in our frail selves—an unexpected sense of distinction—even ennoblement. We made it! Outlaw King Jesus showed us how. So, when I read the harsh report of his coming again in frightening majesty to judge the world, I cannot get myself to interpret this to mean that Jesus is coming at us or for us like a pursuing sheriff. He is coming *to* us. I hear his words to be not a scolding, but an enthronement, "The least of you is me!"

What if we really believed this, your majesties!

Christ the King
(Matthew 25: 31-46)

Index A
LITURGICAL CALENDAR
(Cycle A)

Index B
SCRIPTURAL REFERENCES
(Cycle A)

The Now Testament

Cycle B

Introduction

Testament means "agreement." It could be extended to mean "love letter." The Old Testament is the recorded understanding between Yahweh and the Hebrews after their Egypt exodus.

The New Testament is an updated accord with the Father through His extraordinary representative, Jesus of Nazareth, who emphasized divine love and forgiveness for the entire world—God's love letter.

Now is another word for "eternal." Now is never over. Now is a perpetual present. *The Now Testament* ventures into its second volume of a trilogy of Sunday Gospel readings for liturgical cycle B. Love, old or new, is forever fresh!

Homecoming

It is New Year's Day for the Church—the first Sunday of Advent—as the twentieth century slips farther and farther away. For some, the recent approach of Y2K spelled ominous foreboding. Nor does the gospel today mitigate that tension. . . . "Be watchful! Be alert! . . . You do not know when the time will come! . . . You do not know when the Lord of the house is coming."

Why must this *coming* be seen as a menacing ambush—a snare to the nonvigilant? History records its share of religious vigilantes. St. Paul, for a spell, preached the Lord's Second Coming to be in his own lifetime. Centuries later, a Baptist, Benjamin Leach, predicted the year to be 1689. Methodism's founder, Charles Wesley, pronounced the date to be 1794. An American, William Miller, gathered a flock who sold their possessions, moved to upstate New York and awaited the grand finale in 1846. The passing of the second millennium will no doubt breed its own doomsayers.

The traditional notion of Judgment Day has all the spooky appeal of Poe's "Murders in the Rue Morgue." This hardly jibes with the image of the good Shepherd tenderly rescuing the lost sheep. So, what are we to watch for . . . a hanging judge or a deliverer? The scripture features both—take your pick!

The spirit of the season offers ample opportunity in favor of the latter. Like no other month in the year, December brims with brilliance, color and caroling. The malls are jammed, sales soar, shoppers scurry. It's that magic time again when the focus is on others . . . what gift to get for the folks you care about; what Christmas card says the greeting you feel; what surprise will delight your significant other? People seem more willing to be pried loose from their conventional shyness and enjoy being friendly, convivial, jolly. They like being good-natured. It's liberating!

Then there's the other side to the festival. The perennial complaint that the Yule fuels consumerism; that wide-hearted emotions are outrageously exploited in the holiday hype. The Puritans thought the festal merrymaking a bit much and outlawed Christmas.

Perhaps holly time could be made holy time by preparing a gift list for the birthday child. Nothing extravagant— just things one doesn't need, like temper tantrums, or insisting on having one's own way, or snacking when not even hungry, or working off those extra pounds, or walking those five blocks instead of driving. It's a cozy time—the days shorten and darken—good sleeping weather! But the Advent wake-up call sounds! He has come and we are still becoming.

Virtue cannot be imposed either by authority or by threat. According to Thomas Aquinas, virtue is a habit achieved by repetition. So, Advent can be seen rather as a bidding to be our least constricted selves—good-hearted, congenial, easygoing. Jesus must have been comfortable even in a stable with the warmth of his mother. Maybe even our manger hearts can be another homecoming for him.

1st Sunday of Advent
(Mark 13: 33-37)

Mark Time?

Of the four Gospels, Mark's is regarded as the shortest, the oldest, the most vigorous and picturesque. He was the son of a well-to-do Jerusalem Jewess whose home was a center for the gathering of Jesus believers (Acts 12:12). His cousin was Barnabas and both of them accompanied Paul on his first missionary journey. For some reason, halfway into the tour, Mark returned home. There may have been a falling out over this, since Barnabas also later quit Paul. All were eventually reconciled. Mark's biography of Jesus reflects, therefore, the insights of Paul and the eyewitness highlights of Peter. The essence of his Gospel is condensed in a single sentence . . . the first one.

According to *The Way,* the Tyndale House version of the Bible: "Here begins the wonderful story of Jesus, the Messiah, the Son of God."

Of course Christ was not Jesus' surname. It is a title of Greek origin which meant "anointed." The Hebrew word for anointed is *messiah.* Special people were anointed, who had a special mission, like kings and prophets. Cyrus, the pagan Persian emperor (529 B.C.E.) was given that designation by the grateful Israelites he had liberated. Especially favored intimates of the Almighty were labeled kin to the Almighty. The prophet Hosea referred to his own people as "sons and children of God" (Hos. 1:10).

The Bible thus ascribes "Messiah" and "Son of God" to more than just Jesus. It is the advance man, John, who clearly proclaims the singular transcendence of Jesus, "I have baptized you with water, but he will baptize you with the Holy Spirit."

What can this mean if not that the baptism of Jesus is more than a religious ritual? It has to mean an inner experience, a heightened awareness of the sacredness of reality: a consecration of the common stuff of life, like making a living, raising a family, sensitivity to humanity. Baptism by the Holy Spirit can mean only one thing: the grace to commit to love. What could more infallibly reflect the presence of the Spirit of God than a compassionate human heart?

The Holy Spirit is the *Good News,* and the core of this message is the practice to be kind rather than right. It consistently communicates that connectedness is the essential component of the human condition. Mankind is a network—a complicated original—that does not survive in isolation. Love is a corporate enterprise and needs to be completely inclusive. The baptism of Jesus invites us beyond the desert of separateness into a fresh field of energy—interrelatedness. Why is human connectedness so important? Because humanity is connected to divinity. Human beings all tread the same earth, warm by the same sun, and breathe the same oxygen as Jesus did. To comfort the discomfited is to be his heart and his hands. Liturgically, Mark will march us into the new millennium. Each week in the final year of the twentieth century he will track the steps of that incomparable life that is a blueprint for our own. Time to be on your Mark!

2nd Sunday of Advent
(Mark 1: 1-18)

What's So Funny?

Life is a mixed bag of fortune cookies. Paul recommends that we lighten up about it. At least life turned around for him on that road to Damascus when Jesus happened to him. It must have been a relief for the Apostle mystic to be full of someone besides himself. Gradually it must have dawned on him that religion was not far-right, or uptight, or even being right. It was not the rigid, rigorous, resentful ritual business it had been for him. It most likely was elating to discover that faith was not something, it was Someone. For Saul this new awareness made him Paul, and with this conversion, the personal conviction that "joy is the infallible sign of the presence of God." His enthusiasm eventually spilled out on the Thessalonians: "Brothers and sisters, rejoice always!"

The well-being that flows from a sound spirituality cannot be commanded, or even intended. Like divine grace it happens, unbidden. Saul/Paul had no idea what would befall him on that fated road. He had other things on his mind when the lightning struck. Suddenly it all changed. He began to have new notions of what was important.

No doubt the unfamiliar meanings took time to ripen. Maybe an unexpected tranquility even mingled with his wonderment and an interior harmony was being forged within Paul. It's like when one experiences getting it together. Heightened awareness and the acceptance of life's ups and downs with equal serenity take place after the numbness.

Kahlil Gibran (1883-1931) in his tour de force *The Prophet,* captures the counterpoint in the nature of genuine joy:

> *Your joy is your sorrow unmasked. And the self—same well from which your laughter rises was often times filled with your tears . . . The deeper that sorrow carves into your being, the more joy you can contain.*

This sense of at-one-ment with the universe and with oneself sets in when one lets go . . . lets go of whatever fences one in: erroneous education, harsh religion, suspicion of the physical, the pretense to be number one, the pressure to fit in, the preoccupation to please . . .

In this enterprise, humor helps. If joy is the intimate relative of divinity, then humor is its kissing cousin. Humor needs 20/20 vision in order to perceive life's paradox, contradictions, and ambiguities that are laughable. Humor is holy when it has the faith to accept the incongruities of God's Creation. Whatever gladdens, saddens, or maddens the human heart rates a genuflection. Humor is the harmony that can celebrate our eccentricities, our inhibitions, our prohibitions, our hopelessly unrealizable ideals and still smile.

Laughter is healthy. It releases to the bloodstream endorphins, the body's natural pain controller. It provides six times more oxygen to tissues than deep breathing. It aids the heart, opens the pores, enhances respiration, digestion and relaxation. One cannot laugh and be angry at the same time. Someone once called laughing "interior jogging." It comes from the same sensitive, susceptible side of us that makes our tears. It affirms that of all the missing persons in our lives, God is the most missed. Benita, age 10, caught this insight when she wrote:

> *Dear Mr. God,*
> *Love is a two way street. It's your turn, God.*

Humor does not deny tragedy, any more than the clown, who is consistently tricked, humiliated, stepped-on, but never defeated. So, what's so funny? Life, you, me, maybe even God! After all, *She* put this show on the road!

3rd Sunday of Advent
(1 Thessalonians 5: 16-24, John 1: 6-18, 19-28)

Cheers!

I was waiting for a bus one December day in the mid-'50s. It was a Santa Monica corner where Henshey's department store was located. Two passers-by gazed at the manger scene in the store's display window. I overheard one say to the other petulantly, "They're trying to put religion into everything."

There are those who need no convincing that Christmas is a particularly apt occasion to justify religious expression, and sadly deplore when Christ is left out of it, or when the *mas* (Mass) part gets shortchanged in the celebration. The commercialization of the festival is gravely lamented by the devout. But can commerce really compete with the spiritual magic of the season? The jingle bells of cash registers cannot successfully drown out the bells of St. Mary's. How does mourning the tide of secularism bring the Savior nearer? Can the Creator ever be separated from His Creation? Does the sun need human perception to keep shining, when hidden by clouds?

There is no way to overlook divinity. Even atheists attest to this reality. . . . cigarettes are needed to have anti-cigarette laws! The Divine Presence is everywhere. The English poet Francis Thompson (1859-1902) saw it sublimely in his poem "The Kingdom of God" . . .

> *O World invisible, we view Thee.*
> *O World intangible, we touch Thee.*
> *O World unknowable, we know Thee.*
> *Inapprehensible, we clutch Thee!*

The Now Testament

Does the fish soar to find the ocean?
The eagle plunge to find the air.
That we ask of the stars in motion
If they have rumor of Thee there?

The angels keep their ancient places:
Turn but a stone, and start a wing!
Tis ye, tis your estranged faces,
That miss the many splendored thing.

Churches have always assumed the charge of serving as God's official bodyguard. Yet if God revealed Himself principally by theology, then only Ph.D.s would be believers. In this day's first reading, King David feels obliged to take care of God. His edifice complex prompts him to build God a temple. Through Nathan, the Prophet, God's response to David's offer is, in effect, "No thanks, you need it more than I do."

So, Christmas cannot be submerged by any economy—bullish or bearish. Its message is too unearthly. "White Christmas" and "Jingle Bells" are not competing with "Adeste Fidelis" and "Silent Night." They separately, lyrically announce the glad tidings of love and peace. "Rudolph" or "Frosty" or "Santa" may supplement, but never supplant, the Bethlehem Baby.

Christmas urges us to say *Mary's yes* to life, which echoed the *yes* of the Creator when He made the universe, and liked what He had made. Christmas says God has not changed His mind about this. In fact He wants to be here—in the center of it. So, give the gifts, relish family, hug the kids. We raise our glasses to God's world!

4th Sunday of Advent
(2 Samuel 7: 1-16, Luke 1: 26-38)

Human is Holy

While the twentieth century and the second millennium stagger to their respective graves, dare we, U.S.A., swagger to our self-elected grade of world power number one? Superiority complexes usually mask inferiority complexes. As an era ends, a national inventory reveals a few things we may justly feel inferior about.

Our economy booms and so do our senseless murders. Unemployment is down and so are the pink-slipped victims of corporate merger downsizing. The homeless increase and so do the soaring salaries of corporate CEOs. In 1980, the ratio between the salary of a top executive and the wage of a factory worker was 42 to one. In 1998, the figure exploded to 419 to one. Still the needy try to survive on food stamps.

The Cold War is over, but the Pentagon budget currently amounts to one half million a minute. That is $9,000.00 per second, which could pay a lot of college tuitions. And that's not to mention the hundreds of millions that will be squandered this year for political campaigns by candidates that don't even get elected. Votes do not put aspirants into office—money does!

After decades of the draining integrity of our national leadership, fate chose a place called Vietnam to call in our debt. This humiliation has taught us something about the ultimate failure of massive power. Yet the U.S.A. is our home, where opportunity abounds like nowhere else in the world. Where the races can connect, and where diversity stands a chance. All human history is a legend of progress and decline, of crises confronted and solutions achieved. It can be no surprise to the Creator that His creatures are imperfect. That is how we were made—unfinished, in process! That is what creatureliness means—limited! We dangle between the infinite and the infinitesimal. And with it all the Divine spark glimmers unextinguished in all mankind.

Each generation hints that humanity is only getting started. The species is only beginning to get the hang of what it means to be a human being! Jesuit paleontologist, Theilhard DeChardin (1881-1955), caught a glimpse of the mystery: "Someday, after mastering the winds, the waves, the tides, and gravity, we shall harness for God the energies of love, and then, for a second time in the history of the world, man will have discovered fire."

More and more scientists are sensing the hunch that benevolence is the mystic secret underlying the basis of the universe. Happiness may only be a sometime thing for harassed mortals, but evil can never be the bottom line. Human is not an excuse, it's a privilege!

The holy family had their dysfunctional moments, but they are more than a footnote to history. We all belong to a holy family—mankind. We were born holy—each one of us—because we came from the Hand of God. Human is holy! Whatever the future holds, we know who holds the future.

Sunday after Christmas
(Luke 2: 22-40)

Y2-OK

It was a blast watching TV hopscotch the globe on New Year's Eve 2000. It was a kick to be in on a global party—people enjoying themselves in the sight of the glorious Eiffel Tower, the gleaming Thames, and in Calcutta, Johannesburg, Tokyo, Beijing, and Moscow. It was a break to join in the international countdown to the new millennium with happy celebrants around the wide world. In this colorful diversity, I sensed the majesty of its Creator. Mankind, in all its variegated hues, is the perceptible manifestation of divinity—the Epiphany of God.

What will this new century bring? The first woman U.S. president, automobiles fueled by hydrogen and oxygen, clothing made from anti-bacterial fabrics making deodorants a thing of the past? Painless eye surgery is already eliminating eyeglasses. Computers may make books passé. How about a garage sale for worn out replaced body parts? Will miraculous modern medicine discover cures for cancer, AIDS, the common cold? Improved intelligence and technology hold the promise of undreamed advances for the twenty-first century. State of the art items today threaten to be junk tomorrow.

Problems persist, nonetheless. There is global warming, barely confronted. Folks living at the seashore may need to move to the second floor. War continues to be a national policy. The past century, the bloodiest in human history, records one hundred million dead from this insanity. Civilization and education have not yet liberated mankind from the prison of infectious "isms": nationalism, militarism, materialism, fundamentalism. Ideologies are always dangerous when slogans substitute logic and brainwashing is accepted pedagogy.

Among the agreeable "isms" is optimism—a particularly becoming attitude for a freshly minted millennium. There is solid justification for this as I notice the baby boomers' progeny. The young people born between 1977 and 1994 are seventy million strong, and you parents know that they are brighter, more interesting, more confident, and less apologetic than you may remember yourselves having been. You nurtured them sensitively, respecting their individuality and, thus, they seem more concerned for one another. Socially they are more open. One out of seven among their peers are African-American, one out of seven, Hispanic. Scholastically they are obliged to compete with brilliant Asians who garner the academic prizes. They are more colorblind. They have grown up amid a wider diversity and recognize that women are every bit as competent as men. They have matured with an understanding for gays, for the backward, for the underprivileged. They enjoy social service and are quick to volunteer to build or repair or maintain necessities for the have-nots.

There are always exceptions, and there are some things I will never miss; if these youths finally outgrow baggy pants, spiked hair, pierced tongues, tattoos and punk rock. But I trust their unbigoted minds, their willing hearts, their no-nonsense spirituality that values each human being with the importance of Jesus himself. I raise a New Year's toast to you. This is your century!

Epiphany
(Matthew 2: 1-12)

Decisions, Decisions!

Considered to be the first of the Gospels, written between 55 and 70 A.D., Mark moves fast. He makes no mention of Jesus' birth or childhood years, he just has him appear suddenly—out of nowhere—fully grown, recognized and baptized by John as someone special. This again was ratified by a numinous celestial confirmation; Jesus was ready for his new vocation. It took him thirty years to decide to go public.

Decision making can be awesome, especially if the only options are risky. There are moments when we know what we have to do, but are terrified to do it. . . . Should I tolerate the travail of chemotherapy, or take my chances? Should I just quit or confront the badgering boss? Decisions, decisions! The temptation is to retreat, and ever rue playing chicken. Shakespeare's familiar lines from *Julius Caesar*, act 4, scene 3, describe the dilemma:

> *There is a tide in the affairs of man,*
> *Which taken at the flood,*
> *Leads to fortune.*
> *Omitted, all the voyage of their*
> *Lives is bound in shallows*
> *And in miseries.*

An undecided life is a wasted life. A state of constant, rootless, restless drifting. In Apostolic days, baptism meant taking a stand about one's life. It was a "decision for Christ"—the commitment to believe what Jesus believed.

The rite of baptism has had a checkered career in Church history. Initially it was exclusively intended for adults capable of free choice. In the fourth century, Augustine picked up on the Pauline Theory that mankind was separated from God due to Adam's noncompliance and "original sin" took hold . . . a tenet that is not biblical, but a later theological development. Baptism was seen as a divine presidential pardon. Hence, its focus began to light on infants in order to qualify them for heaven as soon as possible. By the fifth century the mood about baptism shifted from purposeful conversion to passive amnesty.

The ritual of baptism is meant to signify a bonding—a new alliance with God. That is why it is called "Christening," because Christ stands in for the baptizee, giving that person his (Christ's) identity with the Father. It can be likened to the ceremony of naturalization when an alien is made a citizen of the U.S.A. So important is this formality to the Church that it empowers all believers to perform it, not just its currently endangered species, the ordained priesthood.

There are several kinds of baptism. Baptism of water—the conventional version. When this is not available, there is baptism of blood—suffering for the faith, martyrdom. There is baptism of desire—the wish to conform to God's wishes. Let me tell you about still another variety—the baptism of tears.

The hospital's student chaplain was on call. Late one night he was summoned to the room of a mother whose baby had been stillborn a few hours earlier. "We want our baby baptized," the young couple asked, the mother cradling the lifeless body of their daughter. "Her name's Nicole."

The inexperienced chaplain didn't know what to do. In order to buy some time, he asked the couple to meet him in the chapel a few minutes later.

The overwhelmed chaplain frantically tried to find a more experienced chaplain to take over, but none was available. So, he was on his own. Despite his nervousness over his professional inexperience and theological uncertainties about what to do, he tried to think of what to say to the grieving parents.

When the couple arrived, the chaplain realized his words would be inadequate. Instead, and almost without realizing it, he took a tissue, wiped at the tears in the eyes of the parents, then wiped his own tears, and touched the tissue to the baby's head. "Nicole, I baptize you in the name of the Father, and of the Son, and of the Holy Spirit."

The chaplain said nothing else—the tears were more eloquent than any words (John Pattan, *Ministry to Theology*).

Baptism of Jesus/1st Sunday of Ordinary Time
(Mark 1: 74)

Disco

This is the Latin word for "I learn." "Disciple," therefore, means "learner" more than "follower."

Learning can be a joy and so can teaching. When they come together, knowledge happens. But the teacher needs to be willing to see what the pupil does not, and be willing to take all the time the pupil needs to develop curiosity about what is not understood. Thus, the good teacher influences the student to be his/her own teacher. The educated know what they do not know—the ignorant do not.

This day's reading has two of John Baptist's disciples curious about Jesus, and so he asks them, "What are you looking for?" They obviously want more than a casual chat with him, so they invite themselves to lunch—a long one—till four P.M., "Teacher, where are you staying?" Good teacher that Jesus was, he answers, "Come and see." Find out for yourselves!

A pedagogue with all the answers is probably not asking the right questions. Truth is as illusive as is the luxury of certainty. Quick-fix conclusions only promote dependency on the answer-man. The most useful schools and churches are not filling stations where enlightenment is pumped in passively, but where doubt and dissent are not dismissed, but confronted courteously and discussed. "Any authentic community is founded on participation. Its structure is correct only if it admits the practical effectiveness of opposition." Karol Wojtyla said that in 1970. He was Pope John Paul II in 1978.

Ideas need bodies to live in, and that is why "the Word became flesh." Education is sensory as well as cerebral; a collaboration of the concrete with the abstract. Live experiencing reduces unreal theorizing. Students can sometimes learn as much from the class picnic as in the classroom. So Jesus gathered a group around him, as was the custom for master educators of that time.

And what a group it was—a doubter, a denier, a betrayer! In this first Christian seminary class there were three sets of brothers: Andrew and Simon Peter; James and John; and James the Less (meaning younger) and Jude Thaddeus, cousins of Jesus. Andrew seemed to be a good middleman, introducing his brother to the Lord; the youngster with the box lunch of five loaves and two fishes; and some foreigner Greeks who wanted to meet Jesus. Simon Peter was named "Satan" one time by the irked Jesus (Matthew 57: 13). James and John were regarded as aggressive enough to be nicknamed "Sons of Thunder." There is virtually no press on the other two brothers. Then there was Twin Thomas; guileless Bartholomew (John 1: 47); Philip; the quisling tax collector, Matthew; Simon, the terrorist; and the tragic Judas Iscariot, a suicide and the only nonlocal of the dozen. The press, reporting the scandalous behavior of current clergy, would find ample copy in this handpicked collection. Still, they were the apostles of the Good News who Jesus personally selected. As candidates for the ministry today, few of them would probably pass inspection. God does not need moral heavyweights to get His job done!

Despite his magnetic attraction, Jesus must have been a puzzle to these men. He did not resemble a prophet as did the Baptist. He was not an austere ascetic. He liked parties and did not mind dining with the riffraff. To the law and order set, Jesus was a nonviolent provocateur. . . . Except for the time he threw the furniture around in the Temple (Mark 11: 15). For the moral majority, he was too laid-back. To the silent minority, he was too noisy. Jesus was an outsider—

unconventional—but he must have been a gifted leader to hold those disparate personalities together. Undoubtedly he was a good teacher; patient with questions, acceptant of diversity, tolerant for however long it took to get his message. By his civil demeanor he taught that arguments fail when issues are met instead of people. He wanted his disciples to be more on their toes than on their knees. He allowed them to verify for themselves that the wisening experience is something one gets just after one needs it.

We learn most from people who are different from us, and from teachers who give us roots and wings.

2nd Sunday of Ordinary Time
(John 1: 35-45)

Let Freedom Wring

This chapter reflects a smattering of all three of today's readings. The first features the Archie Bunker of the Old Testament—the reluctant prophet, Jonah. Typical of bigots, he is narrow-minded, self-righteous and preoccupied with his own comfort. Reneging on his preaching assignment to the Hebrew's cruelest enemy, the hated Ninevites (present day Iran), he almost kills himself playing it safe in escape. A fearful storm erupts at sea; Jonah's shifty behavior gives him away. The frightened mariners finger him as the reason for their perilous ill fortune and make him walk the plank. In this preposterous story, even the whale that swallows Jonah won't have him. Regurgitated onto dry land, Jonah concludes that he better take the Ninevites job seriously. Surprise, surprise! The detested antagonists get converted, to Jonah's acute chagrin. He is a very sore winner! He is about as happy at this unexpected turn of events, as would be Archie when he publicly, piously denounces a gay-lesbian rally and they turn about and march to the church he attends.

Oliver Wendell Holmes said: "The mind of a bigot is like the pupil of the eye. The more light poured on it, the more it will contract."

The bigot resents the light that binds. He has low tolerance for diversity. He needs an enemy to feel one-up-on. He does not understand that superiority is the obsession of inferiority. To play one-up, he is unaware that he has to be one-down.

What the bigot is down-on he is not up-on, so he belittles. The inevitable consequence is being little! The

Jonah story points out that God even uses bigots for His merciful purpose.

In the second reading, Paul, like many millennialists, did not expect the world to be around much longer. His urge to detach from the "things of this world," including husbands from their wives, is a bit hard to take, unless he is insisting that a line needs to be drawn between self and possessions, if possessions are not to be possessors. Still, Paul knew the value of human beings. Things were to be sensibly used, and people dearly cherished. He understood how one can find oneself by being lost in another. He discovered this in his relationship with Christ. Married couples find this in one another; I doubt if God finds this as unfair competition for His affection.

In the third reading, Mark has the celebrated Baptist in jail. The stage is now set for Jesus and for his opening on the road, Galilee. This is a lakeside province of Northern Israel. Fish is its principal industry and Jesus begins collecting his apostles among its work force. Their response to his call is unhesitating. Impulsive, perhaps—risky for sure—but the adventure that lay ahead of them beats any small town fishing career.

Decisiveness is the mark of a winner. Annie Dillard is a contemporary animated author who illuminates this characteristic in her autobiography, *An American Childhood*. Annie enjoyed playing football with the boys. Her dad gave her some sound advice about tackling: "You've got to throw yourself *mightily* at the runner's legs." Injury more likely results from half-hearted, timid attempts. The lamb who takes on the lion should not be surprised at the outcome. But the lamb willing to stake all has the heart of a lion.

To fling oneself into what one decides to do—the job, a cause, a relationship—is surprisingly invigorating. There are no bad decisions. There is always learning, since good judgment comes from bad judgment. Life may wring us dry, still the Good News insists there is "another life," but it is in this one.

3rd Sunday of Ordinary Time
(Jonah 3: 1-5, Corinthians 7: 29-31, Mark 1: 14-20)

Religion vs. Spirituality

Though tradition bills him as a carpenter, the Gospels make no mention of Jesus ever having done work. They record him only as an itinerant preacher—and a good one. His audition at the synagogue of Capernaum earned a rave review. "The people were astonished at his teaching, for he taught them as one having authority and not as the scribes.... His fame spread everywhere throughout the whole region of Galilee." Jesus was a hit!

Now, who were "the scribes?" They were a professional class of trained copyists, notaries. Duplication of the written Hebrew scriptures gained them regard for being learned in the Law of Moses. From their group, Pharisees (*Peru shim,* derived from the Hebrew word meaning "separated") were recruited. They were notorious for their obsession with the literal practice of the Law in its minute details. This is what happens when a religion becomes a book!

There is no record of written Hebrew until about 1,000 B.C. Around the reign of King David, Jewish oral tradition of the preceding millennium was collected to form the first books of the Bible. Books have lives of their own. Especially important books. They spawn analysts, specialists who assert particular insights about what the books mean. The scribes (*sopherim,* in Hebrew) apparently assumed this claim, but they were dull, as legal wranglers often are. The briefs of Supreme Court judges on a constitutional fine point would hardly storm bestseller heaven!

Jesus was not dull. He wowed the audience according to Mark. What did he say that so stunned them? We only know that he said it with *authority.* He was authentic. Authenticity inevitably commands attention any time the speaker's source is the depths of his inner self rather than the theories from other authorities.

To believe in oneself takes being in touch with that self—all the parts of the self—the glad, the sad, the mad, and the bad. Once acknowledged; and without judgment, one can begin to be centered, to assimilate events rather than be crushed by them. This availability to reality produces a rare security. Jesus seemed to have this assurance. He had come to know himself. His inner struggles are metaphorically dramatized in the Gospel account of his desert temptations. Intimacy with his own feelings and ideas opened his sensitivity to life about him. Self-aware, he could be perceptive of others. That's his *authority!* He was outside what he was inside. Jesus was *transparent,* according to theologian Paul Tillich (1886-1965).

This quality does not come from study, or deliberate intent, or intense religion. It is an unmerited gift of grace— a spirituality that recognizes the awesome sacredness of life. It believes in a Creator that believes in His creatures, who sees them as partners in His nonstop creating process, and not the subordinates of an Almighty Egoist demanding to be pleased.

Jesus knew about the human heart because he knew something about the hungers of his own. He knew rules and ritual were not food enough. The serenity he experienced with his Father was the Good News he wanted the world to be in on.

By-the-book religion attracts the structure-hungry; uneasy with inquiry, they tend to settle for the quick-fix theology of cliché evangelists. They are forever taking their morality temperatures and righteously consign the unchurched to the *pit.*

Spirituality brings a lighter touch to the life of faith. Its attention is on the light, not the road map. The light is the path. Spirituality knows that the universe is in Good Hands, so it can be tranquil about the uncertainties, the ambiguities of existence. The paradoxical ambivalence of the human condition elicits sympathy rather than censure.

In the late '80s a memorable TV series, *The Power of Myth,* featured Bill Moyers interviewing Professor Joseph Campbell, the renowned master of the meaning of mythology. In one of the sequences, Campbell offered his view of the difference between religion and spirituality.

> *I had a friend who attended an international meeting of Roman Catholic meditative orders, which was held in Bangkok. He told me that the Catholic monks had no problem understanding the Buddhist monks, but that it was the clergy of the two religions who were unable to understand each other. The person who had a mystical experience knows that all the symbolic expressions of it are faulty. The symbols do not render the experiences, they suggest it. If you haven't had the experience, how can you know what it is? (The Power of Myth,* p. 60)

The scribes expounded on the external symbols of their religion—i.e. "the label on the bottle." Jesus let the people taste the wine.

4th Sunday of Ordinary Time
(Mark 1: 21-28)

Mission Impassable

Like the man says, no one makes it out of this life either tearless or alive. All three of this day's readings draw attention to the mystery of our mortal travail. Mark, ever in a hurry, records a busy day for Jesus. Most likely disturbed by the suffering surrounding him, sleep eludes Jesus. Rising before light, he seeks solace in prayer and solitude. But no rest for the weary! He is pursued: "Everyone is looking for you." He meets the demand. George Bernard Shaw (1856-1950) applauds this response:

> *This is the true joy of life, the being used for a purpose recognized by yourself as a mighty one: the being thoroughly worn out before you are thrown on the scrap heap: being a force of Nature instead of a feverish, selfish little clod of ailments and grievances, complaining that the world will not devote itself to making you happy.*

Why should the world owe anything to anybody? It was here first!

Paul tries adjusting to his mission by "being all things to all men"—a ready recipe for burnout. However, the Pauline effort may have been less motivated to patronize or to people-please, than to defer his vigorous opinions to others equally opinionated. Boswell (1740-1795) praises Dr. Samuel Johnson (1709-1784) for his "readiness to throw himself into the interest of other people." Such gracious accommodating is to "walk in another's moccasins." An underrated social virtue—this willingness to see another point of view.

Now for the masterpiece—the matchless ancient folk tale—Job! Composed about five centuries before Christ, it is considered to be the longest surviving Hebrew poem. Superbly written, it is a bold tale about divine atrocity; the bad things that happen to a good man.

The drama opens with God conducting a staff meeting with His celestial cabinet, of which Satan (Hebrew for "prosecuting attorney") is a member. The Deity gets hooked into a crooked wager with Satan. They bet on a perfectly honorable dupe named Job: the former, playing Job to win; the latter, to lose. An avalanche of horrors befall Job to test his fidelity to God and to virtue. His faith holds: "We accept good things from God—ought we not accept bad?"

The narrative describes Job as so foul smelling from his assorted diseases, that he is deposited on the top of a (bleep) pile. His agonies are augmented by the annoying advice of insipid friends. His soured spouse urges him to "curse God and die." Still Job persists in his innocence and angrily stands up to an indifferent God: "I will defend my ways to His face. I hold fast my righteousness, I will not let go."

Job respects God enough to confront Him candidly. Exasperated, he pleads "why?" God's answer is no answer, but a snooty-sounding put-down over impugned divine sovereignty. Job is stumped—told off. There is little left to do but accept. A change takes place. Bitterness softens to discernment. A bigger picture comes into focus, reducing his self-pity and resentment. No longer a victim, Job forgives God. In fact, Job comes off looking better than God.

Job personifies a quality dear to the Jewish heart—*chutzpah*, a Yiddish term for audacity, gall, nerve, "guts." God apparently endorses this by restoring Job to even more abundance than before. The legend does not resolve the mystery of why the innocent suffer. Rabbi Kushner, in his celebrated bestseller, *When Bad Things Happen To Good People,* suggests that a more useful question than "Why?" is, "What can I do when disaster strikes?" Job's troubles occasioned the discovery of unknown resources in himself.

The Job story is fiction. The Anne Frank story is fact. The famous *Diary of Anne Frank* recounts this remarkable child's ordeals under the Nazis. A holocaust victim, this bright-eyed smiling youngster showed the world how to stay human in an inhuman existence. She died in the Bergen Belsen death camp just days before its liberation. Her last recorded thought: "In spite of everything I still believe that people are good at heart."

That tops chutzpah!

5th Sunday of Ordinary Time
(Job 7: 1-7, 1 Corinthians 9: 16-23, Mark 1: 29-39)

Familiarity That Breeds Content

If you have ever felt anonymous, abandoned, like a nonperson, you had a feeble hint of what it was like to be a leper in days of yore. Cruelly quarantined from all family and friends, they were forbidden all human interaction. Often repulsively disfigured, they were piously scorned as outcasts by an angry God brutally punishing them for their sins. Their isolation was living death.

Any skin blemish was considered leprosy in those days. That meant that psoriasis, dermatitis, ringworm, even measles or chicken pox, were treated as a leprous plague. Since there was no knowledge that bacteria cause infectious diseases, demon possession was blamed, and priests were put in charge of public health.

Most of us have experienced, at one time or other, the castaway sensation . . . as a child, to be second banana to a preferred sibling. Later, to be passed over for promotion after twenty loyal years while a young hotshot, only six months with the firm, gets your coveted prize. Or to be downsized out after thirty grinding years, and now you are over 55! Or you raised the four kids, supported him to his M.D., and now he wants out for that cute nurse! Why? It's not fair!

Somehow you got through it. You survived. Some even got a better deal. Valentine's Day is the day to celebrate that living "good deal" in our separate lives; that unexpected "break" we could not imagine we deserved. Valentine's Day merits more liturgical prominence than the Church accords it. Maybe it should be a Holy Day of Obligation like Immaculate Conception or All Saints. What other feast day acknowledges more of what the human heart is all about: the need for and the gift of intimate human caring? If you have been rescued from isolation by someone who stopped long enough to notice you—to want to share, to mutually disclose—you know the miracle that set you on the road to wholeness. You have a Valentine!

Thirty-five years ago I ensconced my aging parents in a senior citizen community that happily suited their declining years. They have since passed on and now I live where they lived. I do not find it exciting. The mean age of the residents is 75. There are no children to enliven the stillness. But one feature never fails to move me—the sight of an elderly couple taking their daily walk together hand-in-hand.

As a celibate, I muse to myself about them. . . . All the years of talking together, thinking together, worrying together, the differing, the arguing, the disappointments. I ponder the innumerable forgivenesses, the "I'm sorry"s, the "I didn't mean it"s. There is no place to hide from the full-length mirror that each one is to the other. There can be no hit and run when they promised each other to see it through. They have something durable now. Relationships change, commitments do not. They fell in love many years ago and they have come to know how to stand up straight in it. It was never easy.

Learning to live together yielded a liberating side effect: outliving the narcissism that every infant is born with. People who need people and have what they need, are never bored. There never is nothing to do. There is always something to do for the other. What a break to have something more than oneself to live for! May all you sweethearts continue to enjoy each other as God surely enjoys His "funny valentines."

6th Sunday of Ordinary Time
(Leviticus 13, Mark 1: 40-45)

Through the Roof

Tired from an extended tour of Galilean synagogues, Jesus returns to Capernaum, his chosen home, for a breather and a standing-room-only audience. Mark depicts a scene worthy of the Marx Brothers. While lecturing to a full house, four fellows are tearing up the roof over his head in order to get a paralyzed friend within healing touch of Jesus. What would you do if some strangers were scuttling your roof? I would call the cops, or at least 911! Jesus looks up and he sees faith. He sees marvelous, single-minded, enterprising caring for a helpless friend. He probably smiled as he said to the paralytic, "Child, your sins are forgiven."

For the assembled scribes, the self-appointed assessors of religious orthodoxy, that declaration was too much. "Who does he think he is . . . God? Blasphemy!" Why did Jesus risk agitating these rigid certifiers? Obviously he wished to make a point. He wanted to disabuse people of thinking of God as a hanging judge poised to sentence the wayward with savage penalties simply for being human. In those days, Judaism indissolubly linked sin to sickness. Disease and suffering were God's judgment for sins. Jesus wished to refute sin and suffering as cause and effect. But how could he subvert a venerable religious mindset and not offend the tradition experts? Getting into an argument about it—the "I'm right, you're wrong" approach—would be futile. So, Jesus meets the opposition on their own ground. Using their logic, he reasons, "If sin is the cause of this paralysis, then if the paralysis is removed, so is the sin." God is no longer the heavy!

195

Arguing fails when questions are answered instead of questioners. Knowing their fondness for debating fine points of the Law, Jesus addresses this puzzling poser to the scribes: "Which is easier to say to the paralytic: 'your sins are forgiven,' or 'rise up, pick up your mat and walk'?"

Why this strange query? Could Jesus be implying that to forgive and to do a miracle are the same thing? That one is just as difficult to perform as the other, but both are within human power? Might he be intimating that in God's eyes, to forgive is the miracle cure for the human condition? That the healing in forgiveness gives life back to the forgiven as well as the forgiver? Still, forgiveness is not possible unless the forgiver sees in himself that same capacity for evil he so loathes in the enemy.

This gospel could be making another salient point, namely, that pain is not God's penalty, but God's opportunity. What can deepen, teach, mellow, and strengthen the soul more than suffering endured? The memory of crosses and crises survived provides our most confident personal self-image. Thus, no lifetime is spared them.

That is why Jesus wanted his church to be a sanctuary for the world's rejects: gays, addicts, divorced, criminals, religious derelicts. He wanted it to be the defender, not the accuser of mankind. He wanted his church to be a mystical presence of compassion, hospitable to dissent, gracious to antagonists. He did not need it to be an institutional power broker—a closed corporation of efficiency exclusively reserved for the elect. He wanted his church to be a servant church, but bold enough to go through the roof for us spiritual cripples.

7th Sunday of Ordinary Time
(Mark 2: 1-12)

We There Yet?

In this Gospel I hear Jesus designate what is important to him about life and religion. To him, life and religion are one piece. Worshipping God and making a living are equally urgent. To his scandalized critics, he obviously preferred feasting to fasting and seemed quite comfortable doing the former with the local riff-raff. Who could better benefit? The point is clear that fellowship with Jesus did not exclude moral derelicts who enjoyed his company. In a subsequent age, any church operating in his name would therefore need the welcome mat out for those whom a righteous society looked down its nose at. Might that mean the Mafia, crooked cops, druggies, gays, and streetwalkers? Seems so! The sick are the charges of the hospital, just as the church is a sanctuary for the disreputable.

Relating to his Father was upbeat for Jesus. He consistently identified the kingdom of God—that is, when goodness takes over—as a party. He even styles himself as the bridegroom at a wedding feast who wants his guests to have a good time. With Lent just around the corner, the liturgy cheerfully emphasizes festal nuptial imagery. Fasting is associated with the rites of mourning. Sadly, there is a time for that. But Jesus insinuates that grimness must not distinguish the face of his disciples.

Where did the Church pick up that God somehow is pleased with human corporal austerity? How does severe monastic asceticism bring God nearer? What possessed the buoyant St. Francis of Assisi, so jubilantly relishing the glories of nature, to so cruelly punish his body in the name of the love of God? He apparently repented when he confessed

197

to his worn form at his premature demise, "I have not been very kind to you, have I, Brother Ass?" Jesus may have felt that life was tough enough on people without religion imposing further hardship.

Jesus, therefore, brought a new look to the mien of religion. Solemn is not necessarily sacred. As the environs of Paradise were approached, the epic poet Dante distinguished the sound of the celestial music of the spheres to be laughter. When visiting San Francisco, Mother Teresa was asked by a sober young woman, "What must I do to be a saint?" The holy nun's one-word response: "Smile!"

This lighthearted focus was the Good News of Jesus. He referred to it as "new wine"; new wine that would shatter the shrunken wineskins of weary ritual that routine repetition had rendered stale. In fact, the occupational hazard of organized religion is the illusion that tradition is holy just because it is old. Spontaneity, freshness, and flexibility react to the "now," not the "then." Small wonder that this luminous insight is such a contemporary hit: "The past is history, the future is mystery, that is why the gift of 'now' is called the present."

Old sacrosanct habits die hard. Jesus obviously was sensitive to the incompatibility of the old being imposed upon the new. Applying an old shrinkable patch to a new shrink-resistant fabric made as much sense as medically prescribing former bloodletting to cure modern pneumonia. Still, he pressed his avant-garde message that valued service to human needs over obsessive devotional practices. God does not need the attention that people need, and he knew how difficult change could be. Mark Twain once remarked that the only one that enjoys it is "a wet baby."

For Jesus, living was not a tidy lockstep march to a regimented cadence. It is a journey through a minefield of unforeseen vicissitudes. The pilgrimage on the way back to the Author of Life is a zigzag course of constant adjustment to the unfamiliar. Jesus saw himself as supplying the mature spirituality that this odyssey demands when he promised, "I have come to give you more abundant life"—not more religion (John 10: 10). Are we there yet? Almost! That is when you live life lightly, connect with everything, but belong to yourself.

8th Sunday of Ordinary Time
(Mark 2: 18-22)

The Litter of the Law

If you have visited New York City, you probably visited St. Patrick's Cathedral on Fifth Avenue. It is an uncommon experience to step from the flurry of the noisy Manhattan street into the soft tranquillity of that splendid church. Despite its stately interior, it has the feel of a quiet village wayside chapel. The sense of God is palpable.

The ancient Hebrews invented the Sabbath to enjoy this unruffled serenity within the bustle of a busy week. It was intended to be a rest from daily toil, a one-day holiday of relaxation with the family, an unhurried communion with the Lord. The lowliest drudge was entitled to this blessed interlude of ease and thanksgiving.

How could this regenerative holy rite so twist into becoming a trap of petty prohibitions and repressive restrictions? Lighting a candle, brushing your teeth, combing your hair were proscribed as forbidden labor by the religious authorities. I recall as a boy, the reward of a chocolate from the local synagogue sexton for simply snapping on the lights each Saturday morning. . . . How can such oppressive legalisms become accepted devotional practice? What pervades the psyche of religious leadership that needs to manage its votaries' behavior in such stifling detail? Controlling people can be a heady enterprise, and the clergy are not above this intoxication, especially when justified as enforcing "God's law." The will to power is a natural human impulse, but it's particularly the preoccupation of the impotent.

I remember a psychology class in the '70s conducted by Rollo May, himself an ordained minister. His impression of the cloth: "The clergy reflect two main characteristics for me," he said. "One is positive, the other negative. The positive one is the earnest desire to help people. The negative one is the divine right to be taken care of."

Less than omnipotent, our deplored human dependencies can promote unconscious defenses, such as insensitive authoritarian governance over others. That is why Jesus cut through the legalistic detritus of the rabbinical code by declaring, "The Sabbath was made for man, not man for the Sabbath."

This pithy wisdom is not saying that religious institutions, rituals, rules, dogmas and spiritual discipline are not important. It is saying that they are not sacred; human beings are. If this logic is valid, then the hallowed foundations in our lives—church, school, court of law, marriage, the nation—never preempt the human person in value. They are meant to serve people, not vice versa.

In tune with this theme, how might Lent, commencing again on Wednesday, best serve our individual humanity? What do each of us need more of for fuller living . . . time with family, exercise, reading? What can we use less of . . . tobacco, TV, alcohol, snacking between meals? This Lent is our big chance to go for our best selves.

Another Lenten suggestion: pick out one person you feel needs you most. Invest in that person, focus, listen, relate, take your time, get acquainted. You may decide that one person is your very self. Then let this Lent make you your own best friend. This is not easy, knowing yourself as you do. No mortification is more difficult or more worthwhile. Getting to know you is the surest way of getting to like you. You deserve it—go for it!

9th Sunday of Ordinary Time
(Mark 2: 23-3: 6)

Choice vs. Chance

Yes, there probably was a deluge; floods were quite common in the Euphrates Valley. No, Joan of Arc was not Noah's wife! A recent poll reported that ten percent of Bible readers thought she was. Like life, the Bible is not easy to understand. It is called the Word of God, and it seems to be not so much the word of God about God, as much as the word of God about mankind. In his potent little 1999 volume, *The Heart Is A Little To The Left,* William Sloane Coffin comments:

> *I read the Bible because the Bible reads me. I see myself reflected in Adam's excuses, in Saul's envy of David, in promise-making, promise-breaking Peter. . . . I find a God who not only answers our questions, but equally importantly, questions our answers. . . . If you take the Bible seriously, you can't take it literally—not all of it.*

The Bible is a Jewish book. Both Old and New Testaments were written by Jews, for Jews. It is the Hebrew attempt to figure out God. That is why it reflects so many varied faces of divinity: a militant monarch, a tender shepherd, a testy sovereign insisting on unquestioning obeisance, as well as a playful Creator enjoying His creatures. These are all projections of the Hebrew mind trying to make sense of their God experience in their phenomenal history. Scholars date the beginnings of the written scriptures at about 750 centuries before Christ. Preceding this was the oral tradition—campfire stories retold from generation to generation. The first five books, the Pentateuch, were probably put together about five centuries before Christ. Incidents related in Genesis, like the Garden of Eden story and the Tower of Babel, can be found in Sumerian/Babylonian folktales as far back as three millennia before Christ. The Flood story is one of these.

The sacred writers consistently sought the Deity's personal involvement in Hebrew history and thus interpolated the Divine Presence in their major fortunes. Calamity meant God's displeasure; prosperity, His approbation. Their writing is about religious experience, not a factual chronicle.

So, what's the point of the Noah story? That God has feelings much like their Hebrew selves: truculent, rueful, contrite? The legend reveals the Creator admitting a mistake when He created humans, and deciding to clean out the mess with a Deluge and start over. Like a sensitive parent who deplores overpunishing a child, God regrets His harshness and makes a rainbow as a promise that He means business about forgiveness. The story affirms that a "process God" can change His mind.

In the typical hurry-up style of Mark, this Gospel reading features a condensed version of Jesus' desert temptations. He apparently resolved any dilemma about the nature of God when he referred to Him as "Father." He may not have been that sure about himself, however. He knew he had to go public with this message. How should he present it? Who should he be: celebrity, CEO, commandant? Or just take his chances being vulnerable? It is the typical struggle of identity for anyone embarking on a career. What will assist success—people pleasing, assertiveness, or just being teachable? This vexing introspection, for anyone open to daily experience and to growth, endures longer than forty days!

According to Matthew's fuller account, Jesus resorted to citing Bible principles to guide his path of action. Clearly his traditional religious background offered the advantage of controlling his deliberate choice over random chance or impulsive instinct. Parents who deny their children religious training in the name of sparing them "brainwashing" or "guilt indoctrination," sadly set them on life's sea in a rudderless vessel. Guilt is not irrevocable injury if it prompts amendment for the harm done, or forestalls the harm planned. An unfortunate death row inmate lamented, "I always had choices in my life, but I was never taught to consider consequences."

A cartoon depicts two elderly nuns chatting together. One says to the other, "This is a letter from a former pupil. She says she forgives me for ruining her life." The capacity to forgive sounds like a healthy consequence!

1st Sunday of Lent
(Genesis 9: 8-15, Mark 1: 12-15)

Pluck of the Irish

Among my varied handicaps, one of them is not being Irish. Just hearing brogue, I'm on the floor! Though I boast no relic of Erin in my middle-European heritage, I cannot think of the Transfiguration and not think of Ireland. The incandescent divinity that shone on Mt. Tabor was soon followed by the hideous Crucifixion on Mt. Calvary. The flame of glowing faith ignited by St. Patrick did not exempt the Irish from their centuries of agony.

In his splendid book, *How the Irish Saved Civilization,* Thomas Cahill describes early fifth century Ireland as a brooding, dank island whose inhabitants, while externally carefree and warlike, lived with quaking fear within. Their terror of shape-changing monsters, of sudden death and the insubstantiality of their world was so acute that they drank themselves into an insensate stupor in order to sleep. Patrick provided a welcome alternative. The Christianity he proposed to the Irish succeeded because it removed the dread of the magical world that haunted them. Once Christianized, they enriched civilization with the monastic movement and the laborious copying of valuable books otherwise lost to history.

Nonetheless, the sad threnody of the Irish story laments centuries of British cruelty; the potato blight and famine of 1840; a century-long recession; an uprooting emigration. By 1870, thirty-three percent of the foreign born in the U.S.A. were Irish and painfully unwelcome. "Irish Need Not Apply" greeted their employment efforts. Back home, there was the bloody civil war for Irish independence

(1918-1921) and the continued strife currently between Northern Ulster and Southern Eire.

The poet William Butler Yeats (1865 -1939) sums up the Irishman's soul: "Being Irish he had an abiding sense of tragedy which sustained him through temporary periods of joy."

Still no misery has disfigured that soul. However victimized, they would not surrender to victimhood. Whatever their travail, they refused to cry the "blues." The Irish are simply not a "poor me" society. They have a knack for making a song, a story, a jest of their heartache. In fact, they are transfigured by their troubles. The world rejoices in the mirth and mayhem the Irish have brought to the staid Anglo Saxon culture. How about this twist? "To those who love us—love us. For those who don't—may God turn them. If He can't turn them, may He turn their ankles . . . So we may know them by their limp."

Then there was Bridget O'Malley repairing to Father Grady in tears:

"Ah, Bridget, what can be so wrong as to upset you so?"

"Oh, Father, I've got terrible news. Me husband died last night!"

"God save us," replied the priest. "Tell me, Bridget, did he make any last requests?"

"That he did, Father. Mr. O'Malley asked me, 'Bridget, for God's sake, put down that gun!'"

(Thanks to Father Bill O'Donnell for the above goodies!)

One more time . . .

Paddy is on trial for robbery. For lack of evidence, the judge acquits him. Paddy then says to the judge, "Does that mean I can keep the money?"

So, on this feast of Transfiguration, I raise my Guinness to the nation of saints and scholars. Though I have nary a teardrop of Hibernian blood in me, I feel singularly blessed with a share of their Gaelic wit and whimsy.

Erin Go Bragh!

2nd Sunday of Lent
(Mark 9: 2-10)

Real Zeal

Those turned off by the effete-looking holy card Jesus can have a ball with this Gospel. Gentle Jesus—meek and mild—is throwing the Temple furniture around. "He made a whip out of cords . . . spilled the coins of the money changers and overturned their tables." Why this out-of-control violence from the one who urged turning the other cheek, walking the extra mile, giving your shirt away, and loving one's enemies? A hint is offered as "his disciples recalled the words of scripture: 'zeal for your house will consume me.'"

Jesus was not the first religious teacher to denounce the crass commercialism in the great Temple. The prophets, Jeremiah, Zachariah, and Malachi, all warned that God could not be trapped by codes of ceremonial observance. God was better served by humanitarian solicitude for one another than by ritual procedures. But Jesus was the first to put his actual muscle into his words. Surely he must have known that this eruption would hardly change things. There was probably business as usual the next day. After all, Temple money exchange was sanctioned by the highest religious authority, since Roman coins were forbidden in Temple transactions. The Talmud prescribed a one-half *shekel* tax (almost two days' wage) as an allowed fee for the money changer. Fleecing impoverished pilgrims by exorbitant rates infuriated Jesus.

He also may have felt that it was high time to make a strong statement on the irrelevance of animal sacrifice. Seven centuries before, Isaiah (1: 11-17) declared God's scorn for the bloody custom:

211

What to me is the multitude of your sacri-fices?" says the Lord! "I have had enough of burnt offerings of rams and the fat of fed beasts; I do not delight in the blood of bulls, or of lambs, or of goats. Bring no more vain offerings.

His vehement action announces vividly that heaven is not embezzled by money, nor is God domesticated by ritual.

Jesus was as out of line as the Selma marchers or the jailed protesters of abortion clinics and capital punishment. His startling performance sends the clear clarion call that there are some things we should not stand for; outrages that should outrage human beings . . . such as extravagant defense spending when schools need to be built, or obscene campaign expenditures, or foot-dragging on gun control legislation.

Jesus' white-hot wrath helps clarify confusion about the validity of intense emotions. True, anger can be dangerous. So can food, sun, and water. But emotions are innocent in themselves. Like children, they need to be heard, attended to, if they are to be controlled. Aggressive feelings are often uncomfortable and embarrassing, so the natural tendency is to shove them under the rug. Anger denied can build to volcanic fury. This is the case with many a serial killer, whose neighbors report him as "never any trouble, just kept to himself." Anger needs advertence. When recognized and dealt with, it can be a dynamic advantage to vital living.

One expedient formula for handling upsetting emotion is "Name it-Claim it-Aim it." That is, label the feeling consciously for what it is: annoyance, hurt, or rage. Then, own it as one's own without blaming another for it. Finally, direct what is felt to the offender simply by saying, "I am hurt/uneasy/furious," not, "you make me mad!"

Joseph M. Wadowicz

Anger is a perfectly respectable emotion. In the face of threat, it is far more serviceable than terror. Even the Bible refers to the "wrath of God." This is another way of saying that, unlike Rhett Butler in *Gone with the Wind,* God "gives a damn" about human behavior. We are important to Him. Therefore, anger has something to do with caring. The opposite of love is not hate or anger, it is *indifference.* We are generally angered only by what is important to us. Psychology claims that the other face of anger is fear. One might usefully ask oneself when angry: "What am I afraid of?" It could be the threat of losing something precious.

Passion is a bounteous gift in anyone's life. The late, great Paddy Chayefsky conceives the Creator's evaluation on this subject in his luminous play *Gideon.*

> *It is Passion, Gideon, that carries man to God. And passion is a balky beast. Few men ever let it out of the stable. It brooks no bridle; indeed, it bridles you; it rides the rider. Yet, it inspirits man's sessile soul above his own inadequate world and makes real such things as beauty, fancy, love and God and all those other things that are not quite molecular but are. Passion is the very fact of God in man that makes him other than a brute.*

Our human brain weighs about three pounds and consists of one hundred billion cells, of which, we are told, we use only ten percent. However, this tiny corporeal computer surpasses the one hundred million galaxies surrounding us, because it can think, get exasperated, and love!

3rd Sunday of Lent
(John 2: 13-25)

213

La Vie en Rose

Today is the Sunday of the Rose. In contrast to the somber season of purple, the liturgy injects this flash of color to remind earnest worshippers that lighthearted is as holy as solemn—even more so. It used to be called *Laetare* (Latin imperative for "rejoice") Sunday. In its commanding way, the Church is commending balance to its disciplined followers.

The first reading (2 Chron. 36: 14-23) catches no euphoria of the day. "The anger of the Lord against His people was so inflamed." But it closes on the cheery note as Persian King Cyrus repatriates the exiled Jews to their homeland. The second reading (2 Eph. 2: 4-10) comes closer to the keynote as Paul exults in "the immeasurable riches of His grace in His kindness to us in Christ Jesus."

The Gospel is hard to follow. Jesus sounds more like an abstruse academic lecturing a dull student. His words are abstract, stilted, unlike the homespun plain-talk in the synoptic versions. The generations subsequent to his death were better able to evaluate the impact of that Risen Life in the lives of his followers, much as later generations can more clearly comprehend the significance of deceased presidents and their influence on world and national history. John's Gospel was put together about the end of the first century and reflects a developed Christology. It could be that the author affirmed the divinity of Jesus as a fit competitor for the homage the self-proclaimed *divine* Caesars demanded. Matthew, Mark and Luke do not highlight Jesus as God.

The Nicodemus nocturnal visitation is the same as our story when "what will people think" rules our behavior. Nicodemus was a prominent citizen, a respected religious leader. He was not about to expose his reputation to any suspicion by a detected involvement with the upstart Nazarene. To court public approval usually means abdicating a part of oneself. A performer who depends on the audience to define him will never win an Oscar. The consummate actor is always more convincing when he plays his role as he sees it.

Nicodemus was not sure where he stood. He was stuck with the old time religion: rules, ritual, a God insisting on strict ceremonial observance. Jesus saw religion principally as duty to people and less as devotion to external structure. Nicodemus must have liked what he heard. But it may have been strange sounding to him, possibly far-out, certainly unconventional. Then there was possibly that nagging anxiety about disloyalty to a revered tradition. So, Nicodemus was cautious, if not timid, about endorsing openly the controversial young teacher. Still, to his credit, he made a move. However nervous, it was a baby step out of the dark.

Jesus rewarded this circumspect gesture with an enigmatic response. He was sensitive to the human resistance to change, but he emphasized that there was no growth without it. "Unless you are born again," he states, "you can never get into the Kingdom of God." Another simpler translation of this text: "You must be reborn from above." What does this mean? It mystified Nicodemus as well. One interpretation could be that personal education involves forgetting much of what was learned in the past. Grownups discover eventually that what got them through childhood does not work as well in adulthood. Cooing, cajoling, crying, and tantrums may have been effective once; now mature relating is called for. Jesus' focus on reverence for human beings is as good a lesson to learn as even the most scholarly erudition. Those gifted with this modest understanding have discovered that gentleness is an amazingly durable attribute and its offspring is joy. Want joy in your life? Try a little tenderness!

4th Sunday of Lent
(John 3: 14-26)

Never Say Die . . . !

John's Gospel features Jesus in conversation more than in action. It is thus more abstract and prolix, as theological thinking often is. The death of Lazarus provides the occasion for Jesus to advance his doctrine about mankind's most distressing destiny, the grave. He is touched to tears at this loved friend's passing. Only one other time do the scriptures report him weeping: over apathetic Jerusalem. Death disturbed Jesus, as it does us all!

This episode wraps up for John the public ministry of Jesus and supplies a bridge to the story of his final days. Jesus senses the approaching end and talks about dying as the opportunity for a new and fuller life. He points to nature's rhythm as the buried seed produces a rich yield. "For nothing dies but something lives, till the skies be fugitives," so says the poet. Living and dying are of one piece for Jesus. Death is the entrance to real living; "eternal life" he calls it, for which all mankind was created. Earth's existence is only for openers. The best is yet to be!

Even science affirms this theology when it reasons that physical matter is indestructible. The tiny atom can be shattered, but in its diffusion, it becomes something else—energy. Base quantity is transformed into a higher form—activity. Incredible power is released from battered matter. So it is not so far-fetched to think of the human soul as immortal. To expire is to be transformed from a gross to a purer state—to pass to another time zone, another dimension.

This thinking may comfort the mourner, but it does not displace the aching emptiness that a loved one's loss creates in the griever's life. The deceased may be in a better place—

219

the survivor is not. Why this wrenching agony? How does tragedy improve our lives? After standing tall, why must we be brought to our knees? Opposites seem to feed each other. Negative versus positive gives us electricity. Illness makes health precious. Not having makes having gladder. Suffering is inherent in the nature of mankind because it is imperfect, limited, and in process. Pain is an invitation to transcend, to reach beyond self. Compassion is born of it. When Jesus proclaimed, "Blessed are those who mourn," he was saying, fortunate are they who love enough to grieve.

Death, when it happens, we may no more be aware of than when we fall asleep. It's the dying that frightens us. How long will it take? Will it hurt? Will I trouble others? Will I be "chicken"? The final curtain may include all the above, but it is not the end of the play. It is only the intermission. Were it not for death, life would be an unrelenting soap opera without commercial breaks . . . a kind of perpetual insomnia. Dying takes practice—like letting go of Monday so it does not contaminate Tuesday. Kissing off the good and the bad of each day could well ease the shock of final departure.

Maybe dying is our last chance to get it right—our terminal choice for freedom. Have you noticed the serenity on the countenances of the demised? Worry, if you must, but the issue is in even better hands than Allstate! The popular Lutheran seminary professor, Joseph Sitler (born 1904), says it for me:

The only life I know is this finite one that I live before dying. What life beyond might be, I have no notion. If all life is engendered and created by God, then that relationship will certainly not be destroyed by the periodic appearance and disap-

pearance of this particular person with my name. Something continues but what that will be I'm perfectly willing to leave in the hands of the Originator.

—*Grace Notes and Other Fragments*
Joseph A. Sittler

5th Sunday of Lent
(John 12: 20-33)

King for a Day

The Romans reserved palm waving for their conquering emperors. The Jews brandished branches to commemorate the victorious entry of the warrior Maccabees into Jerusalem to rededicate the Temple. If the followers of Jesus wanted to display how much they thought of him, they did so at his own fatal expense. Ever sensitive to suspicions of sedition, any pretense of local prominence was viewed by the vigilant imperial occupation as politically incorrect. Five days later, Jesus was executed for the capital crime: being "King of the Jews," a claim he consistently and sedulously resisted.

Kingship never seemed to appeal to Jesus, but royalty did. Not the parliamentary variety, but the nobility of humility. Life, for most, is no walk in the park. Our planet is a perilous place. Awake or asleep danger lurks. Holy Week liturgy is a thicket of symbolism—an abridged reproduction of paradoxical human existence. The dramatic final days of Jesus offer insights about handling hurt.

The Passion narrative is remarkable for its simplicity—its matter-of-fact, emotionless recording of a gruesome horror. The stark event is reported like a telegram—without an extra syllable. Strange that the word *passion*, which signifies intensity, is not matched in its Gospel telling. In this Passion Play, we have played all the parts: Judas the betrayer, Peter the denier, Pilate the compromiser. There were times when we were the supporting cast: Mary and John beneath the cross, the merciful Veronica, whenever we attended the needs of a sufferer.

Some of us have known the desolation of "My God, my God, why have you forsaken me?" This soulful sob from tortured lips is the opening verse of Psalm 22. It does not end, however, on this forlorn note. Verse 24 revives hope: "For he has not despised my cries of despair; he has not turned and walked away. When I cried to him he heard me and came." This is faith speaking—the single most indispensable resource when disaster strikes. The temptation to repudiate faith is when we most need to believe—to believe that there is a plan, a purpose, a solution—that evil can never be the bottom line as long as there is a God.

To paraphrase the poet who understood something of the mystery of that Holy Week: Love means to love the unlovable, or it is not virtue at all. Forgiving means pardoning the unpardonable, or it is no virtue at all. Faith means believing the unbelievable, or it is no virtue at all. And hope means hoping in the hopeless, or it is no virtue at all.

Maybe this is what "royalty" means. It can happen to us without our even knowing that it is happening. It simply means playing the hand that life deals us. It often happens best when we feel least about our worth.

A reprise of Sister Mary Clare:

> *Why did you make me, Lord,*
> *the way that I am,*
> *which is just as I would not*
> *wish to be?*
> *Did you perhaps know what You*
> *were about,*
> *And plan me thus for all*
> *eternity?*

Joseph M. Wadowicz

If I had fashioned me,
I would have used a sterner stuff,
and formed a soul more strong,
immune to pains of love
and deaf to tears,
unmoved by sentiment,
untouched by song!
But I, I am a fool; I feel too much,
At every little hurt,
I cringe and whine.
Did you intend that I
should win the cup by just
these handicaps of mine?

Palm/Passion Sunday
(Mark 14: 1-15, 47)

Mini-Resurrections

Headcounters report that more attend church for Easter than they do at Christmas. Why is this, do you suppose? Could be that as appealing as is the miracle of birth, rebirth is even more so. Spring says more about reanimation than does winter!

To elicit more consistent church attendance, a prankish pastor sported a touch of whimsy in his Easter sermon, by introducing a novel "No Excuse Sunday." He announced:

> *Cots will be placed in the foyer for those who say, "Sunday is my only day to sleep late." There will be a special section with lounge chairs and recliners for those who think our pews are too hard and uncomfortable. Eye drops will be available for those with tired eyes from the glare of late night Saturday TV programs. We will have steel helmets for those who say, "The roof would cave in if I ever came to church." Blankets will be furnished for those who think the church is too cold and drafty; fans will be given to those who say it is too hot and stuffy. Score cards will be distributed to those who wish to keep a record of the hypocrites present. Relatives and friends will be in attendance for those who can't go to church and cook dinner too. Ushers will pass around "Stamp Out Stewardship" buttons for those who are weary of being asked for money. One area of the church will be devoted to trees and grass for those who prefer to seek God in nature. Doctors and nurses will be in attendance*

for those who plan to be sick on Sunday. We will provide hearing aids for those who can't hear the preacher and cotton for those who can. Hope to see you there. (*Celebration,* 23 April 2000)

People might be going to church for the wrong reason—to be inspired, when it is more useful to go to be inspirers. This is the wonder of the Paschal mystery—that we can be restorers of life to one another when we stop long enough to care.

Many of us have seen little resurrections . . . not stupendous, like bringing the dead to life, but seeing someone eased from the sepulcher of fear, of despair, of futile guilt. For many years, veterans' hospitals have ministered to the "walking wounded": men entombed in the memory of terror, afraid to move out to the scary land of other people . . . who seek peace in paralysis—emotional rigor mortis—too frightened to feel again. No amount of urging, badgering, or cheerleading could penetrate the petrified barrier, only the patient vigil of persevering attention—reverent, gently waiting. And suddenly the great stone would roll away and a newly risen human being would reach out to touch life again.

We need not be professional therapists, but we are all called to be a friend. All of us have that power. Whenever we pause—not to judge or advise, or even encourage—we need just to listen intently, perceptively. Hear this resurrection of a young woman who lost her way in the tomb of emotional pathology. It is a poem by Bonaventure Stefan entitled "Talitha Cumi," the Aramaic words Jesus spoke to the child he brought back to life: "Young woman, I say to you, Rise Up!"

Joseph M. Wadowicz

I was not dead,
Not death marked by a stone

But I begged for the rest of burial.
Death—
I could not tempt his bony hand.
He looked for better company,
I volunteered for his corps,
Then groveled with guilt for asking.

Others were only human, as I—
Yet I was not,
Only the hull, the sham—
And this man could see it all.

I litanied to him my ills,
My oppressions.
They made me so—these people,
Twisting and contorting
Until my thoughts writhed
Like snakes in hibernation,
Or smaller than that,
Worms in a fishing can.

He listened—
No repulsion veiled his eyes,
No scolding, No hackneyed remedies.
Only the listening.
Intense, knowing, respectful,
With interjected "uh huhs"
That lullabied my fears.

His understanding
Became the hum of a dynamo—

The Now Testament

The throb of another human's heart
Who did not shun me like a leper.
He listened and accepted,
Like the Christ of compassion
Who gave the people bread
When they had enough of words.

I could dare warm myself
At a flicker of hope.
His acceptance
Became an echo of "I thirst"
I saw my soul rise,
The void no longer yawned
With bottomless ugliness.
I felt the spark of life.

My life,
Accepted and meaningful
Another knew I lived
And now I knew it too.
I told the sun and the taxi driver
And shouted the news to the sky.
But the universe was too small for the joy
Exploding in my risen heart.

Easter Sunday
(John 20: 1-9)

230

Thomas Our Twin

Faith, like health, is most appreciated in its loss. Thomas must have been an unhappy camper—lonely, cranky, despondent, as he refused to believe in the new presence of Jesus. But he did not alter his mood to suit his company. He was not a people-pleaser.

Faith improves one's vision of life. It helps one see past the appearance of things and into their depth. Faith is what makes a marriage work when love has worn away—a belief in the other's integrity.

Religious faith can emerge in many assorted ways. For some it comes ready-made, like a prefabricated house. These are born into it, identify with it and have nary the need to question it. For others, arriving at a faith is a complicated journey involving assiduous study and tedious searching, full of detours and blind alleys. When this exploration ends in discovery, a whole new world opens. The celebrated English author, G. K. Chesterton (1874-1936), described his conversion as "turning upside down and coming upright!"

Something like this happened to Thomas, nicknamed Didymus, the twin. In the vernacular of academe, he had "cut class" and missed the fantastic resurrection appearance of Easter Sunday. A week later he was doing a "make-up," probably reluctantly, since he shared nothing of his companions' enthusiastic credulity.

Nonetheless, he showed up and so did the solution to his problem. Jesus happened to him. He was never the same since!

It is worth noting that this embryo church saw no reason to exclude the incredulous Apostle for his dissent; nor did Jesus. The episode points out that questions, doubts, even challenges about himself are welcome by Jesus. Notice how he responds to the person—not the problem—thus eliciting from Thomas the same oath that the Roman emperor, Domitian (51-96 C.E.) demanded of his subjects: "My Lord and My God."

Thomas undoubtedly felt disappointed in the Master. Cynical, let-down, indignant, he was probably driving on "empty" as he pushed himself to join his brothers. What if he had persisted in his dark temper and refused to be with those naive believers? He would not have heard the healing words of peace, forgiveness, and reconciliation. He could not have come alive again!

Thomas' disillusionment in Christ resembles people who have grown dissatisfied with the church. Once a solace, especially when those you needed to care didn't seem to. Now, the church holds little more than pledge drives, dull sermons, errant clergy and embezzling bishops. What's the use? There is nothing in it anymore. Quit attending!

What to do? How about doing what Thomas did—"go on empty"? Something might happen! What's to lose?

Folks go to church for the wrong reason, namely, to be inspired. A better reason is to be inspirers. In the story *The Color Purple*, Shug asks Celie: "Celie, tell the truth: have you ever found God in church? I never did, I just found a bunch of folks hoping for him to show up. Any God I ever felt in church I brought with me. And I think other folks did too. They come to share God, not find him."

A faith is not something, it is Someone. Devotion to a creed is no substitute for intimacy with God. Dogma is not as important as is pragma—the sedulous practice of caring for human beings. A religion that is a quest for certitude is not a search for truth. There is no commandment, "Thou shalt be right."

Jesus gave himself personally and lovingly to doubting Thomas. This same solidarity with humanity continues today in the darnedest places, among the darnedest people, not just to the religious elite who regularly attend church. Check these words from a particularly surprising source. The turbulent, hard-living Irish actor, Richard Harris, wrote this moving appeal of Christ to the world in the early '70s:

I am not in Heaven
I am here . . . Hear Me
I am in you . . . Feel Me
I am of you . . . Be Me
I am with you . . . See Me
I am for you . . . Need Me
I am ALL mankind. . . .
Only through kindness will you reach me.

2nd Sunday of Easter
(John 20: 19-31)

Body Language

The disciples were spooked at first sight of their fallen, now risen, Master. Phantoms frighten, so Jesus came to them as a guest, not a ghost. He dropped in for lunch. Now they could celebrate!

Among the wonders that Easter celebrates is the conspicuous reality of the human body. Western religions have not always been kind to it. The saints of old regarded flesh with grave suspicion—a treacherous tyrant ever demanding forbidden comforts. The appealing Francis of Assisi probably hastened his untimely demise by his pitiless corporal austerities. For centuries the Church encouraged harsh penance as a way of subduing the libido and thus placating its Author. Strictness was the antidote to laxness, but cold showers can stimulate as well as suppress.

Of course there is always the tendency in the human animal to overindulge and to waste inordinate time in the grooming process. Though vanity may be the motive, putting one's best face forward can also be considered an act of charity to the public. Beauty in any form always deserves a second look. So, what can be behind the current costuming craze to resemble a bedraggled refugee from the Klondike? Why are patched jeans more expensive than unpatched? Why are overalls de rigueur at the junior prom, or tennis shoes with a tuxedo? Such style statements are a bold declaration of independence from the older generation, but they are not a blow for freedom from peer pressure.

It is not easy to look nice, especially if one's looks win no contests. One's fragile body can be an annoying nuisance . . . what with its imperious urges, its noisome secretions, its

235

embarrassing excretions. And it falls apart so soon. That is why our bodies deserve the same patient compassion that Mother Teresa brought to the suffering poor of Calcutta. If incarnation means divinity took on a human body, it was surely not just from the neck up!

Why has mortal flesh received such indifferent press over the centuries? Six hundred years before Christ, the Persian Zoroaster proposed the theory that two external principles ruled the universe: light and darkness. This later developed into the Manichean heresy, namely, the dualism of matter (evil) vs. spirit (good). In this everlasting battleground, mankind is stranded in no man's land. Four centuries B.C., Plato resented the human body as a prison of the soul. Jesus taught that the body was innocent and that the mind concocted all manner of evil. Nazism was not invented by a body, but by a distorted intelligence.

The Easter mystery emphasizes the transcending importance of the human body. For Thomas Aquinas, the ultimate fate of the mortal person was the combination of body and soul for all eternity. This means that the Resurrection of Jesus is likewise the destiny of human beings.

To mistrust bodily instincts is sometimes the product of even sane religious training. Sensuality justifiably requires a caution signal. But there is a difference between sensuous and sensual. Jesus was sensuous; his senses worked for him. He felt grief and he wept; he felt terror and he sweat. He enjoyed children, a good meal and wine, laughter with his friends. He could be angry enough to throw the furniture around in the Temple. He was not ashamed of his emotions, including the negative ones.

Sensual is more a mental hang-up. Its focus is gratification and reduces the world to a playpen of infantile pleasure seeking. Play becomes more important than people. It is the offspring of fear and hysteria. Such jaded playboys and playgirls are too uptight to sip the wine of life. They gulp it down and are capable of only extreme, extravagant sensations that inevitably issue in ennui.

The body's five senses are meant to be experienced. They are singular instruments to bring us in touch with the stupefying grandeur of God's world. Physicality nurtures spirituality and vice versa. There is a whisper of wildness in all holiness. John Donne, the sixteenth century English metaphysical poet, caught the passion in the disciplined wholesomeness of the human heart bursting with longing for its Maker:

> *Take me to You, imprison me—*
> *For I, except You, enthrall me,*
> *Never shall be free, nor ever chaste,*
> *Except You ravish me.*

Be good to your body—trust its five senses. These know what your soul needs even better than your brain does.

3rd Sunday of Easter
(Luke 24: 35-48)

Sitcom Mom

Happily or not, the modern media seems to have outgrown the *Ozzie & Harriet* depiction of family harmony. Situational comedy series about dysfunctional families spark the higher ratings. The trauma begotten of maternal extremes between pandering and punishing a child is unblushingly dramatized in the 1982 film, *Mommie Dearest*. The movie star depicted in the picture, Joan Crawford, would hardly win the "Donna Reed" award. A mother can be no more than she is as a woman, though her children expect perfection. Parenting appears to bring out the best and the worst in one's nature. Is there a more demanding vocation or broader education?

Mothers take the heat for parental failure more so than do fathers. But what man would apply for this job description?

WANTED: housekeeper—140 hour week, no retirement benefits, no sick leave, no private room, no Sundays off. Must be good with kids, animals and hamburger. Must share bath.

The irreplaceable Erma Bombeck added her typically matter-of-fact reality. . . . "No man could stand being pregnant. The first time a man lost his breakfast three solid months in a row, he would make plans to have a nocturnal headache for the rest of his married life."

Back in 1958, an indicting writer, Philip Wylie, rocked the public with a bestseller, *Generation of Vipers,* in which he charged that "Momism"—mother worship—was menacing the American Way. He emphasized that children should be raised to leave the nest. "To bring up children who are not dependent on you, it is necessary to indicate, from the start, that you, when you wish, can act entirely independent of them." This can mean that the couple is married to each other—not to the children. As someone sagely observed, "Good parenting is the product of good husbanding and wifing." Marriage and family is nature's seductive invitation to outgrow inherent narcissism. Females seem to have a head start in this process. Little girls are made aware of their future maternity in their early doll playing, but what boy is brought up to think of himself as a father-to-be? Wylie adds, "Fatherhood is the greatest male skill. But it cannot be picked up idly: it is not inborn." Neither is the talent for successful mothering. There is no crash course, no Motherhood 101. There is just the learning by the doing, which includes all the mistakes. Lucky is the mother who has married a father, not just a breadwinner. Some mothers do not have that support and have to go it alone.

Besides troubled marriages, mothers today must stretch themselves between kitchen and career. Fifty percent of modern moms will return to work outside the home before their child's first birthday.

Fittingly, a grateful nation celebrates Mother's Day. Fittingly also, today the liturgy features the Good Shepherd, which our mothers have been in most of our lives. But no place is more uncomfortable than a pedestal. Mothers would probably prefer understanding to applause. It took me 65 years to understand mine. . . . Tiny, weighing in at 110 pounds, she was nonetheless fearless, forceful, fiercely independent, explosive and quick with the hated strap. I could not forgive her for the humiliating sting of it. In her mid-eighties and widowed fifteen years, I knew I would have to look after her. Retired from federal service, I headed for my duty with the enthusiasm of a gas chamber victim. I decided to level with her—to put my lifetime of gripes and disappointments on the table. With the persistence of a prosecuting attorney, I enumerated my list in the face of her denials, defenses and tears. Then, she finally said something that turned me around completely. . . . "Do you want me to confess to you?" she firmly declared. "Well, you can whistle for it. I did the best I knew how to do, and that's the end of it."

Suddenly, I saw my self-centered self-absorption. I had only thought about me and I was sick of it. I felt a new inquisitiveness about my mother: how she saw life, what mattered to her, what her feelings were. I explored her recollections of grinding poverty in her native Hungary, escape to America at age fifteen, learning the language, factory labor, an unfulfilling marriage, the hand-to-mouth depression years, the determination to survive. We became friends. We finally enjoyed each other's presence. She died at 92 and the last five years of her life are a cherished memory for me.

From all this I learned two important facts:

1. You cannot love anyone you cannot be angry at.
2. You are only angry at those you care about.

A mother of thirteen was chided for claiming to love all her children alike. "We all have favorites. Which of the thirteen did you love the most?" she was asked. Her answer: "The one who is sick until he gets well. The one who is away, until he gets home."

We bless you, Mothers, for having so blessed us!

4th Sunday of Easter
(John 10: 11-18)

The Vine That Binds

"Never pass up a kiss," wrote Stan Burroway in a newspaper report some years ago.

In Pittsfield, PA, Roderick Long began to walk across a 50 foot long bridge over Little Broken Straw Creek on his way to work. His wife, Geri, had driven him to the span, but the bridge had been damaged by ice floes earlier in the day and he didn't want to drive across. Suddenly, Long turned around and walked back to his truck—he had forgotten to kiss Geri good-bye. Just then, the 25-foot center section of the bridge collapsed—the very part he would have been on, he said later, if he hadn't remembered the kiss.

This closeness of the Longs saved Rod's life. In the Gospel image of "Vine and Branches," Jesus is highlighting how intimacy with him can safeguard our spiritual lives.

Vineyard tending is a fine art. The University of California at Davis offers doctorates in viticulture—the study of vines, and in endology—the making of wine. Productive vines demand delicate attention. They need a special soil, a special climate and drastic trimming. Young vines are not allowed to produce for three years in order to increase the eventual yield. The implication is that a caring Providence allows life's rigors to prune us humans if we are to achieve adult specifications.

The vitality of the vine comes from its suitable grounding. Nurturance from the soil passes to the branches, which in turn energize the roots by absorbing sunlight and CO_2. The vine and the branches depend on each other. They are one piece. In fact, vine and branch appear indistinguishable. Separated, they perish. In this process, nothing is wasted. Even sour grapes are useful. Withered branches are good for kindling.

This lovely pastoral vinery parallel emphasizes the Creator's unity with Creation. Divinity is embedded in humanity. To see God, one needs only to look around. . . . Having attended church with his grandfather, the youngster asked, "Grandpa, can you see God?" "Billy," replied the old gentleman, "it's getting so lately, I can't see anything else . . ." Looking for God is like looking for the air, when all the time we are breathing it.

This means that no one is ever alone in this universe. Mankind is a mutually interdependent network. All living beings survive by complicity with other living beings. The great eighteenth century poet/preacher, John Donne, illustrated this intertwining hominal fabric when he wrote:

> *No human being is an island entire of itself; every person is a piece of the continent, a part of the main. If a clod be washed away by the sea, Europe is the less. . . . Anyone's death diminishes me, because I am involved in humankind. And, therefore, never send to know for whom the bell tolls. It tolls for thee.*

In John Steinbeck's classic, *The Grapes of Wrath*, a down-home preacher, Casey, utters these profound words:

> *Tain't sayin' I'm like Jesus. But I got tired like Him, an' I got mixed up like Him, an' I went into the wilderness like Him, without no campin' stuff. Nighttime I'd lay on my back an' look up at the*

*stars; mornin' I'd sit an' watch the sun come up;
midday I'd look out from a hill at the rollin' dry
country; evenin' I'd pray like I always done. On'y
I couldn't figure what I was prayin' to or for. There
was the hills, an' there was me, an' we wasn't separate no more. We was one thing. An' that one
thing was holy. . . .*

God is holy because God is whole. We are part of it.

Four Letter Word

Swahili has a dozen words for banana. There are separate names for ripe banana, picked banana, cooked banana, and so on. Why so? Because bananas are important to that culture. For the most important reality on our spinning planet, the English language has but a single overused word: LOVE. People declare "love" for their cat, their canary, and their Camaro; as well as for God, baseball, and lemon pie. Enough, already! How about a moratorium on that indiscriminate term of endearment? Can we explore more exact expressions for our varied affections, perhaps caring, concern, cherish, regard, fond?

John's Gospel is awash with the word love. In today's brief reading, he uses it nine times. How should it be understood? The Greeks had a word for it—*agape*—the unselfish wanting good for another. No easy chore for the self-absorbed. That is why love is a commandment. Were it not an order from on high, our concerns would tend to end with the self. Jesus enjoined it because life demands it. There is simply no human development without love. Deprived of this essential nutrient, an emotional cripple is formed. . . . But can love be commanded? How can loving be a duty?

Nazi holocaust survivor, psychiatrist Victor Frankl wrote:

> *In the living laboratories of the concentration camps, we watched comrades behaving like swine, while others behaved like saints. Man has both these potentialities within himself. Which one he actualizes depends on* decisions, *not* conditions.

Our generation has come to know man as he really is: the being who invented the gas chambers of Auschwitz, and also the being who entered those gas chambers upright—The Lord's Prayer or the Shema Yisrael on his lips.

To love, therefore, is an act of the will. To fall in love is common enough: to stand in love takes soul—resolution— a response to injunction.

A religion that teaches the positive acceptance of the self that I am, not the self I would like to be, provides the firm basis for loving mankind. The thirteenth century German mystic, Meister Eckhart, summarized this topic:

> *If you love yourself, you love everybody else as you do yourself. As long as you love another person less than you love yourself, you will not really succeed in loving yourself, but if you love all alike, including yourself, you will love them as one person and that person is both God and man.*

This is our high calling—why we were born—the shining privilege to be a friend to every human being. This vocation is sure to bring us life's inevitable twin offspring, joy as well as sorrow. But it will bring us to wholeness—another word for holiness. In the words of Kahlil Gibran: "For even as love crowns you so shall he crucify you. Even as he is for your growth, so is he for your pruning. When you love, say not 'God is in my heart', but rather, 'I am in the heart of God.'"

Maybe we overcomplicate this mystery of love. Even a child can understand it. A child is freely impertinent enough to make affection pertinent. . . . Early one morning a little girl tiptoed into her sleeping parent's bedroom and softly touched her lips to her mother's cheek. The abruptly roused mom gruffly chided, "How many times have we told you not to bother us at this ungodly hour?" The child: "I didn't come to bother you—I came to give you a kiss."

6th Sunday of Easter
(John 15: 9-17)

Breaking Up is Hard to Do

A hand for Neil Sedaka!

When Romeo finally bid goodnight to his new flame, he could characterize parting as "such sweet sorrow" because he had just made another date with Juliet for the morrow. He would see her again. It was not so sweet for Bogart and Bergman to say good-bye in the classic movie *Casablanca*. Their farewell was final after an ardent "hello." For those close to each other, it is a wrenching ordeal when the bond is abruptly sundered. When the person who opened your life to you is no longer there, you are once again half-alive.

When Jesus suggested that "those who mourn" are blessed, he could be saying how fortunate are those who have loved enough to grieve for a departed. The measure of one's grief is the measure of one's love.

In the movie, Bogie and Ingrid could opt for their poignant parting, because they were involved in a cause larger than their mutual affection—defeat of the Nazis.

The Ascension story is something like this. The disciples of Jesus had grown accustomed to his space among them. They never knew anyone like him: straight talking, perceptive, profound, unpretentious, astute, transuding God's Spirit. He was their guru. Dependent on his leadership, now he needed theirs. If they were to get his job done, it was necessary for him to go away. It was time for them to take on the world, but on their own.

Jesus' leave-taking was much like Inauguration Day as the outgoing transmits authority to the incoming president . . . or the colorful military change of command ceremony when the former CO hands the flag to the new commander. Jesus knew they would be distressed, but he knew the crisis was not terminal and that it could toughen undeveloped muscle. So he did not "poor baby" his unfledged emissaries, he exacted their marching orders.

Human nature readily tends to distrust autonomy in favor of authority, that is, the surrender of personal independence to a charismatic leader. Such abdication provides a temporary illusion of security. Jesus apparently did not wish his protégés to be easily-led sheep. He, therefore, encouraged questions, dissent, even challenges. He prized frankness. He rebuked Simon Peter for not understanding God's ways, but he never threw him away. Jesus knew it takes time to mature. He gave it all the time the process needed.

The Ascension message attests that the beautiful things of life are built into the ugly. Joy and sorrow are never far apart. In fact, one nourishes the other. It takes an ominous illness to elicit the sweet thrill of recovery. Chaos occasions order. Remedies are the offspring of disease. Glorious flowers bloom from the commonest dirt.

Maybe God's best-disguised gift to us mortals is life's custom-built crosses that never seem at first to match our dimensions. Suffering eventually tenderizes us. Another's heartache is more sensitively commiserated because of our own. Were it not for loss, what would we know of the loneliness that tells us who we really are when there is no one to hold our hand? When we come face to face with emptiness—when there is no place we feel we belong—it is then that faith bids us reach out to touch another lonely exile.

From his *Responding in Gratitude,* Rev. John D. Gondol describes a little boy plying his granddad with questions:

"Gramps, what happens when you die?"

Gramps explained it as best he could. Still puzzled, the boy asked, "Does that mean you won't be here anymore?"

Grandpa nodded, "Yes, that's true."

"Does that mean you won't be able to play catch with me anymore?"

"Yes, it does."

"Does that mean you won't be able to fly a kite with me anymore?"

"Yes, son, it does."

"Does that mean you won't be able to take me fishing anymore?"

"Yes, it does."

"Well, Gramps, when that time comes, who is going to do those things with me, if you're not here?"

The wise grandfather explained, "When that time comes, it will be time for you to do those things for another little boy."

7th Sunday of Easter (Ascension)
(Mark 16: 15-20)

Bombshell Phenomenon

Today is a day for balloons, streamers, and party hats. It's the Church's birthday. Celebrate!

Scripture attempts to describe the spectacular event metaphorically by employing the language of elemental forces: wind and fire. It is the evangelist's way of relating what happened when the Spirit of God zapped a handful of scared people, snapping them out of their frightened funk, inspiring them to turn their world upside down. This festival remembers the hurricane and flame that symbolizes God's Spirit connecting with man's.

Pentecost affirms that God is not a testy sovereign, impossible to please and poised to punish whenever human nature steps out of line. It attests that God is a thunderbolt of animation—boisterous, noisy, a high voltage happening, not an abstraction. God is a verb, not a noun.

The Pentecost God is playful, does not mind being misunderstood, and is not miffed when not taken solemnly. It is hard to imagine this God enjoying being treated as an oriental potentate—worshipped behind silken veils and smoky incense. Pentecost invites the world to lighten up about God, who is for us, not our adversary. That is why Jesus names the Holy Spirit Paraclete and Comforter—our defense attorney and support. Pentecost celebrates a good-humored Creator, perfectly willing to share the secret of sacredness with creatures.

The innovative first Pentecost announced to the wide world that the Spirit of God is not the exclusive preserve of any particular religion. An implication can be drawn that divinity welcomes fresh, unconventional ideas about Itself.

Thus, it is not solely dependent on traditional, organized ritual to make Itself known. "The Spirit lists where it will" (John 3: 8). Religious orthodoxy need be no mental straitjacket. Vitality, originality, naturalness appear to be as prized by the Deity as by ourselves. Whatever their status, Pentecost is a testimony that all human beings participate equally in divine dignity. Which means that groveling in guilt is hardly a tribute to God. Self-debasement can scarcely be praise to the One who cannot make junk.

Why is it so hard for people to appreciate their specialness? Probably, because from birth, some of us have been brainwashed into believing that to feel important is a sin. Humiliation is seen as training for the real world. I, for one, was not taught to trust my judgment, but to prefer that of my "betters." This is standard strategy for a dominating authority that wills to maintain control. Thinking out loud for oneself is taken as resistance.

So, Pentecost emphasizes human preciousness and the latitude it thrives on. It invites the serious, searching mind to break new ground in religious thinking. It suggests that ancient formulations are not cast in cement—that new problems require new solutions. It highlights that God does not condemn us for being human, any more than a parent would banish a child for spilling his milk. If we are born into imperfection, perfection can hardly be expected. Again, we are saved, not because we are good, but because God is.

To believe in the frolicsome, zestful god of Pentecost, one, therefore, need not turn a back on life in order to approach the holy. Living everyday—in the kitchen, the supermarket, the freeway, the office—is where God is encountered. Someone captured this blessed ordinariness in a prayer/poem discovered in the Chester Cathedral almost five centuries ago:

Joseph M. Wadowicz

Give me a good digestion, Lord,
And also something to digest.
Give me a healthy body, Lord,
With sense to keep it at its best.
Give me a healthy mind, good Lord,
To keep the good and pure in sight,
Which seeing sin is not appalled
But finds a way to set it right.

Give me a mind that is not bored,
That does not whimper, whine or sigh.
Don't let me worry over-much
About this fussy thing called I.
Give me a sense of humor, Lord;
Give me the grace to see a joke,
To get some happiness from life
And pass it on to other folk.
Amen.

Pentecost
(Acts 2: 1-11)

257

Mega-God

A fourth grader questioned her rabbi: "Jews say the Lord is one. Catholics say God is three. Can you tell me when He'll be four?" The late controversial Episcopalian bishop of San Francisco, James Pike, once quipped: "Mohammedans have one God and three wives. Christians have one wife and three Gods." So much for informal levity about the Trinity!

Today the liturgy celebrates not a hallowed event, like Pentecost, but a "doctrinal" feast—Trinity. It refers to the fact that this dogma was developed centuries after the last word of the New Testament was written. The Hebrew scriptures have no hint of a triune God. What did the Church Fathers have in mind when they formulated a tenet important enough to begin and end every formal prayer?

As Christology developed in the first century Church, so did belief that Jesus was divine. Assigning divinity to significant personages has not been uncommon in human history. The Roman Caesars were claimants to this august attribute, as were Japanese emperors, until the end of WWII. The oneness that John's Gospel (10: 30) claims for Jesus with the Father, fostered this faith of his co-equality with the Godhead. Bitter were the disputes over this theology and much violent blood spilt, but defining the "Blessed Trinity" insured deity status for the carpenter of Nazareth. The feast of the Trinity did not become generalized until the fourteenth century. It is still unknown in the Eastern rites.

The early conciliar Fathers may have aspired to interpret for the world a God actively involved with it. The Trinity was their answer. "Father" identifying providence, "Son," brotherhood, and "Holy Spirit," the medium joining the

259

divine and the human. It was an elaborate attempt to have God appear more accessible, more personal. In fact, the "person" aspect was so emphasized as to include "three."

Alas, words are feeble. In the rare air of the mind, words are all that thoughts have to start them on their way. Theologians do the best they can with what they have to work with—frail language. Thus, abstruse formulations can result about the divine nature that often obscure more than they clarify. Jesus could best explain who his Father is by what his Father does. He used everyday figures with which his hearers were familiar. How to convey that God is to be sought less in ceremonial ritual than in the humdrum routine of daily life: in the kitchen, the bedroom, the freeway, the mall, the office? Trinitarian theology is a college try to this end, but a clearer message comes through since today is also Father's Day. Now hear this! . . .

Hello there, this is your Father, God, speaking. . . . Do you really want to know what I am about? You can study theology and the scriptures if you like, but I will let you in on a sure-fire secret. Try being a parent. There is nothing that will bring you in closer touch with Me.

I have shared My power to create with you, fathers. Like you, I was not certain what I let myself in for, when I created your kind: free to rebel or obey, to reject or embrace. It was a path you had never been down before, when you first became a dad.

Creating meant limiting My omnipotence, just as generating restricted your liberty. We both did it willingly. We both took a chance, and I'm glad I did.

Trinity Sunday
(Matthew 28: 16-20)

Corporate Takeover

Christendom is doubtlessly grateful that ceremonial religion has outgrown sprinkling people with bulls' blood, as recorded in this day's Exodus reading (24: 8). Jesus instituted a tidier ritual of God bonding when he initiated the Eucharist. Corpus Christi celebrates this event. What was in his mind when he declared the bread he blessed to be his body, the wine he offered to be his blood?

There can be no doubt that Jesus wanted his presence to remain in the world that he was leaving. He had been the Good News; it was now his disciples' turn. He clearly wanted them to be his extended living substitutes. In the 2 March 2000 edition of the Jesuit weekly *America,* F. Gerald Martin wrote: "Jesus did not institute the Eucharist to change bread and wine into his body and blood, but to change us into his body. The Mass is not meant to transform elements, but to transform people." In that same issue, a laywoman, Amy L. Florian, states: "Those who reverence Christ's presence in the Host must also reverence Christ's presence in human bodies." Implicit in Vatican II's Constitution on the Sacred Liturgy is the teaching that the words of consecration are spoken over the elements of bread and wine, as well as over the assembly. Thus, the presence of Christ becomes real through three forms: scripture, the Sacrament, and the believing congregation.

The emphasis is obviously to keep Jesus alive in our everyday lives, so he identified himself with the commonest staples of his day—bread and wine. Which can come down to this: what nourishes and refreshes us is Jesus happening to us. Eucharist, then, is not something we do; it is something we are. We can make Eucharist whatever has meaning in our lives—our loves, our labors, our losses, our longings.

No words are more important than those we say in our good-byes. At the final meal with his beloved Twelve, Jesus might have intended this farewell . . . "When you wine and dine together, when you are sharing and listening and laughing with each other, when you are having a good time, I am there." In fact, the original celebration of the Eucharist in the first century was more like a tailgate party. *Agape* it was called—"love feast." As numbers increased, so did problems. Snobbery in the ranks led to elitism. Some got high on the wine. To insure becoming behavior, the Church formalized the rite with a protective thicket of rules and prohibitions. Initially, lay people were chosen to preside over the Eucharist, including women. Subsequently, ordained clergy claimed that privilege exclusively. In later centuries, detailed auricular confession began to give a courtroom cast to the penitential rite. As the accuser and the accused, only the priest's absolution rendered the penitent "worthy" to commune, though reminded by the Liturgy just prior to receiving, "O Lord, I am not worthy."

This bread for the world was becoming more and more distanced from it. Enclosed in the tabernacle, or enthroned in a golden monstrance, the Sacrament became an object to be gazed at from afar but not consumed. It appeared that Jesus was being quarantined from contamination with the sinners he redeemed, as though getting too close to them would somehow corrupt God's morals. The faithful attend Mass these days not to kowtow to a conceited deity, or to be ranted at for being human, or harangued for money. They come for solidarity with a God that invented the Eucharist in a supreme attempt to humanize human beings.

A devout daily communicant was invited by her pastor to serve as a special Eucharistic minister. She was uneasy about this; would she do it right, maybe spill the Sacred Species? She acceded, however, and was a nervous wreck for her first performance. Gradually, the prayerful devotion of those to whom she extended the cup dissolved her tension. She was deeply moved. Later that week she was asked to help at a community soup kitchen. As she ladled the potage for the elderly needy, she felt the same reverence she experienced that Sunday offering the chalice. From then on, the kitchen stove became an altar for her.

Those blessed with a faith that sees in the Eucharist the Lord's desire for a friendly incorporation with himself, will understand the sentiment in this poem entitled "A Memory and a Hope":

Often, tis true on my day's horizon
I see in the east the clouds arise,
But within my heart I carry a whisper
That brings light o'er the darkest skies—
A memory bright as a golden sunset,
A hope as sweet as the fields in May,
I am going to Holy Communion tomorrow—
I went to Holy Communion today.

Many a time I am weary of labor,
Vexed with a life of work and worry.
Tired of giving myself to others,
Worn with the fret of this age of hurry—
Then o'er my heart's unquiet waters
Comes my Lord's sweet whisper to say,
"We shall meet at communion tomorrow—
We have met at communion today."

The Now Testament

Sometimes others are rough and thoughtless—
Sometimes it may be hard and cold.

I long to pour out on the first quick impulse
All the pain that my heart does hold—
Then my HOPE & MY MEMORY blended
Plead in my soul with a note of sorrow,
"Jesus lay on your tongue this morning,
Keep your story for Him tomorrow."

All day long like a ballad burden
Sings in my heart that musical chime—
All my minutes swing backward and forward,
Between that bliss of two points of time—
And I know the grateful heart on the Altar
Is touched to think my own is gay—
Just because He is coming tomorrow—
Just because He has come today.

Corpus Christi
(Mark 14: 12-16, 22-26)

Ladies' Day

A harried young mother was beside herself when the telephone rang, but she listened with relief to the kindly voice on the line. "Hi, Sweetheart, how are you?"

"Oh, mother," the poor thing said, breaking into tears. "It's been an awful day. The baby won't eat and the washing machine broke down. I tripped down the stairs and I think I sprained my ankle. I haven't had a chance to go shopping and the house is a mess and we have company coming for dinner tonight."

"There, there, darling everything will be all right," the soothing voice on the line said. "Now sit down, relax and close your eyes. I'll be over in a half hour. I'll pick up a few things on the way over and I'll cook dinner for you. I'll take care of the house and feed the baby. I'll call a repairman I know who'll be at your house to fix the washer this afternoon. Now stop crying. I'll take care of everything. In fact, I'll even call George at the office and tell him he ought to come home early."

"George?" the distraught woman said. "Who's George?"

"Why, George! Your husband!"

"But my husband's name is Frank."

There is a pause; then the woman on the line asks: "Is this 555-1783?"

The tearful reply! "No, this is 555-1788."

265

"Oh my, I'm terribly sorry. I must have dialed the wrong number," the voice on the phone apologizes.

Another short pause before the would-be daughter asks: *"Does this mean you're not coming over?"* (*Connections,* June 1994)

Jesus agrees to "come over" to Jairus' house to attend his mortally ill daughter of twelve. On the way, he encounters a desperate woman suffering from a female disorder known as menorrhagia, a profuse menstrual flow, for as many years as Jairus' child has had life. This was an especially mortifying morbidity since in the Jewish culture it rendered the victim "ritually unclean." She was forbidden worship in The Temple. Whoever she touched incurred official pollution. She had to keep her distance. "If I but touch his clothes, I shall be cured." In the jostling crowd she reached for her relief. . . . The Torah recommends no less than eleven prescriptions for healing this ailment. Among them was a superstitious nostrum of carrying a burnt ostrich egg in a linen rag. . . . Her contact was instantly efficacious and Jesus was aware "that power had gone out of him."

Helping hurting people is not without cost. To reduce another's pain, one must be willing to allow it to pain oneself. Compassion means suffering with the sufferer. . . . Jesus did another subtle favor for the recovered woman. He invited her to confront her embarrassment. She did so and enjoyed a richer liberation. A culture that prizes concealment and camouflage over upfront disclosure is a society of disguise and subterfuge. To confront is to care enough not to overlook a problem, but to look it over candidly together. It is the opposite of condemnation.

It is not hard to identify Jesus as a feminist. He had no trouble dealing with women as equals in that repressive patriarchal age. Centuries later the battle of the sexes wages on. Men who are uncomfortable with feminine equality simply are afraid to learn about themselves. Team-person-ship sounds more useful than a competitive stalemate. Samuel Johnson (1709-84) admitted: "Nature has given women so much power that the law has very wisely given them little." In the words of Charles Dickens: "If the law supposes that," said Mr. Bumble, "the law is a ass, a idiot." It is a strain, however, to understand how female fulfillment is enhanced by doing more and more of what men do. Women surely deserve their executive chairs, or even, at last, president of the U.S.A., but firewomen, combat Marines, prize fighters? . . .

Appropriately dubbed the "Womens' Gospel," the next scene is the home of Jairus. On the threshold of woman-hood, his daughter is now dead, and the professional mourn-ers are in full swing, rending pre-torn clothes and wailing to the tune of flutes, would you believe! They jeered Jesus for not joining in, but put-down or applause never seemed to turn his head. He took charge of defining himself and did not abdicate that responsibility to others. This self-assur-ance is noted in his recommendation to Jairus: "Do not be afraid, just have faith."

Faith in what?

It was probably reckless of this respected synagogue official to openly affirm the suspect Nazarene. I hear Jesus urging the grieving father: "Take a chance on what you believe in—however politically incorrect—a miracle can happen!" And it did.

A miracle of our time is the about-face of the infamous apartheid in South Africa. For nearly thirty years, octoge-narian Nelson Mandela was a political convict. He is now Prime Minister of the nation that imprisoned him. Check the Christ-like confidence in his inaugural:

Our deepest fear is not that we are inadequate. Our deepest fear is that we are powerful beyond measure. It is our light, not our darkness, that frightens us. We ask ourselves, who am I to be brilliant, gorgeous, talented, fabulous? Actually, who are we not to be? You are a child of God. Your playing small does not serve the world. There is nothing enlightened about shrinking so that other people won't feel insecure around you. We are born to make manifest the glory of God within us. It is not just in some of us, it is in everyone. And as we let our light shine, we unconsciously give others permission to do the same. As we are liberated from our fear, our presence automatically liberates others.

13th Sunday of Ordinary Time
(Mark 5: 21-43)

Wisdom of Weakness

A hit on the road, Jesus was a flop in his hometown. His neighbors were admittedly impressed by his words, but not with him. How important can a blue-collar person be, or one of questionable parentage, to a snooty audience? "Is he not the carpenter, the son of Mary? To mention only the mother's name, for the Jewish mind, was to imply illegitimacy. Even the Gospel records the conception of Jesus to be out of wedlock. Joseph also had a problem with this.

Novelists find small town narrow-mindedness a favorite theme. Sophisticated urbanites are no less hobbled by this cramping mentality. To restrict one's view of an individual only to the limits of social classification, is to miss the unique surprises in every personality. The town folk dismissed the impact of their native son because they stereotyped him. They labeled him out of a significance which is the malevolent basis for all the horrors of racial injustice: holocausts, lynchings, apartheid, ethnic cleansings!

To the religious right, who regard as sacrosanct archaic traditions of another age, disregarding up-to-date prescriptions for current problems, stereotyping is an occupational hazard. Jesus reducing the 613 precepts of the venerated Mosaic code to a simple three-pronged commandment: love of God, self, and others. This might have been a bit too left wing for the neighborhood. "And they took offense at him."

How did Jesus handle this rejection? According to *The Way* edition of the Bible: "And he could hardly accept the fact that they wouldn't believe in him." He is obviously hurt, but does not sulk. He moves on to a more receptive audience. In fact, he empowers his disciples to go out two by

269

two to see if they can do a better job than himself. And darn if they don't (next Sunday's Gospel)!

Stereotyping is a form of prejudice which decides not to examine the unfamiliar. It is the obstinate conclusion to remain inflexibly down-on what one is not up-on. Pious believers who crave certainty will never search for truth. They settle for a God of no surprises who behaves like they want God to behave: rewarding the "good guys" and punishing the "bad guys." The "hanging judge" type! A faith that needs to know what will happen next is hardly faith. Mature faith does not need to know. It does not cling. It lets go. It takes a chance without a net. It leaps!

Which brings us to another intriguing bungee-jump—Paul's free-fall into the mystic insight of the wisdom of weakness. Again, *The Way* edition: "For when I am weak, then I am strong—the less I have—the more I depend on him." The Apostle is saying that all our mortal flaws, failures and frailty are in God's plan for us. We creatures are the Creator's opportunity to be creative. When God made human beings he created co-creators. Creation is still going on. Check the recent DNA discoveries! God continually shares His creativity with us a little at a time, just as parents share their knowledge, experience, and values little by little with their children as they grow.

No caring parents throw their child away for spilling his milk, hitting his sister, or breaking a window. The lapse provides the parent with the chance to show how to hold the glass, how one is liable to get hurt when hurting others, or that the window will be repaired from the youngster's allowance. Responsibility is the message, not reprisal. When the teenager can't stand the sight of the parent because he or she is reminded of being a little kid, the adult knows this will pass. The adolescent has to revolt to discover how revolting the process is.

Paul is saying God is no less savvy. He is affirming that human imperfections do not alienate God from His creatures anymore than a child's inadequacies separate them from a good parent. It simply elicits greater attention. The good God knows that mortal existence is a delicate balancing act between our assets and liabilities. Lighten up, he urges in his first Corinthian letter (1: 27-29):

> *Instead God has deliberately chosen to use ideas the world considers foolish and of little worth in order to shame those people considered by the world as wise and great. He has chosen a plan despised by the world, counted as nothing at all, to use it to bring down to nothing those the world considers great, so that no one anywhere can ever brag in the presence of God. (The Way)*

14th Sunday of Ordinary Time
(2 Corinthians 12: 7-10, Mark 6: 1-6)

Mission Implausible?

The lifestyle that Jesus imposes on his on-the-job trainees would never rate the "Savvy Traveler's" seal of approval. No baggage, no carry-on, no second shirt, and no extra underwear is certainly the weightless way to go, if hygiene is not a high priority. He did not want them to stall for arguments on the way, or to waste time looking for the "light on" at Motel 6. Keep moving, he insisted, and count on the hospitality of the town folk—a social duty taken very seriously in Eastern culture.

It was not that freeloading had any special appeal, but it presented an opportunity to be on a level with the people—to be with them, not above them; even to be subordinate, needy. Let them care for you, Jesus intended. The exchange is to be bilateral: bread and board for heart and healing. Listen to their perceived demons: anger, abuse, fear, the taxes, the children, the in-laws, the boss! Healing can more readily happen around the kitchen table than from pulpit to pew. Get close to people, be a presence of peace—you need no more than your heart and your head!

I came closest to this communal ministry in the active service. The chaplain lives with the men: sharing their dangers, their discomforts, their longings for safety and for home. He was not always welcome at first, but if he brought the presence of God to their foxholes, and to their ship's battle stations, they did not want him to leave. It reminded me of the description of a missionary given by Bishop James Walsh, a Maryknoll founder: "To be a missionary is to go where you are not wanted, but needed and to stay until you are wanted and not needed."

273

Traveling light takes getting used to. Did you ever have to move out of a commodious dwelling into a tiny studio apartment in a strange city, because the job you needed transferred you? Remember the tearful packing of your precious possessions for storage? A year or so later when a promotion offered you a less cramped existence, you sent for your storage stuff. As you began opening the sea of cartons, you may have wondered, "What in the world was I thinking when I packed all this? I haven't needed any of it . . . the clutter is back." Sometimes life deprives us of what we think we want, so that we can discover whether we really needed it.

Possessions have a way of possessing their possessors. But life's most leaden load is reserved for the stockpile of bitterness. According to William Sloane Coffin (*The Heart is a Little to the Left,* p. 5), "In fact, it's comforting to be bitter. But it's not creative, bitterness being such a diminishing emotion. . . . And some people can't live without enemies: they need them to tell them who they are." There are those who collect injuries like trophies; medals of honor for "mayhem endured." The habitué in line at life's complaint counter might more usefully examine an unconscious need for punishment. The self-imposed verdict of guilt for a past secret shame can keep one's antenna on constant alert for offense, whether real or imagined. The tragedy of an abused childhood can have the same crippling effect.

Jesus advises his messengers not to harbor hurt. "Whatever place does not welcome you or listen to you, leave there and shake the dust off your feet. . . ." He is coaching them not to allow the rejection of one town to contaminate their enthusiasm for the next enterprise. Junk all grudges—find a new start—past poison has no place in the present. Quit playing the victim and give resentments a respectful burial!

Joseph M. Wadowicz

The traveling orders of Jesus are less a program of austerity than a blueprint for freedom. The unladen life takes little comfort in the abundance that spawns demons of worry for guarding and getting more. The contented career is convinced that wealth is not things, but people. Jesus did not command the world to be holy, but to love more. Traveling light is to live one's life lightly, lovingly: to connect to everything, to everyone, but to belong to oneself. There is another world but it is in this one.

To the so-called orthodox, whose tastes tend to the reassurances of institutional, formalized religion, Jesus' proposal for a mendicant ministry must sound highly implausible. But to those heralds who enjoy uncomplicated contact with the locals, it is simply the one Mission Possible.

15th Sunday of Ordinary Time
(Mark 6: 7-13)

275

Take Five

"Come apart and rest awhile" is the old translation of Jesus' invitation to revive weary disciples after their missionary debut. When burnout feels like "coming apart" at the seams, relaxation becomes an illusive luxury. In fact, despite the bounty of leisure endemic to the American way, we are far from a people of rest. Foreign cultures are agape at the frenetic pace of American tourists. They seem to pity what strikes them as an American dread of being still.

Perhaps Americans identify stillness with boredom, so empty spaces must be filled. Oscar Wilde said once: "To do nothing is the most difficult thing in the world." We were trained to value busyness: "idleness, the devils workshop"; "time is money"; "at least look busy." But "rest" is a surprisingly popular four-letter word in the Bible. Even God takes a day off (Gen. 2: 2). The popular 23rd Psalm is a veritable lullaby of sweet repose. Jesus promises rest to the work- and worry-weary of the world: "Come to me you who are heavy laden" (Mt. 11: 22).

Why do we fight being still? Could it be that is when our inner demons are most apt to get our attention? We all qualify for factory recall, but we can never fix what we don't know is broken. I am most restless when particularly dissatisfied with myself: for my impatience, insensitivity, self-centeredness. Formerly, the tendency was to look away, or to futilely resolve to change, or to blame others for the way I react, and disquiet increased. Since, I have learned to hold still: stop, look and listen to me.

A friend shared an acronym describing this holding pattern: HALT, it is called. H stands for hungry, A for anger, L for lonely, T for tired. Whenever these are experienced, stop whatever you are doing, make no decisions, stall and thoroughly feel the mood, however upsetting. Allowing it changes it. Do not argue with it or tell it what to do; let it tell you what needs doing.

When the self does not care to be heard, an emotional fog bank ensues that one can get lost in. Confusion only seems more comfortable than confrontation, but the denial defense is exhausting. Developing an ear that hears oneself is the first step on the journey to the center of oneself. St. Augustine (354-430) thought this trip worthwhile; "Recognize in yourself something within, within yourself. Leave aside the external life: descend into yourself. Go into that hidden apartment, your mind. If you are far from yourself, how can you draw near to God?" Myth maven Joseph Campbell saw centering the mark of a champion; "The athlete who is in championship form has a quiet place within himself, and it is out of that his action comes. If he is only in the action field he is not performing properly. There is a center out of which you act. . . . Unless the center is found, you are torn apart and tension comes." (Interview with Bill Moyers)

In his remarkable study of *The Varieties of Religious Experience,* Henry James (1811-1882) analyzes the profound spirituality of "letting go."

> *Passivity, not activity; relaxation, not intentness, should now be the rule. Give up the feeling of responsibility, let go your hold, resign the care of your destiny to higher powers, be genuinely indifferent as to what becomes of it all, and you will find not only that you gain a perfect inward relief, but often also, in addition, the particular goods you sincerely thought you were renouncing. . . .*

Something must give way, a native hardness must break down and liquefy. It is but giving your little convulsive self a rest, and finding that a greater self is there. (James pp. 98-99)

The healing process of centering oneself can be achieved by way of the meditation process. Simply get comfortable. Put your eyes at half-mast. Turn off any tape playing in your head and focus on your breathing . . . in, out, in, out! If a thought bubbles up to consciousness, make no comment, no judgment, just allow it to drift away as you make a meaningless sound to yourself called a "mantra," such as "Om." The habit of fifteen minutes of daily meditation can effect a gentle restoration that reduces heart rate, metabolism and high blood pressure.

Sometimes we do not slow down until life knocks us down. Should illness make you hostage, may this tranquil advice, from Grace Noll Crowell's poem entitled "For One Who is Tired," come through:

Dear child, God does not say today, "Be strong."
He knows your strength is spent. . . .
And so He says, "Be still, and know that I am God."
The hour is late, and you must rest awhile,
and you must wait
Until life's empty reservoirs fill up—as slow rain fills
an upturned cup
Hold up your cup, dear child, for God to fill.
He only asks today that you be still.

16th Sunday of Ordinary Time
(Mark 6: 30-34)

Catered Affair

It is hard to reconcile this Gospel with Jesus' repudiation of the temptation to bedazzle his public with miracles. Matthew and Luke clearly report this disavowal in their fourth chapters, wherein prior to his public career, Jesus wrestles with the decision to take his chances proclaiming the Good News without attendant bewitchment. He obviously wanted people to believe in his message, not his magic. He wanted to be seen as a teacher and a healer, not as a sorcerer or magician. How then are we to take this loaves and fish story? What are we to believe about it?

This stupendous multiplication account must indeed be important. It is the only miracle narrated in all four Gospels. Most scholars generally agree that it offers a conspicuous reference to the Eucharist. But first, the miracle issue . . .

The Bible is a tidal wave of miracles: the Red Sea parting, the Burning Bush, the Walls of Jericho, Jonah and the Whale. The New Testament perpetuates the plot: water to wine, the dead revived, fabulous feedings of multitudes. Ancient biblical authors wrote in an age of scientific unsophistication. They were not interested in proficiency concerning nature's laws. Their tendency was to surround significant events and personages with exceptional details to highlight their prominence. Fact and fiction were interwoven to the delight of the audience, largely illiterate. Authors used extravagant marvels as a literary device to explain mysterious phenomena—the transcendent, the indefinable! It was their way of dramatizing the awesome presence of the aura of divinity. Similarly, the evangelists employ "miracles" to set Jesus apart as a divine presence and beyond the cosmic standards of the Creator. By arousing admiration to him, attention is drawn to His message.

Miracles did not seem particularly important to Jesus, judging from his advice to his disciples to soft-pedal any publicity about them. He knew that miracles did not change people that much. The 5,000 free-lunchers would be hungry the next day . . . the restored dead would have to die again . . . the celebrants at the Cana water/wine tasting could have awakened to a hangover. To focus on the miracles of Jesus is to separate him from human emulation. The same spirit that filled him was to fill his followers. His same compassionate concern for people that few wanted to deal with—cripples, bag ladies, streetwalkers, criminals—was to be the preoccupation of his church. Kindness is the miracle with which we can identify, not the prodigies of Superman!

As previously mentioned, the loaves and fish proliferation is a distinct referent to the Eucharist, the center and essence of Christian worship. Eucharist is from a Greek word meaning "thanksgiving." This suggests the appropriate attitude for receiving the Sacrament—gratitude! Thankfulness for having made it thus far in life; for a faith that helps make sense of it; for the chance to grow and learn to love.

What qualifies one to receive this sacred gift? Confession, absolution? However devoutly shriven, the Liturgy reminds the faithful just before communing: "O Lord I am not worthy." What prompted Jesus to feed the vast throng? They were hungry! And what human being is not hungry for meaning, for filling the vacancies in existence, for the Goodness we call God? Mary Carolyn Davis glimpses this wistful quest in these lines:

When the sun shines in the street
There are many feet

Joseph M. Wadowicz

Seeking God, and all unaware
That their hastening is a prayer.
Perhaps these feet would
Deem it odd.
(Who think they are on business bent)
If someone went and told them,
"You are seeking God."

It is no surprise, then, that the Eucharist should come to the world in the form of food. What is more basic to life than eating? This fundamental habit rates exceptional space in the Bible. Even the hereafter is described as a "banquet." Eucharist, as bread, asserts that God wants to be our nurturance—to be ingested and assimilated into the most commonplace human activities: our working, our relating, our suffering, our dying, and our enjoyments, like the pleasures of eating.

The miraculous supply of provisions for 5,000 proceeded from a very modest source—a young lad's picnic lunch of five barley buns and two fish. Amazing what God can do with little when given with good heart! On December 1, 1955, Rosa Parks probably didn't think she was doing very much when she refused to give up her seat to a white man on that bus in Mobile, Alabama. Her decision to stay put, respect her conviction, and accept the consequences, sparked the racial justice revolution worldwide.

We may feel that we are not much, but the little each of us have is all God needs to make miracles happen.

17th Sunday of Ordinary Time
(John 6: 1-15)

Peak Experience

A little polar bear in the frigid Arctic questioned his mother, "Am I a real polar bear?"

"Of course you are, dear," she responded.

He then asked his father, "Am I a real polar bear?"

"Certainly you are!" his father answered.

Unconvinced, the little guy put the same query to his grandfather, grandmother, and cousin polar bears. The puzzled mother polar bear confronted her youngster, "Why are you incessantly questioning whether you are a real polar bear?"

"Because," he replied, "I'm freezing!"

This child's waggish bedtime story serves to introduce a notion relative to the gospel Transfiguration story—that not everyone is comfortable in his native environment.

Jesus apparently adjusted to the Roman occupation, but there were some things he did not like about the religion in which he was raised. He obviously objected to a piety that placed ritual conformity above human necessity. Over the centuries, the 613 precepts of Moses hardened into a hidebound manifesto. Every aspect of orthodox behavior often hobbled more than hallowed Hebrew life. The inflexible restrictions, for instance, of Sabbath observance were not taken seriously by Jesus, so he was seen as subverting the Law. By-the-book religions tend to degenerate into legalism. For Jesus, persons enjoyed priority over precepts. He refused idolatry to injunctions. Just as Thomas Erskine of

Linlathen once observed, "Those who make religion their God will not have God for their religion."

Jesus saw religion as a celebration of life, not an IRS audit. His spirituality embraced a God who was an enthusiastic companion to the human condition—a willing copartner in ongoing Creation. For him religion was not a moral code or a system of ethics, by which salvation was earned. Eternal life was a wedding party to which everybody was invited. Nor did he seem convinced that exemplary morality guaranteed divine approval. Prostitutes and criminals warmed to his message more so than the righteous right, who put out a contract on him.

Jesus brought a whole new lightsome touch to the old-time religion. That is one way to think of the Transfiguration on Mt. Tabor. It was a peak experience for his favored cabinet, Peter, James, and John. They understood him at last! They finally put it all together! How could the evangelist more dramatically describe their sudden, glorious insight, than in a blaze of incandescent splendor! The ancient law-giver, Moses, was there to affirm the new covenant with Jesus. The great prophet Elijah, who Jews believed would return to earth to introduce the expected messiah, was on hand. The entire scene receives a resounding "Amen" from the Divine cloud!

This apocalyptic scenario allegorically implies that any living religion is subject to the process of all living things: growth, development and therefore, change. To be animating and relevant a faith needs to be open to newness—to fresh ideas. Jesus emphasized commitment to the brotherhood of all mankind. The Old Law highlighted Jewish exclusiveness. Paul consistently repeated the Christ-vision to the reproach of die-hard traditionalists. "In this new life one's nationality or race or education or social position is unimportant: such things mean nothing" (Col. 3: 11).

Joseph M. Wadowicz

The Vatican II Council had a similar breakthrough impact on Christendom. Many resent the changes, but the Church needed to reexamine its relevance to the modern world. As Mark Twain once remarked, "change is only comfortable to a wet baby." The religious right preferred a church they remembered: strict, sovereign, fixed—frozen! They saw the conciliar Church as "getting soft" when it was actually inviting the faithful to a deeper, more mature spirituality; easier access to the Sacrament, fraternal respect for other religions, fuller involvement of the laity. This church accepted that its theologians do not have the last word on the understanding of God or the mystery of life. It outgrew the fortress mentality and saw itself a wayfaring "pilgrim" in pursuit of truth, not its sole possessor.

In the hilarious one-nun production *Late Nite Catechism,* the audience laughs uproariously at the ritual practices of fifty years ago. Will fifty years from now find the piety of this generation just as funny? Why not! Certifiable pilgrims keep moving. If they are not open to learning, to newness, to growth, to change, they have but one option—rigor mortis!

18th Sunday of Ordinary Time (Transfiguration)
(Mark 9: 2-10)

287

Running Mates

If you were in the audience when Jesus said, according to the evangelist, "I am the bread come down from heaven," what do you think might have been your reaction? I would most likely notify the analogous "911" of the time, to get a net! Can you blame the murmuring? . . . "Is not this Jesus, the son of Joseph? Do not we know his father and mother?"

Why did Jesus make this spectacular claim, knowing full well disbelief was guaranteed. His Twelve were just as dismayed, but they hung in with him. They knew there was more to him than just a local carpenter. They did not understand any more than the others but they trusted him . . . Maybe that is what faith is about! It is easy to believe what is usual and understandable. The "incredible" demands greater investment.

When Robert Frost penned the lyrical lines, "The woods are lovely, dark and deep, But I have promises to keep, and miles to go before I sleep," he touched on the plaintive, human pique about life's unfinished business. There is always more to be done when the journey finally ends. That is why Jesus commissioned disciples to perpetuate his message and instituted the Eucharist to preserve his presence. He saw his Good News as nourishment for the world. He obviously personally identified himself with his message and called it the "bread of heaven." He never hedged from this extraordinary deposition. In fact, he testified to it all the more in the face of the perturbing bafflement from followers. Jesus presented a simple choice: he was either nutrition for mankind or just a nut!

Even more astounding is the correlation to this credence: namely, that whoever acts with the heart of Christ is also "bread of heaven." Wherever there is compassion, consideration, and courtesy for another, his presence comes alive. Jesus insisted on solidarity with those who value what he valued.

> *Anyone believing in me shall do the same miracles I have done and greater ones. . . . You abide in me and I in you. . . . Because I will reveal myself to those who love me and obey me. The Father will be in them, too. We will come to them and live with them.* (John 14: 12, 12, 20, 21).

This is not an appeal for saintliness, just common-place sensitive humanness. A few examples . . .

> *An elderly passenger is holding a bouquet of fresh cut flowers. He notices across the aisle a sad-eyed young woman, obviously troubled and depressed. Each time she glanced at the flowers her expression brightened to a wan smile. As the old gentleman prepared to leave the bus, he dropped the cluster in the young person's lap. "I can see you love flowers," he said, "I think my wife would like you to have them. I'll tell her I gave them to you . . ."*
>
> *From the window the young lady saw the old man enter the gate of a cemetery by the side of the road.* Bread of heaven! (Told by Bennett Cert)

The March 2000 issue of the magazine *Maturity* features an interview with the famous movie star, Martin Sheen, describing some of his charity activities. One of them is a full day service, once each week (when not on location) at a refuge for the homeless in Venice, CA. When elected honorary mayor of Malibu, he organized this elitist beach town to be a sanctuary for the homeless—to the consternation of many of the natives. I recall a memorable evening with the actor when we were both guests at the rectory of another social activist, Fr. Bill O'Donnell, Berkeley, CA. Martin explained: "Acting is what I do for a living—social justice work is what keeps me alive." *Bread of heaven!*

Even tiny tots can nurture. Brenda W. Quinn had this story in *Catholic Digest* a few years ago:

> *It was one of the worst days of her life. Newly separated, she was tired, sick, lonely, hot (it was July) and discouraged. It was all she could do to lift her little boy into his highchair for dinner.*
>
> *She put his food on the tray and began to read the mail. Another bill she could not pay—it was the last straw. She leaned her head against the tray and began to cry.*
>
> *The little boy looked at his sobbing mother very intensely, then took the pacifier out of his mouth, and offered it to his distraught mother.*
>
> *She began to laugh through her tears and hugged the source of such total unconditional love.*
> Bread of heaven!

Teachers can be bread of heaven. As Bradley Miller observed: "Teaching a child not to step on a caterpillar is as valuable to the child as it is to the caterpillar."

Eucharist creates equality with Jesus. It is his friendly, mutual corporate takeover. Recently both major presidential candidates made a considerable fuss about choosing running mates. The Lord is less discriminating—whoever wants to be, is his running mate!

19th Sunday of Ordinary Time
(John 6: 41-51)

Rite Stuff

The midsummer Eucharist refresher course grinds into the fourth week of John's sixth chapter. One more week to go! The recurring reprise: "I am the living bread come down from heaven: Whoever eats this bread will live forever: and the bread that I will give is my flesh for the life of the world." This thoroughly startling language obviously shocked the Jews who heard it, but the pagans familiar with the ancient mystery religions of the near east would barely blink an eye.

In his study of *The Gospel of John* (Volume 1, pp. 221-222), William Barclay describes pagan worship of animal sacrifice.

> *Once the flesh has been offered to the god, it was held that he entered into it: and therefore when the worshipper ate it he was literally eating the god. As the people rose from such a feast they went out, as they believed, literally god filled. . . . The one thing the Mystery Religions offered was communion and even identity with some god. . . . In the Mysteries of Mithra the initiates prayed: "Abide with my soul: leave me not, that I may be initiated and that the holy spirit may dwell within me." In the Hermetic Mysteries the initiate said: "I know Thee, Hermes, and thou knowest me: I am thou and thou are I." In the Mysteries of Isis the worshipper said: "As truly as Osiris is not dead, his followers shall die no more."*

Sound familiar?!

Mithra was the ancient Persian god of light; Hermes, the Greek messenger of the gods; Isis, the Egyptian goddess of fertility. Isis' brother/husband, Osiris, was believed to have come back from the dead. Even resurrection was not original with Christians! Pagan rituals were carefully staged to provide maximum emotional impact: music, incense, lighting. Participants were obliged to undergo lengthy instruction and intense ceremonial purification in preparation for these rites. This historic religious phenomena highlights humanity's everlasting longing for unity with divinity. Times have little changed!

Why this besetting preoccupation? Perhaps for the same reason a child likes to identify with Superman or Harry Potter . . . because the child feels small, impotent, unqualified for independence. Consequently the child assigns outsized superiority to the parent in order to feel safe. Should such emotional deficits perdure into adulthood, authoritarian religion presents a strong appeal. It provides a life plan, a moral code, a system of ethics whereby salvation may be earned. It attracts those who want to be led: left-brain-type-thinking that values structure, dogma, law and order. When directives become imperatives, legalism is bred and minimal compliance evolves, but for free spirits, resistance is activated, while the passive-aggressives content themselves with silent sabotage.

People who do not wish to wrestle with life's absurdities and incongruities will prefer security-blanket religion to launching-pad spirituality. Jesus obviously wanted a more mature faith from his followers. He did not value servile submission to gain authority approval. He taught illustrative stories that elicited right-brain speculation, creative conclusions, spontaneity, and openness to newness. He accentuated ideals over edicts, initiative over habit.

Maybe that is why Jesus made such staggering claims about his "flesh" and "blood" as universal nurturance? Maybe he wanted his hearers to get past his words and to him personally. The world is starving for the compassionate presence of Christ! How could he more specifically will that sacred presence to the world than by integrating his body with our own?

We may never be invited to the White House for a state dinner, or to the Court of St. James for tea, or breakfast at Tiffany's, but John's sixth chapter offers one clear invitation: "Come to my table, I've been saving a place for you. Relax, loosen your tie. Tell me all about it. I am here for you—body and soul, flesh and blood—just yours. Let's put them together!"

20th Sunday of Ordinary Time
(John 6: 51-58)

Staff and Stuff of Life

The exhaustive five week series of John's sixth chapter, in the heat of August dog days, has finally crescendoed. To share something fresh on the subject of Eucharist each Sunday, has been a daunting chore, but eminently worth the candle. Making God partisan and an accessible accomplice to the human enterprise is the reason why the Sacrament exists at the center of Christian worship. Eucharist is entente between God and mankind.

Why the relentless drumbeat of words that shock and disgust? Consuming human flesh and blood is clearly cannibalism—an unthinkable endorsement by Jesus. So, what did the Johanine authors have in mind when they assigned these astonishing statements to the Lord?

A possible elucidation could be the evangelist's effort to counter Christological heresies that were muddling the infant Church. . . . It is quite typical of neo-converts to overdo. Flushed with the fervor of renascence, they often tend to overcorrect for past errancy. Extreme cases make up for lost time by embracing an almost virulent probity.

Puritans are commonly indicted for such militant zealotry. The Puritans of the early Church were a group known as "Docetists." They overspiritualized Christ by denying his humanity. For them his physical body was only an appearance—not real. Another elitist group in the growing Christian community were the Gnostics. They believed that only by special knowledge, imparted to the few, was salvation available. Both factions rejected the humanness of Jesus, thus equating him with an ethereal being that objected to being contaminated by any mortal involvement. The official Church refused to allow Jesus to become an abstract theological hypothesis. His life was not meant to be a mythic fiction, left on the shelf of history. He was a living book, to be thoroughly read, indeed, consumed! So the gospel emphasizes the flesh and blood of Jesus to accentuate his humanity and his total participation in the human experience.

Eucharist is an affirmation of the physical body—the soul's sometimes troublesome but inseparable companion. In the wholesome compound of mind and matter, the communion table does homage to the dinner table, even to the pool table and the card table. Material creation continues to be infused with divine approval. "Then God looked over all He had made; it was excellent in every way" (Gen. 1: 21).

Eucharist celebrates life and lifts vision beyond creaturely touch, taste, sound and sight. Each communion is a rite of passage from self-absorption to awareness of fellow beings—an invitation to adulthood. It highlights "the man for others" and a deity that welcomes coalescence with human nature.

The ritual of communing is no guarantee that the communicant will be magically transformed for the better; no more so than the nuptial ceremony guarantees a good marriage. Each day spouses need to renew their pledge to each other. To receive the Eucharist fittingly is to resolve to value what Jesus values—to love what he loves—people!

True love never runs smoothly. Misunderstandings are simply inevitable.

Many of Jesus' disciples who were listening said, "This saying is hard; who can accept it? . . . As a result of this, many of his disciples returned to their former way of life and no longer accompanied him. Jesus then said to the Twelve, "Do you

298

also want to leave?" Simon Peter answered him, "Master, to whom shall we go? You have the words of eternal life."

As in marriages that last, conflict is the precise time not to split. Disputes confronted and issues openly dealt with can mold a deeper, stronger bonding. The late Malcolm Muggeridge, brilliant editor of *Punch,* was raised an atheist. A sharp-tongued social commentator and television controversialist, this witty scoffer had little use for church or churchmen. Toward his life's close, he experienced an astounding change of heart. Skeptic Malcolm confessed to an invasion of his consciousness by the sheer beauty and sublimity of Christ's life as related in the Gospels. His 1975 book, *Jesus,* is an elegant expression of that improbable illumination. He wrote:

Man's effort to make himself happy in earthly terms is doomed to failure. I have concluded after having failed in past experience, in present dilemmas, and future expectations. As far as I am concerned, it is Christ or nothing.

Simon Peter came to the same conclusion!

21st Sunday of Ordinary Time
(John 6: 60-69)

Tyranny and Orthodoxy

This gospel recalls a *New Yorker* cartoon depicting a very nervous candidate for celestial citizenship. As the pearly-gatekeeper reviews the applicants' life record, St. Peter keeps exclaiming; "No, no that's not a sin either. My goodness, you must have worried yourself to death!"

Religions have a way of making sins of the most harmless human behavior, like ball games on Sunday or hamburgers on Friday. I ruefully recall the church of my childhood. Life was one hopeless rulebook. Whatever seemed to be fun was labeled a transgression. What was not a sin was forbidden. For me, the Almighty was a cosmic schoolyard monitor—forever poised to punish for laughing in church or whispering behind Sister's back.

Seminary training further validated this rationale. Pastoral care focused more on admonishing idealistic perfectionism than solicitude for flawed humanity. Even prayer was taught like a binomial theorem. A mathematical exactitude was preferred to spontaneous, lighthearted accessibility to God. Later, as a confessor, I was stunned by the quagmire of guilt in which so many penitents were mired for just being human.

A penitent myself, I confessed time after time, "unchaste thoughts."

"Are you avoiding the occasion of sin?" queried the confessor.

"No," I responded, "I have to hear confessions, and the only thing I hear are sins of the flesh—I get ideas!"

Experience took its time, but reality eventually set in. I can honestly affirm after fifty-five years of priesthood and thousands of confessions, I have yet to hear a mortal sin. The traditional conditions for committing such are "grievous matter, sufficient reflection, and full consent of the will." I could never certify the coalition of these three requirements as occurring simultaneously.

Clinical psychologist Father Marc Oraison, OP, criticizes the moral theology taught in that past era in his 1968 book *Morality For Our Time* (p. 44):

> ... *(M)orality is defined without the least mention of God. (Mindful of Paul to the Galations and Romans). It is neither the law nor its observance which saves. On the contrary, the law although good in itself actually kills. It is grace, that is to say love, that is our salvation.*

How then did the Church get so hung up on moralistic coercion over the centuries, when Christ's Good News is so plainly humane, balanced, and lighthearted? His parables gush with God's limitless mercy. Guilt and censure are barely in his Father's vocabulary. This gospel episode has something to say about regulatory gridlock .... It illustrates mankind's impulse to relieve painful insecurity by escape to the sanctuary of doctrinaire religion. Here, there is no dirth of official masterminds who mask their own flight from personal inadequacies with their drive to dominate the "sheep," and are perfectly assured of doing God's job for Him! Jesus openly revolts against this style of ecclesiastical despotism. He objected to religious leadership that convoluted rational regulations into meaningless taboos.

The Mosaic injunction for handwashing before eating is simply a healthy caution for nomadic wanderers not too preoccupied with hygiene, much the same as parents persistently hound their youngsters to pre-meal ablutions. But institutions change over time because their leadership does. Authority can complicate by overcorrecting. . . . Not only were hands to be ritually cleansed before eating, but between each course! During enemy sieges, when water was pitifully scarce, devout Jews preferred to die of thirst rather than drink what was needed for ceremonial purification.

Jesus objected to this orthodox tyranny. He trusted the intrinsic autonomy of a good heart more than extrinsic compliance to authority. And so he was a menace to dogmatic traditionalists of a bygone era. Discipleship for Jesus meant responsibility; the ability of conscientious response to human need. He favored deliverance from repressive judgment and morbid culpability. He most likely had no argument with regimentation as a good thing for organizations, but not for fellowship. His church fares better as a household than a powerhouse!

22nd Sunday of Ordinary Time
(Mark 7: 8, 14, 15, 21, 23)

"None So Deaf . . .

. . . as those that will not hear," said Matthew Henry (1662-1714). A century before, the adage aficionado John Heywood wrote:

Who so deafe or so blinde as he
That willfully will neither heare nor see.

Two psychiatrists meet for a drink after a long, hot day. One is utterly wilted and worn out—his hair tousled, his face drawn, his clothing rumpled. His colleague, however, is composed, nattily dressed and completely at ease.

"Rumplemeyer, for heaven's sake," the first psychiatrist says incredulously, "how do you do it? I'm completely done in and you look as fresh as a spring morning. How can you look so great and be so composed after listening all day to peoples' problems, fears, anger, unhappiness and neuroses?"

The second doctor smugly sips his highball and then responds, "So who listens?"
(Connections)

This Gospel deals with deafness and its attendant speech impairment. They are usually concomitant. When sound is not heard neither is one's own voice, which then comes out indistinctly. Deafness is generally more embarrassing than blindness. People are inclined to be more considerate with the sightless than they are with the hard-of-hearing. Having to shout can be annoying. Jesus is sensitive to this condition and takes the deaf-mute aside to avoid any public mortification.

Listening is a very fine art. It takes practice. But it's the way to learn about oneself. Self-knowledge is rarely accurate, since one's opinion on oneself is rarely objective. Many of us would like to think of ourselves as we should like to be—not as we are. We are most often influenced by others' impression of ourselves, which, at best, can only be a partial assessment.

Still, most of us wish to be thought well of, so the tendency is to put our best foot forward and to conceal deficits. This leads to a defensive maneuver—induced deafness—whenever we do not want to hear a negative message. Nothing infuriated my mother more than the deaf ear my father exploited to her nagging.

Self-induced deafness is the protective ploy of the passive-aggressive personality; averse to making waves, too timid to confront, peace is settled for at any price. For such, getting involved spells hurt or at least defeat. Thus candid interrelating suffers, and the leading troubled marriage complaint ripens—poor communication. The exasperating indifference of detached types occasionally gives way to caustic sarcasm and ridicule, but the underlying hostility is seldom met head-on. Collisions are devoutly avoided, and pacifiers are pursued in excessive eating, drinking, sleeping, working, reading, overexplaining and cozy religion, to name a few. These illusory escapes succeed in keeping the desired distance from others, but more unfortunately, from oneself, and do little to improve an inner sense of worth.

The non-confronter sees nothing positive about anger. St. Augustine identified it with hope when he wrote that "hope has two beautiful daughters, anger and courage."

To refuse hearing is to refuse hope. To hear no evil is to close oneself from the real world that is in constant need of renewal.

I create my own deafness whenever:

1. I make fun of you so I do not have to take you seriously.
2. I make myself busy to avoid involvement.
3. I pay no attention to my own negative emotions—anger, anxiety, annoyance.
4. I overexplain an embarrassing moment or mistake when a simple "I goofed" would do.
5. My monologue competes with yours and I refuse to allow your opinion.
6. I'm afraid to try for fear of failing or crying for help.
7. I label you; discount you with a category that prejudice inspires.
8. I seek noise, distraction, or intoxication to drown out what I don't want to hear.
9. I pray for miracles before exploring my own solutions.
10. I forget God and I are partners.

We learn to love by listening—to ourselves as well as to others—however faint the whisper or frightening the thunder. All of us need hearing aids in this world's cacophony of sounds. One that works for me is the belief that when I harken to the one that wants to talk to me or shout at me, I am listening to God!

23rd Sunday of Ordinary Time
(Mark 7: 31-37)

How to Win for Losing

The setting for Simon Peter's inspired declaration of Jesus as messiah occurred in the heart of pagan territory. Northeast of Lake Galilee, Caesaria Philippi, once called Balinas, was the center of Baal worship. Up on the hillside was a cave believed to have been the birthplace of Pan, the Greek god of nature. Further up the slope gleamed the white marble temple dedicated to the ruler of the world, the Emperor Caesar, now regarded as god.

At this time the Jews dreamed of a messiah, an anointed, menacing, militant monarch who would reduce the enemy to its knees in homage to conquering Israel. Longing for a liberating messiah is everyone's dream, especially for the oppressed. And deliverers do appear—a Lincoln, a Gandhi, a Martin Luther King. Awesomely, they seem to share a common lot—liquidation. When Jesus knew this would happen to him and talked about it, Peter was upset to think that the repugnant enemy could overcome an invincible messiah.

Life is just not fair! There are consequences to human behavior, but sometimes evil deeds escape retribution and good deeds are capriciously penalized. The sacred writers attempt to make sense of the puzzle of why the innocent suffer by introducing the involvement of God. Still, the mystery persists. While it is impossible for me to applaud a parent who wishes pain for a child, it is just as unthinkable to worship a God who wills the cross for His "only begotten son." I can, however, honor a parent whose heart breaks as he chooses to allow an errant offspring to do jail time for speeding tickets ignored, or for selling drugs, or for repeatedly driving under the influence. Youngsters need to learn. "Tough love" may be as instructive a mode as any. Does a loving Father witness His creatures suffering knowing that tragedy is never the bottom line? We count on a God that will somehow extract victory from the jaws of defeat.

Calvary unravels the mystery: good is made out of evil. God's bewildering providence is a clear sample of "tough love."

Jesus knew that the mind of God values the valor of the "suffering servant" over the heroics of the victorious warrior. He believed that when the chips were down, the dark forces of entrenched power would not be allowed to prevail finally over its victims. Does God then will suffering? Does the caring parent? Both recognize that ordeals can be redemptive, in fact, ennobling, so they do not protect their charges from whatever can lead to the triumph of the human spirit. That is why Jesus could say that losing one's life in a good cause is a way of finding one's true self. Sydney Carton, of Dickens' *A Tale of Two Cities,* comes to mind. He substitutes himself for the guillotine so a condemned friend can escape to marry the woman they both love. Graham Greene's moving *Power and the Glory* tells the story of a failed "whiskey priest" who finally finds reconciliation when he knowingly risks a trap to arrest and execute him, as he ministers to a dying man during the brutal Mexican persecution of the 1920s.

But these are tales of fiction. The martyrdom of Central America's Archbishop Romero is grim fact. So is the murder of Father John A. Kaiser, a 67-year-old Mill Hill missionary, who was an outspoken advocate of human rights in Kenya, where he worked for 36 years.

Since martyrdom is neither hoped for nor foreseen in the sunset of my days, I shall attempt penetration to my best self by abandoning the impulse for self-importance. I should like to accept who I am—as I am—and let go the self I wish I was.

The world-renowned cellist, Yo Yo Ma, demonstrates understanding of this insight. Among his many glorious concert achievements, he is proudest of his appearance on Sesame Street, where he taught Elmo how to play the violin. The wife of one of his friends, Gert, lay dying of cancer. With his cello, Yo Yo visited her in the hospital and played one of her favorite Bach fugues. For her husband he brought a flask of fine scotch. Gert had a notorious penchant for pickles. Again Yo Yo visited her with his cello, but this time she was in and out of consciousness. The husband announced to his drowsy wife, "Yo Yo is here with his cello. What would you like, Yo Yo or pickles?" "Pickles," she responded sleepily.

Yo Yo left his cello and returned a half hour later with six jars of assorted pickles. The vanity of genius was swallowed by sensitivity to suffering. Yo Yo was never more of a virtuoso!

24th Sunday of Ordinary Time
(Mark 8: 27-35)

Teacher Children

The tenderness of Jesus to children actually flew in the face of the common values of his time. In the Roman-Greco civilization of that day, children had zero status. They were the sole property of parents who could dispose of them as they pleased. To exterminate them or to sell them into slavery was not illegal, in fact, the word used in the New Testament for child is the Greek word *paedion,* also the word for "servant." Most servants were slaves in that era. Since children enjoyed even less rights than women, Jesus, in his gospel, assigned them for top priority care and attention.

The disciples argued about who was the most important among them. Jesus selected the most vulnerable "nonperson" in their presence to highlight the precedence that powerlessness rated with God. Numero uno or last place appear to rank on a par in divine appraisal.

As a compulsory celibate, I watched my sisters' families grow, and often felt deprived of the education raising children could afford. Having retired from federal service in 1980, my chance to be a deputy dad presented itself. Friends were going on a three-week cruise and offered their house for me to babysit, along with their two children. This episode is reported in the "Father's Day" chapter of the A cycle in this series. Suffice it to say, I flunked my paternity audition. Kind neighbors that I had appealed to for advice in my parenting dilemmas smilingly comforted me: "Don't feel too badly, Father, no one can take over in the middle of another's chess game!"

But I learned a few things. Typical of first-time parents who are anxious to do it right, I focused more on me than understanding the children. I wanted another chance.

At a recent overnight hospital stay, sleepless, I chatted with the night nurse. Interested in my points of view she finally asked, "What is the one thing you most want to do in your life?" I think she was expecting me to say, "Be pope, or bishop, or the chaplain on *Love Boat*." She seemed surprised, but pleased, when I answered: "I should like to care for a child."

I learned the following from my abridged surrogate parent venture:

1. The one thing that frightens children most are adults.
2. The saddest tragedy for a child is to be belittled. If a host would not think of humiliating a guest in their home, why a child?
3. The parent that does not allow a child privacy dooms the child to it forever.
4. The parent needs to be a good teacher. Teachers teach subjects; good teachers teach students.
5. The young need firm authority. As in handball, there's no game with a spongy wall.
6. Parents cannot expect children to appreciate the sacrifices they make for their young. Children never asked for them.
7. Real education is finding out for oneself. Children learn least when taught most.
8. The parent acts most like a child when the child is expected to be an adult.
9. It is not useful to teach children to be phonies, demanding they kiss someone not trusted, or to make a fuss about a gift not liked.

10. Never shush a child's questions. The universe fascinates them.

Children are quite at home with the idea of God. A mother asked, "Why is God hidden?" Her ten-year-old responded, "Because He wants you to look for Him." An eleven-year-old wrote:

> *Dear God,*
> *I think You should listen to confessions in person. That way bad people would not try to get away with murder.*
> *Hi,*
> *George*

I have to agree with G. K. Chesterton in his uncommonly fresh *What's Wrong With The World,* written at the turn of the past century. According to G. K., what's right with it is that women are superior to men, not because they outlive us, but because they are closer to children, therefore, to life and nurturance. He decries the feminist ambition for equality with males. He deems this a step down for females. He also laments women who deplore the restrictions of domesticity. For to him there is no more important spot on the planet than a home. No government can be more supreme than a household and no wealth richer than a child. Each one born is God's testimony that He is not finished with us yet!

25th Sunday of Ordinary Time
(Mark 9: 30-37)

Clique Club

This is one industrial strength gospel! In the first part, Jesus claims no exclusivity in demon expulsion for himself or his affiliates. The second part is stark Mark, headlining millstone drowning, terrifying endless torture and ghastly self-mutilation. Mark has Jesus speaking a language of jolting hyperbole, thus accentuating the enormity of malevolence. The words are not to be interpreted literally.

Drowning by millstone was especially offensive to Jews since it was a form of Roman execution. . . . Gehenna was the garbage dump outside of Jerusalem. It was situated in the valley of Hinnom, just south of the city, where the hideous sacrifice of infants to the god Moloch had been practiced. Gehenna was the Jewish figure for the nether world of retribution for evil behavior. The smoldering trash heap was used as a metaphor characterizing the consequence of a corrupt and wasted existence, much as when we describe a misspent life as "going down the tubes." Such a reprisal is no more the direct punishment of an offended deity than is a hangover from overdrinking. Nature has its own inflexible justice system.

The repugnant recommendations to self-mutilate in order to obviate evildoing persist in saturating the reading with extreme overstatement. This excessive language is intended to emphasize the resolute decisiveness vital for avoiding evildoing . . . the Galilean healer of the blind, crippled and lame could hardly advocate seriously such self-violence.

Back to the "members only" part of the gospel! The Christian churches of history have not been notorious for

317

their sufferance of each other. For more than four centuries the Roman Catholic Church has been a "closed shop"—a tight union refusing to recognize the validity of any other faith. Sixty years ago seminarians tastelessly nicknamed their washrooms "Martin Luthers." Thanks to the Vatican II Council of the early sixties, this contemptuous intolerance died the death it deserved, and amicable ecumenism flowered forth. In 1986, Catholic churches joined their Lutheran brothers and sisters in celebrating the 450th anniversary of the birth of Martin Luther. In 1999, Pope John Paul II published his encyclical *Ut Unum Sint* ("that they may be one"), soliciting input as to how the papacy might proceed for the new millennium in the interest of Christian unity.

The Sunday *Los Angeles Times,* 28 Nov. 1999, printed a book review on a biography of the current pontiff by its religion writer, Larry B. Stammer.

> *In John Paul's Christian humanism, human dignity is inherent because we (and all creation) are created by a living and sovereign God, the First Cause. Even non-Christian religions, the pope wrote (stirring up much consternation within the Vatican), are reflections of one truth. Though the paths may be different, John Paul believes that, to the extent that they tend toward God, they reflect the deepest aspiration of the human spirit to find its fullest dignity in God.*

It comes as a surprise, therefore, that the Vatican should issue a recent 36-page document, *Domine Jesus,* accentuating the superiority of the Catholic Church over other denominations. Because it is the "mother" of all Christian churches, the Church of Rome claims the fullness of

Christ's Spirit, consequently preeminence, and the monopoly on salvation.

The issue is not whether the claim is valid, but how important is it in this day and age of growing mutual deference and interaction among the churches? Vincibility would seem more conducive to empathic dialogue than infallibility. Bridges are not built by one with all the answers and needing no discussion.

Why is it so hard for the human animal to tolerate the outsider? Is the turf worth the flak? Does not every independent soul march to its own drummer? Was it Martin Sheen who said: "Choose your enemy carefully; who he is you will become." Jesus, the ecumenist, along with Moses, had no trouble sharing religious authority: "For whoever is not against us is for us."

The English statesman John Morley (1839-1923) put it well:

> *Toleration means reverence for all the possibilities of truth. It means acknowledgment that she dwells in diverse mansions and wears vesture of many colors and speaks in strange tongues. It means frank respect for freedom—the indwelling of conscience against mechanical forms, official conventions, social force. It means that charity is greater than faith and hope."* . . . *Religion need not be afraid of liberty and its lovely sister tolerance! The word "catholic" still stands for the opposite of clannish narrowness.*

26th Sunday of Ordinary Time
(Mark 9: 38-48)

Hearts That Part

The Lord God said: "It is not good for the man to be alone."

Did this first line in this day's first reading ever spark an argument among the legendary desert hermits of old? They were solitaries, but they did not feel alone. They lived with God. It is interesting to note that in the Genesis Creation story, before Eve, in Eden Adam walked alone with God, and God concluded that even God was not enough for Adam. Neither were pets. Human beings need human beings, if they are to learn to be human.

So the story goes, God made a woman from the rib of Adam. To court a tired pun, she is not a side issue. She is every bit the equal of her man; bone of his bones, flesh of his flesh. Another interesting point is the usage of the word "rib." In Arabic, *rib* is the word for "close friend." Unfortunately, history has not always supported the biblical contention of male and female equality. Women enjoyed virtually no legal status in Jewish culture. They could be divorced for the flimsiest whims, which could account for the strict constraints Jesus urged in the matter of divorce.

Things are quite different for women in this day and age. Today they can make their own living and survive quite comfortably without dependence on the male of the species. It was not so in Jesus' time. Without family they were without protection. Jesus' stern stand on divorce was likely an attempt to safeguard feminine social stability. With the eventual cultural shift toward independence, and less need for a protective policy for women, what might be his attitude about unhappy marriages today? In his day marriage partners were commonly selected by parents. That system seemed to work as well as today's free choice. In fact, statistics indicate that the option to freely choose marital mates presents a higher risk for failure. Three out of five marriages are currently legally dissolved. For Catholics the number is one in five.

Affection dies, communication dead-ends, and relating dries up—how would Jesus handle these things? When all reconciliation efforts are beyond repair, surely Jesus could understand the heartache of a marriage turned sour. The reversal of an adult life's major investment is no minor tragedy. Human beings have a built-in longing for a fulfilling life-love—one that lasts. So why is this appetizing aspiration so rarely appeased? It certainly takes a grownup to see him or herself in the daily full-length mirror that conjugal relating involves. Once the "I do's" are ventured, there is no place to hide!

A California rabbi, who is a skilled counselor, has rescued many a foundering relationship. For the irreconcilable he has devised a "ceremony of parting" in order to obviate cold legal dissolution and bitter courtroom wrangling. In the presence of some close friends or family, the couple stands before him. He reminds them to cherish the good moments of their union and to forgive the hurts. He charges them to part as friends and to pledge themselves to caring parenting (if they have children), and never to speak ill of each other. They return tokens of their marriage, such as rings. He invokes a blessing for the past and for their future, and they part.

The Church could well use this pastoral concern for the separated. Divorced couples need help in dealing with their children. Studies show that the effects of a divorce influence the offspring more in adulthood than as a child. They have trouble trusting lasting relationships. Emotional stability comes more slowly, though they tend to be more successful in professional careers.

Divorced couples need help in the matter of candor with their children. Adolescents especially want to know the issues that were tried and why they failed in their parent's marriage. Youngsters often resent being treated as calendars, having little to say about scheduled weekends with the absentee parent. Advice about a collaborative divorce employing a single lawyer for both parties is also useful financial information.

Some think that the Church's annulment procedure is a canonical cop-out for divorce. Actually the word "annulment" is a more accurate term for marital dissolution. In the Church's thinking the validity of the Sacrament depends on conditions of freedom from force and the adult ability to make a permanent commitment. When either condition is lacking, there simply never has been a sacramental marriage.

The only relic of Eden older than sin is marriage. It is the school for maturing; the best chance to outgrow human nature's inbred narcissism. The one element that makes a human being human is personal relating. Intimacy needs more than a physical body; it needs heart and head and soul! The world is swamped with disposable products—disposable diapers, dishes, even underwear—everything but disposable people. As a plant that has withered through neglect can never be brought back to life, so marriages can run out of gas. Though many may opt for divorce, there is one thing for sure Jesus will not allow—divorce from himself!

27th Sunday of Ordinary Time
(Mark 10: 2-16)

Sad About Bad? Good!

Back in the '30s a *New York Times* featured an obituary. A deceased wealthy Park Avenue dowager had rated several columns, along with the widespread curiosity: "What did she leave?" Everything!

On a back page a lone, scant paragraph reported the passing of a very popular Little Sister of the Poor. What did she leave? Nothing! She took everything with her—her scrubbing the hovels of the needy, cooking their meals, attending their children, nursing the dying. She took it all with her.

This Gospel, about the rich young man, revived this story. He had everything going for him: wealth, success, and even virtue. He even had the spontaneous affection of Jesus, who offered him something he did not offer many—a personal stake in the share of spreading the Good News. But his possessions possessed him and he passed up the invitation of a lifetime.

Imagination tends to range about this fellow; he appears to be a portrait of a nice guy. Proverbially they rarely finish among the winners. He must have been sincere, however, if Jesus liked him. But what moves one to ask the question he asked? Was he bored, disenchanted? Was "Is That All There Is" his theme song? He seemed successful until that fated query: how do you get to heaven?

If one has to ask that question, one better be prepared for some unwelcome advice. There is never a dirth of gurus who are sure they have the right answer. When one does not trust one's own judgment about a life path, one can easily be duped by a charmed shaman ever ready to lead the way. As the suicides of Jamestown, Waco, Texas, and La Jolla, California tragically attest . . . The enormous success of stellar star Elvis Presley was marred by a baneful life flaw. A biographer alleges him as a "momma's boy," which led Elvis to a passive dependence on parent figures. Maturity trumps worldly success every time!

What makes life rich? Probably not possessions. Rabbi Harold Kushner wrote in his book *When All You Ever Wanted Isn't Enough:*

> *Our souls are not hungry for fame, comfort, wealth or power. Those rewards create almost as many problems as they solve. Our souls are hungry for meaning, for the sense that we have figured out how to live so that our lives matter, so that the world will be at least a little bit different for our having passed through it.*
>
> *If a person lives and dies and no one notices if the world continues as it was, was that person ever really alive?*
>
> *I am convinced that it is not the fear of death, of our lives ending, that haunts our sleep so much as the fear that as far as the world is concerned, we might as well never have lived.*

Robert Louis Stevenson had this to say about living:

> *That person is a success who has lived well, laughed often and loved much; who has gained the respect of intelligent people, and the love of children; who has filled a unique niche and accomplished his or her task; who leaves the world better than before, whether by a perfect poem or a rescued soul; who never lacked appreciation of the earth's beauty or failed to express it; who looked*

for the best in others and gave the best he or she had.

Simplistic, perhaps, these quotes, but as artless as wisdom!

The most promising element in this rich person episode is his dejection: "And he went away sad, for he had many possessions." The depression he experienced for declining Jesus' offer could be the beginning of his maturity. As unwelcome as depression is, it deserves attention. It has much to say about what is missing in life. When not a pathology needing clinical treatment, sadness needs going into, not around. It is as natural to avoid feeling sad as it is to detour a bad conscience. If one is sad because of a bad conscience, it is not because one is bad, but because one is good . . . The malicious lose no sleep over their evil. Only good people have bad consciences!

28th Sunday of Ordinary Time
(Mark 10: 17-30)

Power: A Means, Not an End

"The meek shall inherit the earth, because they won't have the nerve to refuse it" quips the wag, and adds that pushy people will get the parking places. Such is life in the big city! James and John, cousins of Jesus, were more this pushy type. They were not nicknamed Sons of Thunder because they were wimpy lightweights. They were nervy enough to lobby for the premier parking spaces, next to the Lord himself. "We want to sit on the thrones next to yours in your kingdom," they said, "one on your right and the other on your left."

As with most aggressive asserters, this brazen cheek does not sit well with the other brethren. Mark has Jesus using this situation to teach a lesson in bonafide *chutzpah* (Yiddish for "boldness"). "As you know, the kings and the great men of the earth Lord it over the people, but among you it is different. Whoever wants to be great among you must be your servant." This is not to advocate shrinking or cringing, but taking charge at being useful. To be in command is to guide, not subdue; to direct, not dictate. Authority, for Jesus, is the ability to be useful.

This Gospel implies that the luxury of winning the top spot is only for openers. This status involves willingness to dare, to depart convention, to reexamine tradition, to suspect applause. It means consulting constituents, but not being controlled by them. It suggests constant evaluation of what is lawful for what is good; of what worked in the past but doesn't work now. Character trumps charisma. (Hitler had the latter.) Superiority ministers to inferiority.

There is no drug more intoxicating than power. We are well advised to beware of those who have to have it. City hallers regard challenges to their authority as civil rebellion. Nor do they trust a competency that can supplant themselves.

Leadership is a function and a relationship. The function deals with the situation; the relationship, with people. People tend to follow the leader they know knows them as well as the situation. There needs to be a bonding between the leader and the led. They do not necessarily have to have a beer together, but subordinates need to know that they are cared about. In the military, officers are rigidly segregated from the enlisted, but a good officer is prized by the men. Marine Corps officers, for instance, receive the same rigorous training as do recruits. The officers do not eat until the men are fed. When a trooper requests an audience with the chaplain, his officer is on the phone: "This is no invasion of confidentiality, padre, but is there anything I can do?" The men know they are cared about and will not be abandoned. Wounded are never left alone. Even the dead were carried on the long, frigid trek from the Chosin Reservoir to Hungnam, Korea in 1950.

The Gospel is saying that for special privilege there's a price tag. . . . Want the height, can you handle the heat? Can you look at the worst and get to work? The future is no more secure for the top dog than for the underdog. The sweet smell of success evanesces about the same for both.

Some young people find churchgoing a bore, but are genuinely spiritually oriented to offer themselves for solid humane intervention. A group of teenagers conceived an extraordinary ministry. They agreed to look after muscular dystrophy victims so that their fatigued parents could get a break and the handicapped teenagers could have a chance to be with their own peer group. Wheelchairs were loaded into vans and off they went for rock concerts or camp-outs.

If Jesus is believed to be the true image of God in human form, then his values are God's. In his own words: "I am here not to be served, but to serve." Could God be interested in doing less? It is, therefore, hard to understand how God rejoices in being worshipped as Almighty and Omnipotent, unless God's power means limitless love. Therefore, believers glory in the Power not as an end to be worshipped, but as a means—having the capacity to love totally, unconditionally.

29th Sunday of Ordinary Time
(Mark 10: 35-46)

Twenty-Twenty

Blindness is oppressive, but then, so can be sight. The assertive Jericho blind man probably found that out for himself when cured of his sightlessness. Pleading for sight from the passing Jesus, he got what he wanted. In fact, it is the last miracle recorded before the death of Jesus. Bartimeus now had eyes to see this hideous spectacle. What would his life be now that he had to earn a living? Begging took no talent. Apparently he had spirit, since he was not embarrassed to make a noisy ado for what he set his heart on. Jesus habitually rewards persistence. "What can I do for you?" he asks the blind man. He addresses the person, not the ailment, and asks nothing from him.

Bartimeus refused to cop out to the crowd demanding him to hush up. Like an ignored hurt child, he cried all the louder. It paid off. . . . For those who equate insistence with arrogance, the tendency is to discount their own needs and consequently live under their potential. They are inclined to relegate themselves to the unthreatened bench and never get in the game. To want not, is to be not disappointed. This wary logic arrests the daring challenge to go for it, and passion idles in neutral.

Seeing is a sensory stimulus that elicits varied reactions. Some sights induce automatic denial. Jacqueline Kennedy's spontaneous words at the first sight of her mortally wounded president/husband: "Oh, no!" Some sights paralyze action, others activate instantaneous animation. It quite depends upon the nature of the beholder. As the sage observed, "we do not see things as they are, but as we are."

Vision, therefore, is a highly selective process. We see only in fragments. Terrorists see mainly their cause, not the agony they cause. Blamers can notice your faults, but not their own. Violators grow apathetic to their violence. Cultured SS officers, at the Nuremberg trials, testified how they got used to the atrocities they inflicted. Our own gun-goofy nation has its own perception distortions. The killer Bowies and Billys of frontier fame are not only celebrated in folklore, but even in musical comedies. Sports fans pay top dollar to witness violent mayhem in the boxing ring, the gridiron, the roller rink, and at the speedways. One of the worst terrorists in American history, who killed 168 people in Oklahoma City, was a decorated serviceman. Masses of Native Americans and African Americans have tasted extra-judicial retributive American violence—lynchings. Current gay bashing, thrill crimes, child and spousal abuse enflesh the mystery of evil that has perpetually cursed the human race.

The big picture is generally the work of a committee of eyes, each contributing that separate detail that captures an individual's attention. Awareness of the universe is a global enterprise. Scientists, poets, and aborigines each have something to say about it. Living and surviving is a corporate venture and blind spots are a collaborative concern. To look is not always to see. Blind spots obscure vision.

Blind spots are ineffectual, often unconscious, defense maneuvers. Take overreacting, for instance, which involves an exaggerated response to a perceived threat. The tension could be sex, or alcohol, or authority, or mother-in-laws, but this enemy must be attacked and vanquished if the overre-actor is to feel safe! Such a person is blind to the uncon-fronted fear within. The scapegoater is blind to the unrecognized "chicken" within. "Mr. Milk-toast" on the job, "Attila the Hun" at home; hostility is vented on the intimidated. The rationalizer does not see the deceit in spurious excuses. "I don't go to church because of all the hypocrites there."

Seeing is not all that comfortable. There are those who watch, with aching hearts, the disfigurement and deterioration of a slowly dying loved one. The ordeal of daily attentiveness exceeds the courage of battlefield bravery. Their conscientious caring plumbs new depths in their humanity, conferring a sensitive conviction of the inestimable pricelessness of human life. . . . This is to stand in the Holy of Holies!

Faith is a visual aid. Faith wants to see what God sees, to believe what God believes. Seeing is believing. Like Bartimeus, when the blind spots dissolve, we are surprised at what we really look like. Faith says, "Getting to know you is getting to like you." As God does. It's even a bigger surprise to discover how worth knowing each one of us really are!

30th Sunday of Ordinary Time
(Mark 10: 46-32)

335

The Greatest of These

Can love be commanded? Can one be ordered to love a cad, or even not to behave like one? Do commandments work? . . . Only when they are affirmed! The doctor's order for bed rest is especially efficacious with an exhausted patient.

But is it possible to render unstinting devotion—heart, mind, soul, and strength—to the Unseen? How can God, the great Unknown, be thus loved? For this to be *fait accompli,* it is entirely up to divine initiative. Saintly mystics know the rush when God takes over. For the rest of us spiritual pedestrians, the commandment to love totally is at least a start in the process; a target to aim at, a value hoped for, a direction. We believe Jesus to have sounded the depths of this affection in his relationship with his Father. He no doubt sensed the difficulty for others to experience the same intensity of his sentiment, so he linked loving God with loving the neighbor and oneself. And so, God is loved only as much as one's worst enemy.

When you are good to me, it is no trick to be good to you. But when you are a cad? . . . I can love me when I am brave, but when I'm a coward? . . . That is precisely when benevolence to me is needed most. That is why love is a commandment. Even under pressure, to try it is to like it. John's words sing with the buoyancy of the understanding heart. Churchgoers who do not make caring for others and self the point of their lives, miss the point. "Anyone who says he is walking in the light of Christ, but dislikes his fellow man, is still in darkness" (1 John 2: 9).

Alas, history's ruthless replay is a tragic saga of man's inhumanity to man. Human beings are simply not very good at loving their fellow humans. In his book *Humanity,* Jonathan Glover writes how the system of depersonalization induces an indifference to the enemy's humanness, so that the barbarism of war can prevail. At his court martial after the My Lai massacre, Lt. John Calley testified: "An enemy I couldn't see, I couldn't feel and I couldn't touch: nobody in the military system ever described the enemy as anything other than communism. They didn't give it a race, they didn't give it a sex, they didn't give it an age." Glover further asserts that Mao, with Marxist chill, was "willing to lose 300 million Chinese people in the atomic war. This would be half the population but would be no great loss as the country would always produce more people." Life is cheap but for the Great Commandment!

Regard means "to look at." What I become aware of takes a place inside of me. It is no longer an other, an object. Looking and seeing unites the observer and the observed. Two antagonists paid attention to each other and became useful neighbors. Together they won the 1993 Nobel Peace Prize: F. W. DeKlerk and Nelson Mandela. This could happen to Croats and Serbs, Arabs and Jews, Hutus and Tutsis, North and South Ireland.

In a 1990 conversation with the Dalai Lama, an American psychologist stumped his Tibetan Holiness with a familiar modern expression, "low self-esteem." Though the Dalai was fluent in English, he had no clue as to the meaning of "low self-esteem." It was an unknown concept in Tibet. Tibetan culture is dedicated to social courtesy, personal consideration and serviceable concern for one another. With this importance that Tibetans freely give each other, no native can feel insignificant. Poor self image cannot survive where attentive civility is a way of life. The Dalai concluded, "My religion is kindness."

To love God is to love His world. The world as it is, the bitter with the sweet. It admires the rose, and does not curse the thorn, nor does it caress it. It respects it. It listens to life. It expects only what is and asks for nothing, but is open to everything.

For the lucky ones, to fall in love is finally to confront one's realist self. Self-absorption starts to wane, along with pretense. Caring for another automatically expands the carer beyond self-centeredness. The mystery of loving unfolds—God happens . . . no need to seek Him. He is as close as the one beside you. An ancient Persian proverb says it all:

I sought my God, my God I could not see.
I sought my soul, my soul eluded me.
I sought my neighbor, and I found all three.

31st Sunday of Ordinary Time
(Mark 12: 28-34)

Mite But Mighty

In this First Kings excerpt, the prophet Elijah strikes the note of a callused caller ordering pizza. He appears to take advantage of his prophet position by imposing his wants on a reverent and indigent widow. But then, generous hospitality has ever been a sturdy eastern tradition, even among the poverty stricken. Sometimes insensitive clergy exploit this benefaction.

The gospel has Jesus excoriating religious show-offs and the pitiless extortion of conscientious believers. Even today, unscrupulous evangelists have not ceased to prosper from an unsuspicious following. He does, however, endorse church donations, as he recommends the virtue of the impoverished widow's contribution of two coins, worth about one-fifth of a penny—all she had.

The largesse of the faithful to their church has been consistently legend. I recall an Ohio parish family of nine. The father was a laborer for the county at a very modest wage. They struggled to make ends meet, but they agreed to tithe. Every payday, right off the top, ten percent went to the church. But they never missed a meal or an installment on a bill. All seven children went to college. Their unselfish liberality had been bounteously blessed.

Write-off or not, people are usually serious about giving to charity. Once given however, subsequent appeals maturate to monuments of junk mail. Father Ernie Brainard shared this predicament years ago in the Oakland diocesan weekly, *The Voice:* "I once sent $5 to a Save The Whale group," he said. "I like whales. They are huge, amiable, playful mammals that sing joyfully in their watery dwelling.

They revel in blowing water into the air and pounding the sea with their titanic tails . . . never have I met a vindictive whale . . . they practice the live and let live motif." What Father Brainard got for his five bucks was a whale of a surprise: "Shortly after my meager contribution, I was put upon to save the condor, the yellow-nosed salamander, the pink-eyed earthworm, the pigeon-toed sloth, the red-rumped shrike and the shrinking violet." The pester deserves a jester!

Philanthropy comes in assorted categories. Take Brian Bruckbauer, for instance. When he was ten years old his family went to Jamaica, West Indies, on vacation. An avid soccer player, he watched young Jamaicans play the game. Having brought his soccer ball with him, they invited him to join in. A real soccer ball was a luxury for them to kick around, since they were making do with old bottles and taped-up cardboard boxes. Brian let them keep his ball; when he got home he decided to take action. He collected 23 balls and delivered them to the Jamaicans. Later two hundred balls went to them along with pumps, cleats and jerseys. The benevolence has grown nationwide.

While possessions are not the lot of everyone, each human being is a separate treasure available to an emotionally hungry world. Everyone has founts of patience, gentleness, and understanding to share with the tired, the lonely, and the dispossessed. We surprise ourselves sometimes at the powerful impact of a simple, momentary courtesy.

Prior to WWII, for ten years a Maryknoller toiled in a remote China province. With his own hands he built a chapel, school and clinic. He was dearly loved. Then, the dread Japanese invasion occurred. Days and nights of incessant shelling reduced his mission to rubble. He was heartsick, exhausted from the sleepless nights of terror, but the worst was yet to come. As troops occupied the area, he was too spent to care if he lived or died. Bayonet in his back, a soldier prodded the missioner to pick up his meager belongings and move into file. Death on the spot would have been welcomed. For him life was over. But the priest decided to reach for the impossible—a smile for the enemy! So moved was the surprised soldier that he picked up the padre's bundle and politely escorted him to a place in line.

Burnout is washout for the oppressed who succumb. In this void, the victim feels that there is precious little to give. But even a little is a lot when given with the heart of the gospel widow. Anyone can run out of gas . . . but when the fuel gauge registers "empty," there is still a gallon in the tank!

32nd Sunday of Ordinary Time
(1 Kings 17: 10-16, Mark 12: 38-44)

Final Curtain?

Gazing at the gentle photograph of a seated Pablo Casals bending over his beloved cello, one can almost hear the melody he is playing. So moved by his music, the legendary photographer, Yousouf Karsh, arranged a pose he had never requested from a subject before or since. He asked that the cellist not face the camera, but just play.

In the Boston Museum of Fine Art where this photo is exhibited, an elderly gentleman daily stood motionless before the photograph in rapt attention. Observing this routine day after day, the curator finally approached the devoted beholder and inquired, "Why?" "Hush, young man, hush, I am listening to the music," was the reply he received.

This incident, reported in November 2000 issue of *Connections,* suggests a useful way to better understand the Bible. That is, not to face the words head on—literally, but to see beyond them to their meaning. It is like not fixing on the lyrics of a song in order to better hear its melody. The Bible is limited by language. The written word is ever an inconstant variable in any communication. What its writers meant when they wrote what they wrote, scholars have given their lives to decipher. The Bible can be seen as an impressionistic painting, highlighting the artist's insights. The canvas is not a photograph. To emphasize a momentous message, ancient authors employed a literary technique known as "apocalyptic writing." This device uses extreme, exaggerated language to make a point. This is similar to a person accentuating a pledge by adding the apocalyptic words "until hell freezes over." The language is inflated and not to be taken literally.

Mark is writing around 70 A.D. Jerusalem lay in ashes, the Temple is dust. The Jewish world was falling to pieces. The new Christians had bloody persecution to look forward to, but deliverance was expected in the second coming of the Lord. Mark had Jesus himself foreseeing this event and appears to put the foreboding words of the prophets in his mouth, as he predicts dire calamities of a world winding down. Pagan cultures were also gripped by such baleful forecasts, as the Sibylline Oracles attest. But it is difficult to associate Jesus with these scare tactics. He seems to put a positive spin on the ominous warnings by introducing the fig tree figure. Whatever the barren winter of discontent, its leaves promise a fruitful summer. It can be another way of saying that with God, disaster is never the bottom line. So, faithful people, do not lose heart—Providence is on the job. Our God is the God of a second chance!

Here is a second-chance story that appeared years ago in a San Francisco newspaper. On a warm, clear day, 28-year-old Kenneth Baldwin stood mid-span on the Golden Gate Bridge and said good-bye to the world. His decision to kill himself somehow elated him. He gripped the guardrail, vaulted over the bar, and plunged more than 240 feet toward the frigid waters and what he believed would be certain death. In his own words:

> *When I got to the bridge I believed I had made the right decision . . . And I felt more happiness than I had experienced for months. But I panicked when I pushed off and saw my hands leave the guardrail. I instantly knew I had made a big mistake, but there was nothing I could do but live through those agonizing seconds knowing I would be gone as soon as I hit the water.*

But Kenneth Baldwin didn't die. Despite the 1-in-100 chance to survive the impact, he was not only alive and virtually unharmed after the ordeal, but treading water with a renewed vigor for life. "I should have died. But I didn't," he said. "And today, all I know is that I'm thrilled to be alive."

End-of-the-world scenarios have ever fascinated preachers. The dullest of them can wax eloquent on the spooky text: "The sun will be darkened, and the moon will not give its light, and the stars will be failing from the sky, and the powers of the heavens will be shaken." Preachers can feel a distorted illusion of power by alarming people. Every generation has its self-styled soothsayers prophesying the planet's demise. In upstate New York, William Miller insisted doomsday would be 20 March 1843. Scores of followers sold everything, donned white gowns, climbed a hill, and shiveringly waited to be the first to greet the Lord "coming amid the clouds" at first light. When nothing happened, they showed up on the same date again the following year. 1920 was the year of the Lord according to Judge Joseph Rutherford and his Jehovah's Witnesses.

To some scientists a "runaway universe" is not too far-fetched; what with supernova explosions, global warming, the greenhouse effect, and ozone layer damage . . . not to mention seven decades of nuclear threat. They report energies permeating space beyond current knowledge. Astrophysicists maintain that our crucial main star, the sun, has about five billion years to go. Then it will expand immensely and burn out, taking with it the planets of its solar system, including Earth. Still, this is not the end of the cosmos, since our solar system is a mere speck among measureless galaxies.

So, what to think about the biblical Day of the Lord? Will He be coming for our scalps, or like a lurking traffic cop to surprise us with an eternal traffic ticket? Whatever the blazing imagery of the scripture, when he comes, just judge that he is, surely he will see how we have tried to love him.

33rd Sunday of Ordinary Time
(Mark 13: 24-32)

Poll Politics

In 1925, when kings were losing popularity contests worldwide, Pope Pius XI solemnly declared Christ the King for the universal Church. Though never interested in that title, according to synoptics Matthew, Mark and Luke, Jesus was nevertheless executed for precisely claiming it. Pilate seemed amused to apply it freely to the battered defendant, to the obvious infuriation of the scorned Sanhedrin. He thought it a good joke on the haughty Hebrews to name a mangled crucified corpse as their king.

Revered colleague, Father Bill O'Donnell, of St. Joseph the Worker, Berkeley, CA, also had a hard time assigning kingship to Jesus, as he wrote in his 1991 parish bulletin:

> *If I were king I'd eliminate the title, especially from Jesus' name. Kingship is one of those abominable inventions the powerful concocted to keep people enslaved. Just look at what kings have done to Ireland . . . the colonies . . . King David of the Israelites was scandalously corrupt and he was one of the good ones.*

A similar sentiment was expressed in the Old Testament by Samuel, the last of Israel's Judges, when the people pleaded for "a king like those of other nations."

> *If you insist on having a king like those of other nations he will conscript your sons and make them run before his chariots, some will be made to lead his troops into battle, while others will be slave*

349

laborers. They will be forced to plow in the royal fields and harvest his crops without pay. He will take a tenth of your harvest and distribute it to his favorites. You will shed bitter tears because of this king you are demanding (1 Sam. 9).

In the Book of Judges, chapter eight, the victorious general, Gideon, is offered the crown. "But Gideon replied: 'I will not be your king, nor shall my son; the Lord is your king.'" And didn't "king" prove to be a dubious benefit for an Israel that prided itself on being a league of tribes with a great deal of local freedom and equality, since their rights were rooted in the covenant with Yahweh!

Back to politics and procurator Pontius Pilate! His charge, as it is today, was a much troubled land. Palestine was considered a backwater nuisance to Rome. Second-class provinces only rated procurators to govern in Caesar's name. The first was assigned to Palestine by Augustus when Jesus was six years old. Pilate took over when Jesus was 26 and ruled indifferently for about ten years. According to Jewish historians Philo and Josephus, he was contemptuous of Jewish religious customs, thus aggravating civil unrest and the seeds of sedition. Public tumult was dealt with quickly and severely.

John's Gospel features a puzzling dialogue between Pilate and Jesus. Some critics doubt that it even took place, since Jews enjoyed no legal right before a Roman tribunal. According to the noted New Testament scholar, the late Raymond Brown, the evangelist aimed at lifting Jesus above an itinerant preacher to the status of divinity. Hence royalty was appropriate for Jesus, which in John, he does not deny. However perplexing, the scene John describes is singularly dramatic. In an attempt to clarify this exchange, the Johannine account is herewith paraphrased hypothetically in today's idiom.

Pilate (bored with having to deal with another Jewish religious nut): Are you the king of the Jews?

Jesus (inwardly—let's get the question straight): Are you asking from your personal curiosity, or are you repeating local gossip?

The tables are turned; Pilate is now on trial.

Pilate (really roiled): Am I a Jew? Your own people have turned you in—what is your crime?

Jesus: Your kingdom has nothing to fear from me. Mine is out of this world.

Pilate: Then you are king.

Jesus: That's your word for it. Royalty for me is saying it like it is. Whoever appreciates what is—facts, reality, God's truth—understands me.

They are talking on two different levels. Pilate emphasizes the power of the state; Jesus, the power within honest people. Samuel Adams articulated the issue when he said, "We may look to our armies for our defenses, but virtue is our best security."

It is not hard to sympathize with Pilate. Responsible for keeping the lid on the Palestinian powder keg, he nonetheless seeks to set Jesus free. He passes the buck to Herod—to no avail. He ventures the choice of liberating Barabbas or Jesus—another stymie. Maybe scourging will get Jesus off his back . . . dead end! The Ethiopian Church canonized these efforts by naming June 25th St. Pilate's feast day.

Pilate was a politician who played the polls. He sold out to the public, not to principle. Though it is important for the civil administrator to know what the people are thinking, it is a mistake to make their opinion a core value.

We have played the Pilate part whenever our job took precedence over justice; the party over principle; petulance over pity; whenever we withdrew from a tough decision, or washed our hands of a mess that needed cleaning up. History is not clear about Pilate's ending. He could have been remembered for the sentence of deliverance to the Unjustly Condemned, instead of the terrible words that have echoed through the centuries: "and he suffered under Pontius Pilate."

Christ the King
(John 18: 33-37)

Index C
LITURGICAL CALENDAR
(Cycle B)

Index D
SCRIPTURAL REFERENCES
(Cycle B)

Cycle C

Introduction

The world's bestseller is not easy reading. The Bible is more than a book. It is a library of books, written by many hands, in many ages. Some of it is shocking. Some of it is contradictory. But all of it is the work of people who believed that God prompted them.

Whatever its power to inspire or to confuse, no one can safely read the Scriptures and not experience an almost uncanny energy—a sense of fraternity with the evolving consciousness that composed them. If ever the mysterious movement of God is discernible in the flux of human affairs, it is in this book. All the brutal bungling, the crafty conniving, and the spontaneous intrepid nobility in the human condition frankly flower in its pages. Nothing human is soft-pedaled. Neither is Divine irritability, nor the Creator's delight in His creatures. Here is told the story of a down-to-earth God of feelings, of changeableness, of self-correction, and not above equality with humans.

In the weltering jumble of texts, this hands-on, involved God welcomes the familiarity of being a *thou*. In the Martin Buber sense of "I—Thou," once experienced, all the other "thous" of the world take on the relevance of the Supreme Thou.

On Your Feet!

The gospel repeats a rerun of the spooky collision of the planets. Two Sundays ago, Mark mounted his version of the world's ending. In case that alarm didn't go off, the liturgy sounds another one by building the Church's new year on the back of the old one. This time, Luke has a crack at it by making the destruction of Jerusalem sound like the dissolution of the universe. This whole focus, however, seems a bit out of sync with the yuletide good cheer. The discrepancy brings to mind a dissonant modern parable of earth's perennial waywardness.

St. Peter and the Angel Gabriel are peering over the parapets of heaven, shuddering at the wantonness they behold among the earthlings. "That is disgraceful," protests the perturbed gatekeeper. "According to my accounting, seventy percent of the population is grievously immoral. Maybe we should send another deluge."

Gabriel, more lenient, tempers that suggestion. "But that would not be fair to the righteous thirty percent."

"Why not send a letter to the thirty percent naming the time and place?" modulates Peter. "So they can avoid the flood?"

The letter is dispatched via the Vatican. Two Archbishops are having a friendly drink and discussing the mysterious communication of such limited circulation. Archbishop I to Archbishop II: "What did the letter say?" Archbishop II to Archbishop I: "Oh my goodness, you didn't get a letter!" . . . I wonder if I would have gotten one? On second thought I've gotten many "letters." Ranging over six decades of assorted ministries: campus priest, parish pastor, editor, retreat director, radio/television producer, Navy chaplain, clinical pastoral educator—many were the pluses and minuses. Rich are the remembered messages from each commitment that widened the heart and broadened the mind. But nothing has been more humanizing than the lessons learned from the disabled: the fragility of life, the loneliness, the fear, the courage, the indomitable spirit to survive.

The hospital has been the most outstanding graduate school. The splendid French words for hospital are *Hotel Dieu,* meaning the "hospitality of God." Someone once wrote, "There is no place on God's earth where, per square inch, people are struggling more with the meaning of life, than in the hospital."

Here, the hospital, is the daily tableau of amazing grace in the direst of circumstances.

Changes can be devastating, particularly when unwelcome. When changes come swiftly, repeatedly, and relentlessly, adaptation falters and ingenuity fails to keep pace with innovation. The safety of what used to be appears more appealing than the complex present. The reforms of the Vatican II Council have jarred the religious tranquility of many a faithful. The vernacular sounds less solemn than sonorous Latin. Banjos and bongos cannot compete with the prayerful tone of Gregorian chant.

Still, the modifications have had positive effects. The pulpit has outgrown the fire and brimstone mentality for a kinder, gentler approach. Terrorist nuns of the past are subject of current comedy. Clergy are more pastoral and less chastening. The laity is more parish-oriented and involved. They are less sheep-like. Even the nature of God is better understood. The worshipping community reveres a deity that is not vexed by questions or doubts about faith, but like a patient parent, pauses to let the child think for itself.

Advent reveals a God that urges believers to get off their knees—"Stand erect and raise your heads because your redemption is at hand." The message is that His Kingdom will not magically fall into our laps. Jesus has come and gone and has left His followers with the task of being His presence in the world.

"Are you still waiting for me? Well, I'm waiting for you. It's your world—get with it!" This is Advent advice.

The planet has seen much destruction. I've seen Hiroshima, Berlin, Beirut, and Hanoi—just in my lifetime. Barbaric inhumanity to fellow humans still rages in the name of national, racial, and even religious sovereignty. Advent bids us stand up to cruelty anywhere. Would a benign Creator design a condign calamity for His misguided, capricious creatures? The apocalyptic gospel language emphasizes that nothing lasts—only God! Is this a problem? If not, then it doesn't matter when the world ends.

1st Sunday of Advent
(Luke 21: 25-36)

Electoral Collage

Contested elections are nothing new. But dimpled, pregnant, and hanging *chads* are. They've occupied a phenomenal rank in the presidential election of 2000. In England during the seventh century, the abbot of a North Umbrian monastery suddenly disappeared. A new one was elected. Would you believe his name was Chad? Well, three years later, the missing abbot shows up and contests the election of Abbot Chad. But the humble Chad declined dispute and willingly surrendered his miter to the original claimant. So impressive was his unassuming meekness, that he was awarded a bishop's see, as well as canonization. Our English cousins report their prayers to St. Chad in behalf of the American electoral snarl.

In his Gospel, Luke introduces another snubber of elevated status, the fiery John the Baptizer. John was the Billy Graham of his day. Enormously popular, hordes flocked to his preaching and tended to regard him a candidate for Messiahship. But John refused the nomination and ceded it to his cousin, Jesus, who was not as well known at that particular time. The Hebrew historian, Josephus, mentions John, but not Jesus.

Luke sets up the emerging supremacy of Christ against a background of the petty power brokers of that day—psychotic Tiberius Caesar, vacillating Pilate, and the quisling sons of Herod. Royalty has customarily demanded preferential treatment. Before traveling and at enormous expense to local subjects, Queen Elizabeth I insisted that roads be spread with gravel to provide her carriage with a smoother ride. If ancient times required such elaborate provision for an arriving dignitary, how much more fitting the spiritual preparation for the expected Messiah! Eight centuries before Christ, the prophet Isaiah employs this road-repair image to symbolize readiness for the hallowed visitation: "Every valley shall be filled and every mountain and hill shall be made low, the winding road shall be made straight, and the rough ways be made smooth." Luke assigns this message to John, the final Hebrew prophet and the immediate preliminary to history's major event.

John was a reformer. His extraordinary popular appeal was not inconsistent with the fire and brimstone preachers of yore. Cotton Mather packed them in at Boston. In 1682, Haley's Comet appeared and Reverend Mather harangued a cringing audience with the assurance that this manifestation was a definitive sign of "The Wrath of God." In 1741, Jonathan Edwards, who became president of what would become Princeton University, preached a hair-raising sermon known as "Sinners in the Hands of an Angry God." Again, in Boston, grown men were reported to have cried for mercy.

Being shaken appears to have entertainment value, judging from the success of films like *The Exorcist,* but reformers generally elicit a more fickle reaction. They disturb the status quo. Warnings about environmental pollution or global warming are ominous, but usually inoperative until crisis time. Though religious reformers are sometimes rabble-rousers, John the Baptist's behests were reasonably entwined with everyday common sensed living—healthy living.

The word salvation is from the Latin *salus* meaning "health," from which are derived the words *whole* and *holy.* To be whole is to be holy. To be whole means to integrate all the disparate parts of the self—the shadow sides, the mean self, the judgmental self, and the self-centered self.

All these live in most of us and show up at the most embarrassing moments. No amounts of prayer, penitence, or re-resolve have succeeding in eliminating them. No self-nagging works, either. Elsie Landstrom confesses in her poem "Inward Light," #67:

You are there, lurking under every kind act I do, ready to
defeat me.
Lately, rather than drop the lid of my shock over your
intrusion,
I have looked for you with new eyes
opened to your tricks, but more,
opened to your rootedness in life.
Thus I would disarm you.
For I have recently learned,
learned looking straight into your eyes;
*The holiness of God is everywhere.**

In the voice of the ancient prophet, Advent celebrates the singular election of all human beings. With God, there are no invalid ballots. The franchise is universal to all mankind; neither class, nor gender, nor race is excluded. Whether propertied, pauper, or parolee, the vote is confirmed—there is no need for recounts.

"And all flesh shall see the salvation of God."

*From the book *Our Many Selves* by Elizabeth O'Conner.

2nd Sunday of Advent
(Luke 3: 1-6)

367

Jarred by Joy

It's Rejoice Sunday again and the church invites its faithful to look at the world through rose-colored glasses. The vestments are a rosy hue and so is the Advent candle. But a Merry Christmas is too tall an order for many folks down on their luck. A Methodist pastor shared this report with his flock:

I'm not sure about this Joyful Sunday business," one harried mother was overheard to say at this time a year ago, as she was getting ready to go home after the Third Sunday of Advent worship service. "Seems to me that joy is reserved for the well-organized who have their shopping done, and the cards and packages sent, and for the rich who don't have to worry about how much their presents cost. I get Christmas cards that say Joy, and in church we light the third Advent candle, the candle of joy, but I'm not feeling much of it right now. My husband and I aren't getting along very well, our oldest child can't stay out of trouble, we are absolutely buried in debts, and last week our pipes froze and split. Everybody in the family has a bad cold that won't go away. I've spent more time in my doctor's office this month than I have at home!

Another woeful appeal went like this:

I'm calling from my neighbor's house because I don't have a telephone. I'm a single parent. My

*'ex' hasn't paid his child support in over a year,
even though our thirteen-year-old has to go to the
medical center across the state every month for
radiation treatments for his bone cancer. We don't
have any food in the house, last year's winter
clothes don't fit the kids this year, and I just found
out that my case worker forgot to turn our names
in for a Christmas food basket. Is there anything
the church can do to help?*

The crowds that thronged to John the Baptizer's preaching were probably looking for a brighter day also. His commonplace counsel was basic social justice: give to the needy and don't embezzle. He urged no heroic virtue, simply honest consideration for fellow humans. The satisfaction such behavior may elicit, is a joy look-alike, but there is more to joy than contentment.

Joy generally comes as a surprise. Joy can be wished, but not willed. It can be sought, but not wrought by dint of effort. It is often a momentary flash, a peak experience, a sudden awareness, an unexpected discovery, a connectedness not noticed hitherto. Nothing feels more like the presence of God, because joy is God's gift. It is the strong sense that the universe is in good hands—God is in charge!

Joy and sorrow are not opposites. The opposite of joy is cynicism; the need to be one-up, in control, where hurt is not allowed in—vulnerability is for losers! Such guarded aloofness leaves the cynic a convinced victim of life's perpetual unfairness.

Joy is neither mirth, nor humor, nor giddy gaiety. It is more the solid confidence that has looked suffering in the eye and has decided to learn to live in and with it. In fact, sorrow makes joy possible. The most tearful goodbyes can be the reason for the most exuberant hellos. Jesus understood this contrast. In His farewell to His disciples He said, "You are sad now, but I shall see you again and your hearts will be full of joy . . . All this I have spoken to you that my joy may be in you and your joy may be complete." Thus, joy has a connection with understanding the heart of Christ. It savors the Good News that God is for us, thus giving us a heart for all mankind. The mystic apostle Paul could thrill to this awareness even in chains. Facing execution, Paul exhorted the Philippians, "Brothers and sisters, rejoice in the Lord always. I shall say it again, rejoice!"

Joy stands in the doorway of the ordinary. The commonplace goes unnoticed most of the time, except for the lowly shepherds. Bethlehem missed an extraordinary birth. The star could be guessed, not the stable. Joy is no stranger to those who can drink from the bitter cup when it comes their turn. George Eliot's masterpiece, *Silas Marner,* tells such a story. The desolate miser, Silas, has only his hoarded gold to obsess over. When this is stolen, life is over for him. An infant foundling left on his doorstep by a heroin-overdosed mother, who dies in the snow, interrupts his agonizing grief. An unexpected richness invades his hermit life. Silas responds to this intruded bundle of needs. He begins to discover that something far more than gold has come to him. The growing child's delight in life awakens his delights, as any animated youngster can brighten a home.

Is this why the savior was born a baby?

A Silas Marner Christmas, all!

3rd Sunday of Advent
(Luke 3: 10-18)

371

A Pregnant Pause

This Gospel selection features an all-women cast. It also highlights the first official pre-Christmas party. An authentic Advent spirit of penitential moderation does not commend partying, as does the Yuletide mood. The former was generally observed by the Canada of old, but then after Christmas Mass, the celebrating began with gusto. For the twelve days until Epiphany, the typically large French-Canadian families had *beaucoup* relatives with which to party hardy.

This tradition seems so much more fitting than crowding in Christmas parties prior to Christmas day. Folks are usually so swamped with gift shopping, wrapping, greeting writing, decorating, baking, and preparing, that 25 December finds them bleary-eyed. Holy holly time can be a joyless letdown!

However, this was not so with Mary and Elizabeth, also pregnant after a long childless marriage. Neither had expected to be expectant, so they had much girl-talk to do about the wondrous miracles they were both carrying. They must have liked each other. It is always refreshing to share the company of someone that one enjoys. There is no hanging back, no reluctance to be useful. No service is a chore. Whether a hand or a hand -out, an ear or an earful, a shoulder to cry on or an arm to brace, affection can't wait to offer what is needed. Christmas is that magic time to indulge extravagantly and unashamedly our appreciation for those we like. Parents skimp on themselves to buy a bike for the young one. He goes in debt for the stereo she has her heart set on. Kids scrimp on their lunch money to save up enough for Dad's fishing reel and Mom's hairdryer.

Maybe this is as close as we get to resembling divine largesse—an eagerness to give without concern for return. This is not easy for those whose emotional wounds have scarred any trusting in human relating. The rejections of childhood are expected repeats in adulthood. Too frightened to be hurt again, defenses harden against tenderness and fabricate an aloof facade that needs no one. Holidays can accentuate loneliness.

Christmas is the one time of the year to venture past these obsolete and thoroughly useless precautions. In Christopher Morley's words, "The stupid harsh mechanism of the world runs down. We permit ourselves untrammeled common sense; the unconquerable efficiency of good will."

Another poet adds, "Give gifts, speak the kind word once again. Deck the trees, bake new and frosted cakes of festival; pour wine, weave legends, kindle fire. All this is worthy. This is Bethlehem, and she would have it so, who bore the child."

While some will be inclined to "deck the halls with gin and tonic," others, in keeping with Mary and Elizabeth, will gather for a good time together in honor of His birthday. Celebrating this event is fitting whenever or wherever . . . Upon pondering this mystery, a second grader asked this unrelated question to her religion instructor: "Before God made anything, what did He stand on?" The teacher might have answered: "Nothing—God rests in your arms whenever you hug your brother."

As the year winds down, it is important to review what is important in human affairs. If there is anything more important than human beings, the understanding of why His birthday is celebrated is missed entirely. Every human being is capable of caring for fellow human beings. Like Mary, every caring human being is pregnant with Jesus—not for holding on to, but for giving away. Wherever there is love, there is Bethlehem. Because of Bethlehem, human and divine became so commingled as to be indistinguishable. The seventeenth-century English poet, Richard Crashaw, understood this idea and wrote the following in his poem "Nativity":

> *Welcome all wonders in one night*
> *Eternity shut in a span,*
> *Summer in winter—day in night,*
> *Heaven in earth and God in man.*
> *Great Little One, whose all*
> *embracing birth*
> *Lifts earth to heaven, and stoops*
> *heaven to earth.*

When we love, God gets born again. Whenever we give love away, it becomes the best part of us. Let the Noel bells ring!

4th Sunday of Advent
(Luke 1: 39-45)

At the Crib

I wonder, did He cry? For babies cry . . .

But what made Him cry? Was He frightened by Herod's outrage, the bloody sweat, the watching olive trees, the traitor's kiss, Pilate's scourge, and the upright deathbed?

What made Him cry—the hunger, the cold? No empty stomach could hurt as much as His hunger for the hearts of men too filled to give Him room. No winter wind could sting as sharply as the selfishness of men too flesh-centered to follow a star.

But did He smile? For babies smile . . .

No infant snuggled in the arms of a sweeter mother, nor a braver guardian than stalwart, silent Joseph. Then there was the vision of those others. There were the heroic eleven, Magdalen, armies of young men and women consecrated to Him, marching fearlessly into unknown lands with His name on their lips and His love in their deeds.

Does He smile this holy eve as war drums throb across the quivering world? There is the young mother kneeling at the edge of the adorers over there. The tot held on her left arm is reaching a chubby hand for the little plaster sheep looking so unconcerned as it sits on the thorny straw. With her free hand, she guides, in the sign of the cross, the stubby arm of her three-year-old daughter, packed solidly into a bright red snowsuit, her blonde curls spilling out from under the scarlet hood.

There is the gnarled laborer in the heavy lumber jacket kneeling there. He is telling Him how he had not touched a drop throughout Advent, and asking Him to bless his victory for the advent he intends to make of the rest of his life.

There is that handsome woman in a fashionable fur blinking back her tears as she holds out the heart He has just filled for the first time in fifteen years, since her marriage was finally blessed.

There is the gray-haired convert kneeling in wordless wonder as he recalls that just last August his whole life turned upside down and came up right in safe harbor at last. The little bald man with the rimless glasses, who has not missed the 6:30 mass since his son was reported missing in Korea, was pleading God's mercy for his boy's soul, and pledging a life of more vivid sanctity.

Here are the little of the earth . . . the ordinary people whose passing tomorrow would hardly cause pause to a world busy on its way to . . . to . . . wherever. But here at the crib, somehow the world is forgotten. Here the victims of its tyranny turn tired hearts to God in search of His smile. Confined by the walls of daily routine, engulfed in the welter of detail, submerged by the unebbing tide of the material, embattled small people search for release, for the key, for the meaning of their bewildering toil. And here lies the answer, shivering on straw in a doorless cave.

Here in the manger, the mystery of the values that matter is suddenly explained with icy clarity. Here is greatness of soul, where the pettiness and conceit of the worldly spirit appear in ridiculous reality. Here the Savior brushes aside all show, frippery, and tinsel—all that drugs the senses. The soul is veritably shocked at the picture of the severely cheerless circumstances of the Divine Child's birth—no drowsy comfort, no intoxicating luxury. For this is the setting of the soul, and this precious commodity did the Redeemer come to rescue.

The mission of Christ is to the spirit. Every detail of His life is a sermon to the soul—simplicity, poverty, misunderstanding, pain, and failure. All these notes are stubbornly obvious in the tableau of the Savior's birth in the manger. He is come to save the soul—and in suffering does it achieve its salvation, its poise, and its greatness—indeed, its peace.

Still, in this comfortless setting, the unearthly spell of Christmas was cast. It was an enchantment that no Korean bullet or A-bomb threat can somehow efface. And caught in the full sweep of its tide—the depths of which no other mortal ever has or will experience such silent music, and veiled beauty as was that cave when He was born. In Mary's soul glowed the predictions of the prophets and the songs of the Psalmist as they blended in mighty crescendo to come to rest at last. Her entire being overflowed with thanksgiving, sweetness, and harmony. God led her away from the rowdy inn, out to the silent, rocky hillside, and there in stark poverty and solemn solitude He gave Himself to her.

Here then is the spirit, the enchantment, and the magic spell of Christmas—the immanence of Jesus. No other substitute, however precious or priceless, can match Him. And for those who share Mary's secret, what terrors of a world in collision can dismay them?

It takes the night to bring out the stars. And in our own darkened times, the mystery and the beauty of Christmas shine more lustrously than ever. It guarantees us that everything—everything that darkens our horizons today—is destined for judgment and expulsion.

These are lessons of the crib. Here, life's meaning is somehow mysteriously, but eloquently, interpreted. Here, for such a pitifully little while, a weary world looks into the face of its Savior and forgets its fears in His baby smile.

A Blessed Christmas, all.

The Now Testament

From the column "Incidentally" by Father Joseph Wadowicz, printed in the *Steubenville Register,* December 15, 1950, just prior to reporting for active duty as a chaplain in the U.S. Navy.

Christmas Day

Family Valuables ~ Children

If not crystal clear, this Gospel selection has its own appeal. It may be reassuring to note that the Holy Family experienced typical family problems like worry and misunderstanding. Maybe it was even dysfunctional from time to time. Mary and Joseph must have been beside themselves with anxiety over their son's three-day AWOL. I can hear the argument, "I thought he was with you!" Then, the boy's standard teenage response, "What were you worried about?" Cavalier, almost indifferent! After all, Jesus was of Bar Mitzvah age, when Jewish tradition conferred manhood. Testing for independence would come as no surprise to the seasoned parent, nor would their parental reaction. In today's parlance, "Get in the car, we will talk about this later." They most likely did discuss it later, since the Gospel tersely remarks, "And he went down with them and came to Nazareth and was obedient to them."

Three days is a long time to anguish over a missing offspring. Jesus may have been insensitive to time because He was enjoying impressing His elders in the Temple. Precocious children are no easy chore for average, hardworking parents. Nor is it a snap for gifted children to feel understood by adults. Mary and Joseph did not comprehend their son any more than beleaguered parents today make sense of teenage tendencies.

This is the time to ponder, as Mary did—to let things simmer—to be open to inevitable changes. It must have been as painful for her, as it is to most parents, to see the gulf widen between themselves and their teenager. But, developing adolescents seem to need to push every button and to challenge every belief of their parents in order to find out about life, themselves, and their place in the world. No manual simplifies the process, nor could it prevent mistakes. It is the time for fully conscious attention, willing listening and frank conversation about feelings. The tendency to argue, to convince, and to persuade, comes more readily than thoughtful regard. This is the time when the respect that parents accord their growing youngsters will pay off.

In the home where courtesy has been taught by being polite to one another, differences are part of interrelating. If it is unthinkable to embarrass a guest, it is just as unthinkable to humiliate a child. If maximum demands are made on the child, then maximum respect is its due. The child's work is to be criticized, not the child. Where questions are encouraged, it is better to answer the questioner than the question, and to allow the questioner the search for one's own answers. Children who are protected from difficulty become adults who can't get out of it. Still, a child never cries so much as when it knows no one is listening.

The most deprived child is the one who does not have to do anything to get what he/she wants. But the child must be allowed to be a child so as not to be one the rest of his/her life. Adults behave most like children when they expect children to behave like adults. The same grown-ups who do not understand the young of today, probably could not understand adults when they were young.

What can be a bigger job in the entire wide world than parenting? What enterprise effects the profoundest transformation, the most surprise lessons in living? Few parents think they deserve an Oscar for their efforts, and many are grateful for what their children have taught them. Their children have been their school—one moment, a lump in the throat, the next moment, a pain in the neck. No possession can match their worth. Aware mothers and fathers would never expect their children to be grateful for the sacrifices they, the children, never asked them to make. Children will most likely pick up on this when they face raising their own. Grandparenting gives the old-timers a chance to do it right. They have, at last, learned to say "no" gracefully, so that they do not have to say "yes" begrudgingly.

So, home is where the hurt and the heart are. Family is where humans learn to be human—the setting of sweet consolation and of unbearable torment. The family photo album is a veritable prayerbook recording the likenesses of the bestsellers that each life has been. Right or wrong—all of us have been both. As the famous Senate Chaplain, Peter Marshall, once prayed, "When we are wrong, make us willing to change. When we are right, make us easy to live with."

Holy Family Sunday
(Luke 2: 41-52)

Blunder Bravely!

It is easy to imagine Matthew with tongue in cheek as he wrote this Gospel story of the Magi. Might he have been poking good-natured fun at the wise men of the east who managed to get lost and seek directions from an uptight, paranoid, puppet king? Nonchalantly and undiplomatically, they boldly inquire, "Where is the newborn king of the Jews?" Their reverential visitation was not without calamitous consequences. "When Herod heard this, he was greatly troubled and all Jerusalem with him." The Holy Family had to flee for their lives and the Holy Innocents had to pay with theirs.

The reported gifts of gold, frankincense, and myrrh were the reputed tributes by visitants to royalty of that era. Matthew is obviously intending to impress the convert Jews of first century Christianity, that Jesus was legitimately the royal Messiah in strict accordance with Old Testament expectations. Their expensive offerings might be possibly evaluated at about two thousand dollars on the market of that day . . . a generous going-away present for the fugitive family! A jocular jest on this regal acknowledgment has a current greeting card depicting Mary and Joseph in their manger cave gazing at the premium windfall and remarking, "I can't believe no one gave us a crib."

Webster defines *epiphany* as "a sudden insight into a greater reality." The Eastern Church celebrates *theophany*—manifestation of God, which more literally describes the feast day, and which may suggest the question, why is God such a secret? In the nature of things, mystery seems more intriguing than the familiar. Mystery invites search and investigation of clues. Clues are small insights leading to larger discovery. The universe is still a cipher that scientists are learning to decode.

The Magi story is fraught with insights. A discernment might be that in the sincere pursuit of God, the seeker could easily get lost. It is a regrettable fact that charismatic gurus are able to influence willing believers away from sensible persuasions. But, like the Magi, even being misled can be a step in the eventual right direction. The truism bears repeating: People find God when God finds them.

The famous author and Trappist monk, Thomas Merton, sought God for many years within the walls of the Gethsemane Monastery. A medical appointment one day brought him to nearby Louisville. There on a busy street corner, amid a throng of people, he experienced the awesome presence of God more powerfully than in the hallowed cloister. Divinity seems occasionally to interrupt habitual human routine with a gentle "Ahmm" to signify nearness!

The Magi were considered learned men, but had a harder time discovering the Lord than did the unlettered shepherds, which introduces another Epiphany insight—namely that superior intelligence gains no better access to the knowledge of God than is available to the rudest peasant. From this implication, another inference flows— nothing God has made is profane. As the fruit from the tree, the Creator cannot be far from His creation.

If Epiphany highlights God's manifestation through nature, then God's exposure is even more dramatic when it shines through human nature. People are epiphanies of God when they pause to care . . . A Vietnam veteran had both his legs blown off in a helicopter explosion. Massive head injuries destroyed his sight. In triage examination, medics agreed the near-death casualty was better off dead. One young medical officer rejected that decision and worked eight straight hours to reverse the near-death fatality. The doctor agonized over his intervention, until some time later when they both rejoiced over restored life. The doctor had a faith others did not. Epiphany time!

The inventor, Thomas Edison, labored long and patiently on the first electric light bulb. Finally, at last, the operational product! Edison beckoned to a young worker to deliver the treasure to staff on the second floor . . . "Be careful," he admonished. You guessed it—the youngster tripped on the top step! The inestimable prize lay shattered. It was back to square one and consequent success, but the young man wanted to die of shame. Edison understood there was something more important than the fabulous bulb—the feelings of the youth. He invited him again to deliver the matchless wonder upstairs. The boy did—competently this time and he was alive again! We kindle dying embers to flames when we give second chances.

Maybe baseball is a favorite national sport because errors, fouls, and strikeouts are part of the game. In an imperfect world, Epiphany affirms that bloopers are part of the game. They make it more interesting.

Epiphany
(Matthew 2: 1-12)

Coming Out Party

Few Gospel narratives match the charm of the Cana event. Weddings were the premier social occasions in the Palestine of the time. The celebrating went on for days. The bride and groom were royally feted by frolicking neighbors. Any sparsity in the fuel for merry-making was an unforgivable humiliation for the couple, that would never locally be lived down.

Mary and son were among the guests. Mary might have been related to the newlyweds, since she was involved with arrangements and had authority to order the servants. Jesus appears to have brought a few party-crashers with Him—five recently acquired disciples. Could that be one reason why the wine ran out?

It is interesting that Mary reports this problem to Jesus and not to the hosts. Maybe she saw Him to be somewhat responsible for it? At first glance, the response of her son appears indifferent, in fact, curt. "Woman, how does your concern affect me?" Here again His independence is asserted. Her being a "Jewish mother" never worked on Him! Addressing His mother as "woman" seems impersonal, remote, even severe. However, in the classical literature of the ancients, the term reflects considerable courtesy and respect. Homer has Ulysses so address his beloved wife, Penelope. As does Augustus to the Empress Cleopatra. There is no argument from Mary. She trusts His responsibility. "Do whatever he tells you," she tells the servers. Authority does not have to nag, just take charge!

"Bring Your Own Bottle" is a popular economy measure among partygoers willing to share expenses. If what Jesus did with the water at Cana got around the neighborhood, no doubt He would be the number one guest invited to everyone's BYOB party. Picture, six water jars, each containing twenty gallons. That measures out to 120 gallons, or fifty cases, or 600 fifths of choice vintage. In poet Richard Crashaw's words, "The conscious water saw its God and blushed."

Teetotalers are understandably embarrassed at this extravagant supply. Surely, Jesus must have known the properties of alcohol. He would not be surprised if a big head greeted any of His five followers the next day, but He trusted experience to be a valid teacher. He did not shun the consequences of free choice. Irregularity disturbed Him less than domineering control. Freedom to be human was a hallmark of His Good News. A waggish interpolation of the post-Cana scene could have one intemperate celebrant cautioning another—"If we go to another party with Him, keep Him away from the water!"

The Cana episode is rife with meaning about the Good News. The marriage backdrop is a fitting introduction to the public ministry of Jesus. He repeatedly styled Himself the "bridegroom" in love with His nascent church. In keeping with the prophet, "As a young man marries his bride, so shall God delight in you" (Isaiah 62). The narrative suggests that believers in Christ can also be agents of the miracle of transformation in casual, trivial interrelating, when they are sensitive enough to forestall embarrassment, chagrin, and frustration in another. As Jesus did for the newlyweds.

Most emphatically, Cana reveals the heart of Jesus and how much life and people matter to Him. He is obviously willing to perform a miracle, out of due time, in an obscure domestic setting, so that people could continue to enjoy themselves. He understood how important it was to have recess from stress, to restore balance, to awaken humor, and

Inaugural Address

Inaugurations generally feature a common theme, a promising future. Jesus' first speech in His hometown was no different. For His text, He chose the prophet Isaiah who defined a job description for the expected Messiah.

"The spirit of the Lord is upon me, because He has anointed me to bring glad tidings to the poor. He has sent me to proclaim liberty to captives and recovery of sight to the blind, to let the oppressed go free and to proclaim a year acceptable to the Lord."

To His neighborhood audience, He drops the bomb; "Today this scripture passage is fulfilled in your ears!"

He is announcing to His neighbors, "I'm it—I'm the one you've been waiting for!"

The audience may have politely applauded and commented how well the neighborhood kid grew up to make such an astonishing impression, but being a hit can be a bit much for some locals. The admiring spectators suddenly turned into a lynch mob. (There will be more of that in the next chapter.) "Who does he think he is?" Jesus won one on the road last week at Cana, then lost the home opener.

What Jesus was declaring in His neighborhood debut was the venerated Jubilee—year of the Hebrew tradition. According to the Torah, after seven sabbatical cycles of seven years—that is, seven times seven equaling forty-nine, the fiftieth year was proclaimed Jubilee. Debts were forgiven, the interned were liberated, and property ceded to the impoverished. It was an honored humanitarian interval of second chance for the victims of life's unlucky breaks. In His inaugural of the Good News, Jesus is announcing that every year is to be Jubilee. The happy hour tone He set at Cana is now reaffirmed in His saving message, that His Father is the champion for rejects, the paladin for washouts; not an intimidating IRS auditor. His emphasis is not on religious externals, but on benevolent caring.

This message was not new. Prophets repeated it for over a thousand years. Now there was a fresh voice. How well has it been heard over the centuries? Welfare agencies invented by the ancient church are now the charge of governments and philanthropists. Still, a third of earth's population goes to sleep hungry. Slavery has been abolished, but not sweatshops. Churches offer spiritual sight while churchmen stumble. Twelve-step programs set junkies free, while hordes lie enchained to their addictions. Christianity has been a panacea to some, an anesthetic to others, a placebo to a few, but thank God, a stimulant to many! The Good News has not been entirely overlooked, though not always understood as its originator had in mind. An unknown poet notes the gap:

> *Long tracts of time divide*
> *those golden days from me.*
> *Your voice comes strange o'er*
> *the years change.*
> *How can we follow Thee?*

Still that voice resonates in every one that has a heart.

A favorite CBS television program is called *Sunday Morning*. It documents the triumphs of little people, not celebrities. Commonplace victories over adversity, especially in small town living, are generally featured. One such comes to mind, entitled "Postcard From Nebraska." Tragedy struck a rural farming community when a tractor tipped over and crushed a young farmer. He left a wife, three youngsters, and a large harvest to get in. Crops do not wait. The day after the funeral, the despondent widow looked out from her window at 6:30 A.M. and could not believe what she saw. Dozens of tractors and combines were gathering, with a small army of manpower. In one day, they brought in a harvest it would have otherwise taken three weeks to accomplish. The Good News was heard!

Less than a twenty-minute subway ride from Wall Street, the money heart of America, is one of the poorest neighborhoods in the country. The Mott Haven area of the South Bronx is an enclave of poverty, asthma, depression, homelessness, AIDS, and assorted drug addictions. The jammed tenements are iceboxes in winter, roach and rat infested firetraps in summer. There, children struggle to grow and survive. There, the little church of St. Ann, an Episcopal parish, runs a thriving after-school program for the youngsters, an evening recovery program for addicted adults, a food bank, and a Sunday noon soup kitchen—more like a family dinner. The hero of the scene, or rather, the heroine, is the pastor, Reverend Martha Overal, who gave up a promising career of trial law for the ministry. Her schedule goes from 5 A.M. to at least 10 P.M. She takes the sick to the hospital, attends court with the defendants, and deals with building managers, absentee landlords, loan sharks, drug dealers, and city bureaucracy. None underestimate her street smarts.

Reverend Martha is the Good News!

Courtesy *Connections,* January, 2001.

3rd Sunday of Ordinary Time
(Luke 4: 14-21)

Falling Out Party

More popular at the wedding party last week than He is this week at His neighborhood synagogue, Jesus, nevertheless, gets off to a good start. "And they all spoke highly of him, and were amazed at the gracious words that came from His mouth." He had them dazzled! Why not quit when you're ahead? Sometimes small town narrowness gets in the way. "Isn't this the son of Joseph?" How can a hometown boy shine brighter than any other local they have known? Jesus does not let this nearsighted insularity get by. He launches into an argument about God's historic, unbiased impartiality: even infidels rate God's attention. "When the people in the synagogue heard this, they were filled with fury."

An occupational hazard for the religious-right is the tendency to want God exclusively for themselves. Only churchgoers need apply! According to the traditionally orthodox, God singularly chose the Jews for sacred citizenship. Non-believers were not eligible for green cards. Jesus had to challenge this elitist thinking. His brinkmanship brought Him to the brim of a cliff. "They rose up, drove him out of the town, and led him to the brow of the hill on which their town had been built, to hurl him down headlong."

"We have just enough religion," wrote Irish born satirist, Jonathan Swift, "to make us hate, but not enough to make us love one another." A religion that closes the mind is about as functional as an unopened parachute to the jumper. The dangerous issue is the sincerity that it can breed in the "true believer": a sincerity that "persuades the zealot with the unfounded conviction that he is right." Oscar Wilde once

397

gibed, "A little sincerity is a dangerous thing and a great deal of it is absolutely fatal." It was almost so for Jesus at the cliff edge! "That God managed to survive the inanities of the religious that do Him homage, is truly a miraculous proof of His existence," jeered the American playwright, Ben Hecht (1894-1964).

What to do about this liberal theology of Jesus? "What's wrong with the way we believe? That's what we were taught," His hearers reasoned . . . "Get rid of the trouble-maker! Hang him . . . burn him . . . throw him off the cliff!" Should Jesus be surprised at this violence? He warned His twelve, "Don't imagine that I came to bring peace to the earth! No, rather, a sword. I have come to set a man against his father, and a daughter against her mother, and a daughter-in-law against her mother-in-law. A man's worst enemies will be in his own home." (Matthew 10:34)

Surely that astounding pronouncement cannot justify history's record of the slaughter of heretic Albigensians, the massacre of defiant Huguenots, the sixteenth century Wars of Religion, and the barbarous Crusades! . . . All in the name of religion. But those were "crude and cruel days and human flesh was cheap." Civilization has yet a way to go to soothe the savage beast resident in human nature. Our own advanced U.S.A. stands virtually solitary among progressive nations of the world, in its devotion to authorize legal state murder: capital punishment.

A 2001 World Almanac study, released 12 June, concluded that the judicial administration of the death penalty in the United States is "fraught with error."

The current sitting president presided over more than 130 executions while governor of Texas. Only thirteen of the fifty states repudiate capital punishment. The Savior Himself was its victim eventually, and it would have been sooner if His neighbors had their way.

Eliminating the opposition often shuts out valuable discoveries . . . like Narcissus, the Nazareth townies could not get past their own image. Non-conformists were misfits and deserved punishment. Father Joe Nolan illustrates this sad fact in his *Good News,* "Short Homily," 29 January, 1989.

Consider Bob Geldof ("We Are the World"), the rock singer who organized Live Aid in 1985. In his autobiography, he tells how he left his native Ireland as a young man because he experienced his home country as a 'place where ambition and talent were denigrated. The cardinal rule was to know your station, where to try to rise above that, to attempt anything ambitious was to invite derision and to court failure.' He complained of 'a parochialism and a morality so stifling it literally manifested itself in him as an inability to breathe.' He left home filled with self-doubt. He was a high school failure with little career prospects. His long hair and scruffy appearance were disconcerting . . . yet he had much to offer. He raised over one million dollars for food and agricultural projects in West Africa. He became a knowledgeable and forceful advocate for the hungry and the helpless. Many of the projects initiated by Live Aid are long term and will continue helping for years to come. Fortunately, he did not buy other peoples' estimate of himself.

"The reasonable man" claims G. B. Shaw, "adapts himself to the world. The unreasonable man persists in trying to adapt the world to himself. All progress depends on the unreasonable man."

4th Sunday of Ordinary Time
(Luke 4: 21-30)

399

Guilt-Edged

That people are scandalized when the preacher fails to practice what he preaches, is generally no surprise. The first one to admit this discrepancy is no doubt the preacher himself. At least all three principals in this day's Scripture readings exhibit a sense of personal delinquency in contrast to their high calling. Isaiah frets that the prophet function is out of his reach. "Woe is me, I am doomed! For I am a man of unclean lips, living among a people of unclean lips" (Isaiah 6). Paul confesses to the Corinthians (1st Corinthians 15), that he is "not fit to be called an apostle, because I persecuted the church of God." Simon Peter, suddenly aware of his baser self, "fell at the knees of Jesus and said, 'Depart from me, Lord, for I am a sinful man.'"

In the presence of the best, *pretty good* is an embarrassing deviation. The acned youth is more conscious of his blemishes as he approaches a good-looking coed. Deficiency tends to hide. To the ashamed, recognition is always an unexpected, unearned surprise. Imperfections are regarded as disqualifiers, rather than potentials for growth. This distorted logic of the idealist did not appear to apply to Jesus. He was a realist. This was an imperfect world and so was its populace. The contradictory elements in human beings for Him seemed to be powers for vitality. Much like the positive/negative poles of electricity that generate energy.

This is what He may have seen in Simon Peter—a thoroughly human, ordinary man, blue-collar, impulsive, outspoken, with a warm heart and cold feet. He probably never got over his triple denial of the master when the chips were down. But this never disqualified him from leadership of the church; in fact, it may have enhanced it. The forgiven are better at forgiving.

Holy events happen not only to holy people. Gentle intimations of God's gaze insinuate into the most casual events of life . . . a tear at a funeral, an insight at a wedding, the clutch at a baby's smile. Or the blessed ease provided by the hospital nurse when she went out of her way to bring warm bath water. Or the artless lift from the supermarket checker, "I like your earrings." Modest instances of God's intrusion surround us almost unnoticed. The big fisherman caught this glimpse in this wonderful Gospel fish story when a carpenter showed him how to fish.

Wiped out from an all-night washout of futile fishing, Simon Peter was brought to his knees by an astonishing catch. The sense of unworthiness that suddenly gripped him, prompted an empathic response, "Do not be afraid. From now on you will be catching men." The pathetic weaknesses of human nature may touch the heart of God more than does blameless probity. Simon's acknowledged frailty did not render him ineligible for the ministry mission Jesus offered to him. Flawed individuals would be henceforth the agents of the Good News. The message is important, not the messenger.

The initial impact of the phrase *catching men* sounds disagreeable and tricky, suggesting the scheming intrigue of the sales huckster. But Luke employs the Greek word for catch that translates into rescue—more in keeping with the Salinger novel, *Catcher in the Rye,* who protects children gamboling near the cliff edge. In Jesus' inaugural Jubilee message to His hometowners, rescue is the emphasis— deliverance from impediments to wholesome living. Guilt is one of these burdens, and human beings are never far removed from its weight, especially if one has sought refuge in a coercive, confining religion. Jesus was especially antagonistic to the idea that guilt was the essential basis on which a love of God is founded. Because the Christian message is one of love, it is only reasonable to conclude that Christ aimed at freeing mankind from the torture of guilt by "taking away the sin of the world."

Guilt can be constructive when it leads to amendment, damage repair, and responsible rehabilitation. To be engulfed in paralyzing remorse is, however, of use to no one, and is the penalty for a hypertrophied self-consciousness that might well reveal a subtle spiritual pride.

For human nature, the deck is stacked. No one has a full hand. Incompleteness is the human condition. Therefore, deficits are endemic. Like dust and dandruff, they are embarrassing facts of life, but are more effectually modified by patient attention than by drastic denunciation. Christ's method was essentially to lift the burden of guilt and sickness as soon as possible. He could not support the focus on law as understood by the Scribes and Pharisees. This is why Christianity spread more overwhelmingly among the Gentiles than among the Jews. This inclusive religion of love for universal mankind was quite novel for the world of that era. This was the net Jesus wanted people to be caught in, and He did not mind who the retrievers were as long as they were loving and human—really human—like Peter—even guilt-edged!

5th Sunday of Ordinary Time
(Luke 5: 1-11)

Plain Talk

The Beatitudes compose history's most famous sermon. The Gospels dramatize it at two separate settings. For Matthew, it is delivered on a mount, for Luke, it is delivered on a plain. These places symbolize its sublimity and its simplicity. What could Jesus have had in mind when He taught this upside down theory of values?

The Scriptures, he had learned, had God administering the world by blessing with good fortune and cursing with ill. Jesus might have looked out at His audience and felt their straining struggle to survive. Life's grim burdens were heavy enough without the consciousness that God was mad at them as well. How could He induce the hope that sound religion was meant to supply? So, He opened to them the great heart of His God.

Blessed are you who are poor, for the kingdom of god is yours.
Blessed are you who are hungry, for you will be satisfied.
Blessed are you who are now weeping, for you will laugh.
Blessed are you when people hate you, and when they exclude you and insult you, and denounce your name as evil on account of the son of man. Rejoice and jump for joy on that day!
Behold, your reward will be great in heaven.

This is revolutionary stuff! Here is an attitude destined to make new history. What sane teacher ever taught that suffering is a source of success, indeed, happiness! Here is a belief that insures that no tragedy can be the bottom line of human existence. Paraphrasing Gerard Manley Hopkins, the grandeur of God cannot be limited only to the glaze of glory, but gleams refulgent from even the crush of grief. In all human experience, there now lives the mystery of a *dearest freshness* that lies deep down in things. The Beatitudes affirm that no frustration or heartache justifies giving up on God. They reassert that human thinking is not likely to be God's.

Jesus does not come off as a warm fuzzy! In fact, His Beatitudes might well be regarded as a tough love program for mankind. There is in them a profound understanding of human nature and what occasions its growth. The inverse standards for happiness that Jesus highlights, such as poverty and hurt, are to Him blessings in disguise. Precious few have acted on this logic, but the strong souls who have risked it, have tasted the wonder of its payoff. Few have lived poorer lives than that intrepid rescuer of the hungry and the homeless, Dorothy Day. Yet, few have lived happier lives. The selfless sisters of Mother Teresa's order, laboring among the poorest of the poor, undoubtedly live more fulfilling lives than have the Gabor sisters, who according to Oscar Levant, do a "kind of social work among the rich." Mother Teresa once remarked that the "spiritual poverty of the West is much greater than the economic poverty of the East." Our worry about cholesterol intake must be a joke to a Calcutta beggar!

Luxury can be a bore. Matter of fact, the body is built for strenuous activity. Stevedores have no need to budget for gymnasium workouts. It is unsettling to note how widespread substance abuse is among the well-to-do; like high-priced athletes and entertainers, who seem to need higher and higher highs.

Another subtle insight implicit in the Beatitudes is the reality that enjoyment is most enhanced by its opposite.

There is no better appetizer than hunger. Fitness is never more relished than after recovering from a grave illness. Being without things makes having things more elating. Contrast enriches zest. Opposites enhance each other.

Though humans naturally cringe from misfortune, the memories of the past most prized are the hardships endured and outlasted. Confronting travail offers a deeper look into oneself, a discovery of a tenacity hitherto unsuspected, a more humane understanding of others' agonies. The Beatitudes remind the world that the inescapable crosses of existence are no less redemptive than the Calvary gibbet. Hence, no suffering, however undeserved, is to be despised or even deplored. No pain is wasted. The sturdy perspectives inherent in the Beatitudes intimate that the unavoidable may just as well be born with a smile. When God breathed His breath into His creatures, He trusted them with His power. F. R. Maltby put it this way, "Jesus promised his disciples three things; that they would be completely fearless, absurdly happy, and in constant trouble." It is reassuring to know that the darkest hour still has only sixty minutes!

6th Sunday of Ordinary Time
(Luke 6: 17-26)

407

Return of Plain Talk

As if by popular demand, last week's great Beatitudes sermon continues a sequel with the Golden Rule. This is Jesus' peace-plan for the world—non-violence. Surprisingly, this is not a popular strategy among civilized nations. Sigmund Freud regarded civilization as a pressure cooker where the repressed id regularly boils over. *Id* is the Latin impersonal pronoun meaning *it* or *that*. Impersonal it certainly is; ruthlessness does not attack people, only its!

In a bully world, how reasonable is turning the other cheek or giving the shirt off your back when being stripped of your jacket? When your car is being stolen, do you offer the hijacker ten dollars for gas? Isn't that playing the patsy—being a doormat? Is patience passivity? Is non-resistance neutrality? Is Jesus recommending that unjust aggression be tolerated?

Two fifth graders were fighting in the schoolyard. The monitor teachers break it up. "Who started this?" a teacher demanded . . . "He did," replied the bloody nose, "when he hit back."

Maybe Jesus is advising against escalation. Force inevitably breeds more force, unless the process is interrupted. Non-violence breaks the chain of violence. It worked for David. This day's first Scripture reading, (I Samuel 26), describes the hunted David fleeing from the homicidal King Saul and sneaking into the sleeping enemy camp with his cousin, Abishai, under cover of night. Abishai whispers to David, as they hover over the slumbering Saul, "God has delivered your enemy into your grasp. This day let me nail him to the ground with one thrust of the spear; I will not need a second thrust!" But David said to Abishai, "Do not harm him, for who can lay hands on the Lord's anointed and not remain unpunished?" Whatever David's motive, the spared Saul returns the favor to David. Non-violence inspired further non-violence. Saul recants, "I have sinned. My course has been folly—my error grave. Never will I harm you."

It worked as well for Gandhi, whose unswerving non-violence brought Great Britain to its knees. Who would have dreamed that a black man could be the mayor of Atlanta, Georgia, if not for the persistent non-violence of Martin Luther King and his heroic followers? Retaliation only inflates catastrophe.

The Pan Am 747 explosion over Lockerbie, Scotland in December 1988 killed 270 people. Terrorists had avenged the April 1986 bombing of Libya for its imputed terrorist activities. A grieving father, a former Pan Am pilot, urged further bombing of Libya in reprisal. Most mourners agreed with him except for a mother whose victim son had objected to the 1986 aerial assault. "This is wrong," he confided to her, "someone will pay!" . . . He did!

For Jesus, all human beings, without exception, enjoy the unique privilege of the Lord's anointed—even the enemy. As hostilities ended in the Persian Gulf War of 1991, a chaplain described the U.S. servicemen's grizzly task of searching through hundreds of burned out enemy tanks for the charred remains of Iraqi soldiers. "Carefully they wrapped the corpses in the green blankets issued to all Iraqi military, and a reverent committal service was pronounced over each. 'It was ironic,' observed the padre, 'that the dead received greater care than the living.'"

The Golden Rule has had a long, distinguished, intercultural history. Five centuries before Christ, Confucius felt that *reciprocity* should characterize human interaction;

"What you do not want done to yourself, do not do to others." In the following century, the Athenian orator, Isocrates, taught, "What things make you angry when you suffer them at the hands of others, do not do to other people." These are all negative injunctions. The Christian ethic is strongly positive. Jesus bid His followers not just to avoid doing ill to others, but also to do good for them.

Love your enemies and do good to them . . . Forgive and you will be forgiven . . . Give and gifts will be given to you; a good measure, packed together, shaken down and overflowing, will be poured in your lap.

A fine film, *Pay It Forward*, depicts a young seventh grader acting out this philosophy. For a school assignment about creating a plan to make the world a better place, the youngster comes up with this design. He selects three people to do something for them that they cannot do for themselves. He asks no payback, but requires his beneficiaries each to do a good thing for three others and they in turn to do the same for three other people. In the short span of two weeks, the project multiplies to a staggering 4,782,969 benefactions.

Utopian? Perhaps, but this idea of Jesus was to liberate people from the dungeon of hatred into the free air of seeking the good of the offender; thus detouring the predator/prey deadend. He understood that if the wicked are not worth saving, the just are also lost. Compassion may not change the aggressor, but it surely will alter the aggressed. If the business of human life is to survive endless and pointless blood baths, then revenge must never be chairman of the board.

7th Sunday of Ordinary Time
(Luke 6: 27-38)

Blame Game

Did Jesus have a sense of humor? This is a trivial question, perhaps, but an intriguing one. If humor is wit, and wit is intelligence, then God must have the supreme sense of humor. Two discrediting bits of information that seem to arouse fighting denials in most people: that one has not suffered; and that one has no sense of humor. Since humor is such a subjective matter (what gets a laugh in New York is not always funny in the Smokies), Jesus probably used it sparingly. It takes digging for!

In the finale to His Sermon on the Plain, Luke has Jesus stringing together four separate observations about human behavior. It can be imagined that Jesus might have approached these issues with the amusing touch of a stand-up comic. "Ever hear the one about the two blind guys leading each other into a ditch? Or the one about the student who thought he was smarter than the teacher? How about the one about the nitpicker who can spot your splinter, but can't see his own two-by-four? Or the one about the bad apple on the family tree?" The optimistic faith of Jesus could interpret the inconsistencies of the human condition as deserving more levity than lament. The condition was never hopeless to Him. Creaturely weakness, He taught, elicited the Creator's compassion more than condemnation. What Jesus is panning is perfectionism, the occupational hazard of the over-anxious. He appears to be poking fun at this particular madness when He asked, "Why do you notice the splinter in your brother's eye, but do not perceive the wooden beam in your own?"

413

Perfectionists are rarely very emotionally secure. Their logic insists that being above reproach will assure the public approval they so desperately crave. But such either/or thinking allows for no failings. Critical fault-finding then becomes a natural sequence. Jesus is talking about this type of ceaseless critic who needs things to go wrong so he/she can take a bow for setting it right. Correcting gives them an illusion of superiority. Perfectionists take infinite pains and give them to others. In childhood, their bids for affection were probably rebuffed, so as adults they are never quite comfortable with giving or receiving it. Berating comes more easily than relating and the blame game becomes habit forming. It was Abe Lincoln who observed, "He has the right to criticize who has the heart to help." Blamers lack this heart. The rose has thorns only for the picker, not the admirer. Sometimes the breach of the law is far less malignant than observing it to the letter.

Naggers are not happy campers. They are needy people. They hardly notice that the deficiencies they note in others are the same deficits in themselves. That is why Jesus gibed the flaw-fixer for the faulty "plank" in his/her eye. The rashness for which the Moral Majority vehemently reproach uninhibited youth, may well be the subtle reprieve they secretly would not mind for themselves. There is a morbid impulse in human nature to punish those for doing the things that critics themselves have a repressed interest in doing. The demon, invisible inside the accuser, only becomes visible in the accused. The sliver detected in another is but a chip off the detector's block.

Blame-gamers are hooked on curing others of the blamer's faults. While intent on another's problem, they feel excused from dealing with their own. Still, the soap is diminished in the cleansing of others. Lent is a good time to get the cleaning right. It is a good time to get to those inner cobwebs we have been neglecting, like the things that send us up the wall. Look at what angers you! You might find an overlooked hang-up of the past that was buried alive. Though forgotten, the ghost comes to haunt you in the person's behavior that sets your teeth on edge. The tip off is the strong emotion aroused—the anger!

For your Lenten devotion, instead of giving up something, try doing something positive for yourself. How about examining the things that bug you? Is one of those, people who talk back, who challenge your authority? Which, while growing up, you were never allowed, nor ever risked successfully since then. Maybe autonomy—initiative—needs attention. Maybe the slumbering rebel needs a stretch.

Whatever aggravates blood pressure deserves a friendly inspection. Just look at it gently, tolerate the possible embarrassment, and let that suffice for your Lenten penance. Don't try to repair; let the problem speak to you, tell you who you are, and why you are the way you are. It's not all your fault. Make your Lenten project to be your own best friend. Here's another reprise from wise Abe Lincoln, "People with few vices, probably have few virtues as well."

8th Sunday of Ordinary Time
(Luke 6: 39-45)

When Bad Looks Good

That's temptation! "Ya got trouble in River City" . . .
"Lead us not into" *it,* we supplicate the Almighty in the
Lord's Prayer, because mortals are not that good at mastering the tantalizing. A line in a popular ballad defines the
problem:

> *My little demon's makin' me choose . . .*
> *Makin' me an offer I can't refuse.*

Temptation! A moment of truth—a choice—the high
road or the low road!

At the juncture where the blacktop ends and the fur-
rowed rural wayfare continues, this road sign appears:
*Choose your rut carefully, you'll be in it for the next twenty
miles.* Temptations are confrontations with choice. They are
not sins, just invitations in that direction. Temptations are,
therefore, important. They occasion clarification of values.
There is no maturation without a duel with evil.

A cartoon pictures a little boy tucked away in bed, asking babysitting granddad to tell him a bedtime story. The
elderly gentleman reluctantly complies:

> *Many years ago, an old Gypsy woman told me*
> *to withdraw all my savings and put the money on*
> *Fancy Gal in the fifth at Belmont. I did, and Fancy*
> *Gal came in seventh. Later, we lost our house in a*
> *hurricane. Your grandmother divorced me, and I*
> *began to drink and lost my job. Now go to sleep.*

417

Grandpa obviously made some poor life choices, but probably became the wiser for them. This Gospel suggests how to pass the temptation test.

Luke employs the allegorical literary technique to describe the struggle of Jesus with the force of evil. He personifies this influence as the devil, in much the same way as Father Time and Mother Nature are poetically identified. It is to be noted that Jesus is not coaxed to any base immoral irregularity, such as lust or larceny. His temptations are those typical of VIPs—self-glorification, control, transcendence. It is no sin to eat, especially when famished (first temptation). Nor to manage a world, as is expected of political leadership (second temptation). Nor to want to bypass physical pain (third temptation). The solicitations are to attitudes that can corrode a serviceable life.

Before this desert contest, something happened to Jesus at the Jordan baptism by John. At age thirty, He knew He had to make a career change. He had to do something with His life. Moved by the Spirit, He made a forty-day retreat to figure it all out. He had animating Good News for the world. How to promote it—who would He be—a magician, a mogul, a manipulator? Or just take His chances, saying it like He saw it, come what may. He opted for the latter.

Most people want to be somebody. They have varied decisions on how to go about it, and the options are rarely over in forty days. Trial and error marks the human march to maturity. Sometimes good judgment blossoms out of bad, and one discovers there is more to life than being comfortable, controlling, or a flash in the pan. It helps to have a background in values. Jesus seemed to find His religious training useful in His identity crisis.

"It is written, one does not live by bread alone." America has little lack of *bread,* but our consumer society makes life more convenient, not more wholesome. In *Lear's Magazine,* Barbara Ehrenreich writes:

Joseph M. Wadowicz

Morality is no longer a prominent feature in civil society. In the '80s, politicians abandoned it, Wall Street discarded it, televangelists defiled it. (But) as virtue drained out of our public lives, it reappeared in our cereal bowl . . . and exercise regimens . . . and our militant responses to cigarette smoke, strong drink, and greasy food. We redefined virtue as health.

"It is written, you shall worship the Lord your God and Him alone shall you serve." That takes care of the false idols of fame, fortune, power, and popularity. None of these keep their promises.

"It also says, you shall not put your Lord, your God to the test." This one is aimed right at us churchgoers who feel that God should be sitting up nights worrying about our heart condition. To test God is to put God *on,* that is, to expect God to behave like we think God should behave; to suit us, for instance. So, when catastrophe strikes, we groan, "Why me—after all I've done for You!" God's rejoinder might well be, "And why not you?" But, when God flunks our divinity test, He is no longer to be believed so, we quit on God!

Temptation is a fact of life. It was as realistic for Jesus as for all human beings. Annoying though it is, it can nevertheless be a learning experience, if it leads to a clearer view of what is important to living. One such value is the robust faith that asks nothing of God, but just reports for duty by playing the hand that life deals. With this point of view comes the promise that whither one is led, ultimate deliverance from evil is assured.

1st Sunday of Lent
(Luke 4: 1-13)

419

Magic Mountain

Tabor is the evangelists' setting for the report of the luminous transfiguration of Jesus, only days away from His gruesome crucifixion. To the attentive Gospel reader, this glittering display before the favored Peter, John, and James, may register an unsettling affect. In last Sunday's account of the desert temptations, Jesus firmly renounces any glamorous exhibition to make an impression. He clearly chooses artless naturalness over the strategy of spectacle. Apparently, the evangelists did not see Jesus with the simplicity that He saw Himself. Their intent was to make their "Messiah" worth believing in. He, therefore, had to be more than an executed outlaw, and so they resorted to the literary style of their time when dealing with a historic personage, hyperbole. Any extraordinary event was consequently allegorically exaggerated in order to emphasize its importance. Something extraordinary happened on that mountain!

The countenances of mystics have been known to glow radiantly when in ecstasy. Jesus ascended the mountain with His friends to talk to God. It is highly likely that such a transport transpired there, and the evangelists recounted it in typical inflated prose. The momentous episode moved Peter to exclaim, "Master, it is good that we are here." Only days later, the memory of it seemed to evaporate in his triple denial of that Master.

Even skeptics would envy witnessing such an ethereal scene. Though celestial surprises are hardly commonplace for most mortals, modest touches with the awesome are less rare. Life's steady transfigurations pass almost unnoticed. In this day's first reading (Genesis 15), Providence figuratively snatches senior citizen, Abram, 75, by the scruff of the neck and deposits him in unfamiliar, bewildering circumstances, for the adventure of his life. Alive a thousand years before Christ, this man of faith is claimed as father of three major world religions: Judaism, Christianity, and Islam.

Husbands and wives transform one another—spousal spats not withstanding. After a particularly baleful altercation, and all the poison has been spent, a sudden gentleness intrudes. A fresh depth moves in and the other is seen with new eyes. The wordless wonder of making-up is a momentary brush with the divine. Parents have a taste of this alteration. It's been raining for three days and the restless kids are driving you up the wall! "How many times have I told you? No skateboards in the living room!" You punish, maybe spank. Before retiring for bed, you slip into their room to check if they are warmly covered. Your heart melts as you gaze down at those innocent, sleeping faces. It's another gentle caress of God.

Human beings have the power to transfigure or to disfigure each other. Simple moments of kindness work miracles on mood and morale. Fr. Joe Nolan tells this story in his *Good News* "Short Homily" of 6 August 1989.

A small boy traveling alone was seated on the aisle and the only empty seat left on the plane was the middle one beside him. A late passenger finally took it. He was a big man and carried a big briefcase, probably bulging with work he hoped to do during the flight. He never did. The boy asked questions like, "How fast are we going?" and (at least every half hour), "When will we get into Los Angeles?" And, "Where is the bathroom?" and "When do you think we will eat?" He wasn't a pest; he was a delightful child, and his companion—who certainly hadn't planned all this—talked to him about many things. When the youngster took out his coloring book of Bible stories, they talked about that. When the food finally did come, he helped him cut the meat. Once he made a brief attempt to open the briefcase and take out some work, but then he gave it up. The boy was in love with life, all this was high adventure, and he had found a friend. What happened then? When the plane landed, he had to wait to be escorted off by the hostess (because he was traveling alone). The big man with the briefcase shook hands and said good-bye. He moved up the aisle (and must have felt a certain relief. It had been a long flight!). Then suddenly he heard the boy call out, "Mister! When are you flying back to Chicago?" He turned and said hesitantly, "Saturday." The youngster's face lit up like the sun and he cried, "So am I! Maybe we can get the very same plane!"

Moments of gladness are hints of eternal life. Instants of kindness are like letting one's best self out of jail. It is deliverance from the confines of timidity and defensiveness—the willingness to stretch inside another self. In the moving film *To Kill a Mockingbird*, Atticus Finch, played by Gregory Peck, explains kindness to his children, "It's climbing into someone's skin and walking around for a while." Robert Browning understood its redeeming quality, "'Twas a thief said the last kind word to Christ; Christ took the kindness and forgave the theft."

2nd Sunday of Lent
(Luke 9: 28-36)

Act of God

The expression sounds more theological than juridical, but it is a valid legal term to explain a happening beyond human causation. Even atheist attorneys seem perfectly willing to employ it. Tornadoes, floods, lightning, and firestorms fit this category. Murder and mayhem are more readily attributed to human criminality. This Gospel deals with both issues: human malevolence and chance accident. The ageless dilemma persists–what is God's part in disaster?

In Jesus' time, catastrophe was regarded as divine retribution on sinners. This thinking continues to our modern era. When an offender fired her ire, the emphatic Maude, of television repute, would ominously predict, "God'll get you for that!" Although the audience would laugh, the threat, nonetheless, had a certain intimidating impact. What if God is the *get even* type?

To this question, the response of Jesus was loud and clear . . . "By no means!"

Could it be that when calamity strikes, the human mind is so appalled at its absurdity, that it instinctively cries out "Why?!" Senseless tragedy searches for meaning. If suffering is God's punishment for sin, then, at least, the sinner can be *paying up,* and hopefully, the scales can be balanced again. Jesus would have none of this logic. His God forgives *debts*.

Such is the reasoning of faith, which is God's gift to a wandering, wondering world. The Lithuanian born Polish poet, Czeslaw Milosz, who witnessed the unspeakable horrors of wartime Warsaw, could still conclude, "Only Paradise is authentic—the world is only temporary." With a mystic's insight, he sees something wondrous, sad, even comical, but touchingly grand, in civilization's noisy passage through time.

In this day's first reading (Exodus 3), the fascinating mystery of God happens to a shepherd on the lam from Pharaoh, for killing an Egyptian who was beating up on a Hebrew slave. Moses means *water baby* and it is difficult to like him from Charlton Heston's film portrayal of him— grim, humorless, self-important. The biblical version of Moses is quite another thing. The story has God using an unconsumed burning bush to get his attention. The voice of God lays a heavy trip on this shepherd of the hills, against which Moses protests for a whole chapter and a half. To no avail. He is tapped to be the reluctant agent of his people's liberation.

In this direct encounter with Divinity, some ambiguous disclosures are confided. This Deity is not to be taken lightly.

"Come no nearer! Remove the sandals from your feet, for the place where you stand is holy ground."

Could this be an invitation to intimacy? "Let nothing be between your skin and My good earth." Perhaps emboldened by this trust, Moses asks God His name; an important ratification of friendship to the Hebrew mind. God replies, "I am who I am."

Though scholars have wrestled with this mysterious answer for eons, its meaning may not be as vague as it first sounds. It could be taken as one more evidence of God refusing to be cornered, or it could be understood as the Creator's identification with His creation. "I am who I am" might be translated to, "I am what's happening . . . What's going on is Me . . . I am reality . . . If you want to know Me, look at what is fact—not what you imagine or fantasy, or what you would like things to be, but what actually is!" This reasoning led Paul Tillich to call God "The Ground of

Being." If this thinking is sound, then when reality is respected, God is honored. That means ugly facts as well as lovely ones. If religion is anything, it is obedience to awareness, and it takes darkness to see stars. To worship God is to enter deeply into one's experience—without anesthetic. The realist relates to the universe and does not make a universe of the self.

Why bad things happen to good people is still the best-kept secret in the universe. Job got nowhere in his direct confrontation with God about the matter. The nearest solution to the puzzle came on a certain Black Friday that the world calls Good, when a hideous tragedy turned into a glorious finale—Easter! God made good out of evil. This transformation is known as Redemption, which means that misfortune can never be the final curtain to God's program.

There is always a little extra something God can do to revive whatever appears to be languishing. And like God did with Moses, He uses ordinary people to get His job done. So, Jesus concludes this Gospel with the parable about the fruitless fig tree. "I shall cultivate the ground around it and fertilize it," the gardener intercedes . . . "Give it another chance," is the message. Jesus' God does not give up on human beings, because love cannot give up, or retaliate, even when evil is done to it. In the marvelous comic strip *Peanuts,* Lucy is crying the blues about how unfair life is. Linus interjects, "But you have a brother that loves you." Lucy snaps out of her *poor me* mood and affectionately hugs her little brother. Impressed, Linus muses to himself, "Every now and then I say the right thing." Every now and then people do the right thing. That is why it is no accident that each human being is an *act of God!*

3rd Sunday of Lent
(Luke 13: 1-9)

Oscar Winner

As the limos line up for the Seventy-Third Academy Awards, votaries of the Gospels have their own nomination for the best parable. "The envelope, please . . . and the winner is . . . *the prodigal son!*" This masterpiece has everything—script, cast, storyline, surprise, visual effects, even a hit song—"Who's Sorry Now?" The plot finds similitude in Neil Simon's award winner *Come Blow Your Horn*. In this play, a Jewish father also has two sons—one is steady, hardworking, and reliable, the other is a rebellious, undependable playboy. This one suddenly takes off without a word. The father kvetches, "I used to have two sons. Now I have one son and a bum." Subsequently, the other son deserts, leaving the father solitary with the family business, but he has the courtesy to leave a note. The father laments, "I used to have two sons. Now I have a bum and a note."

The parables of Jesus illustrate familiar situations and are rich in psychological subtlety. The younger wastrel brother seems more appealing than the duller, dutiful elder. If they were both candidates for office, whom would the electorate most likely vote for? Jesus told these stories to stimulate non-conventional thinking and to highlight characteristics common to the human condition. In this particular tale, most human beings reflect all three principals, at one time or another: reckless self-centeredness, self-righteous resentment, as well as gracious understanding. They each deserve a closer look.

Junior wants his own apartment. Dad can guess for what, but he prefers to trust rather than control. The boy has to find out for himself—whatever the heartache. Life normally does not allow callow youth to get far along the fast lane without a sobering "sig-alert." An empty stomach helped this young swinger to his senses. "Even my Father's slaves have more than I. Why not return home and sign on as a hired hand?" Good thinking!

The elder brother did everything that was expected of him and he winds up as the heavy in the piece. He has been likened to the image of a right-wing, ultra-reactionary, straight-laced clergyperson; law and order mentality, routinized, righteous, and immovably safe. According to Mark Twain, "A good man in the worst sense of the term."

Parenting takes practice. Many parents agree that they made the most mistakes with their first-born. It could have been the case in this story. Maybe the father was stricter with the senior son. He might have withheld approval until the boy produced satisfactorily. This could make the lad performance-oriented, lonelier, more structure-hungry, and dependent on security. Note the words of his long overdue outburst to his father (*Good News Bible*):

Look, all these years I have worked for you like a slave.

(Sounds reluctant, servile, people-pleasing— humor the old gent.)

And never disobeyed your orders!

(Too timid to assert feeling?)

What have you given me? Not even a goat for me to have a feast with my friends!

(An echo of Red Buttons' "Never Had a Dinner").

Did he ever ask for one or was he too busy earning approval?

And that son of yours . . . (not "my brother.")

Joseph M. Wadowicz

The elder's contempt for his junior sibling is typical of one lacking the nerve to scratch his own itch, too diffident to match his brother's brass.

The father takes the eruption of accumulated bitterness and disappointment. Neither of the boys understood him, but he is without judgment toward them. He accepts each for who he is. Neither one's faults disqualify them from his affection.

By this parable, Jesus apparently wishes to demonstrate how extravagantly enthusiastic God is when the wayward at last come to their senses and find their way home to Him. Quite appropriately, this day the Church celebrates another Rose Sunday, as she reminds Lenten penitents to lighten up and put on a happy face. Traditionally, this day has been known as Laetare Sunday—the first word of the ancient Mass—the Latin imperative meaning *rejoice*. The parable suggests that there is much to cheer about—especially for a God that is too radical, too lavish to figure out —a God whose heart is an inexplicable puzzle of prodigality. A God whose own heart is possibly cheered that ours is in the right place, when even a bumper sticker can offer our earnest prayer, "O Lord, help me be the person my dog thinks I am."

4th Sunday of Lent
(Luke 15: 1-3, 11-32)

Extreme Penalty

. . . says it more vividly than *capital punishment*. What could be more extreme than death, and death is exactly what the Mosaic Code prescribed for adultery, kidnapping, worship of foreign idols, false prophecy, a bride lying about her virginity, cursing, and striking or disobeying a parent. Later, witchcraft and sodomy were added to the capital crime list. The Books of Leviticus and Deuteronomy are explicit in their death dealing sentences.

How did Jesus feel about capital punishment? This Gospel episode about the woman caught, *flagrante delicto,* in the act of adultery, is evidence of His dissent. Each year, opposition to legalized state killing seems to be mounting. One hundred and eight European countries have currently cancelled the death penalty, and this includes nations of the former Soviet Union. As far back as the eleventh century, Czarist Russia eliminated capital punishment on religious grounds. This lenient legislation has been since repealed, as it has been in the modern United States. In 1992, California resumed carrying out death sentences. In 1846, however, the state of Michigan progressively voted against the death sentence. In that same century, English parliament introduced a bill to abolish capital punishment for stealing five shillings . . . it lost! On 18 December 2000, the distinguished United Nations secretary, Kofi Annan, announced this personal statement, "The forfeiture of life is too absolute, too irreversible, for one human being to inflict on another, even when backed by legal process. And I believe that future generations throughout the world will come to agree."

It is not unreasonable to want brutal murderers to pay with their lives, but what does this accomplish? Safety from further brutality? Life imprisonment accomplishes this. The latter at least affords the opportunity to learn, to be useful, even serviceable, like "The Birdman of Alcatraz." It is cheaper to house a prisoner for a lifetime, than to execute him after years of costly appeals that the law sanctions.

Studies made of the backgrounds of capital offenders most frequently reveal that the outrager has first been outraged. Robert Lee Massie died by lethal injection at San Quentin in the last days of March 2001. He was born of teenage parents who fed him liquor and drugs until he was taken from them at age five. He passed through eleven foster homes. When he stole a car, he was sent to juvenile hall where he was gang raped. Emotionally, he never made it to adulthood, but he was punished as one.

Joseph Odell, on a Virginia death row, pleaded for DNA testing to prove his innocence. He was denied and executed. Women also have been written off in their death house watch, no matter how much they may have changed for the better. Karla Faye Tucker, at the Mountain View unit in Gatesville, Texas, won the esteem of the warden and inmates. Everyone that knew her agreed that she had become a loving human being and that a newly found religious faith had made the difference in her life. She was killed anyway! Betty Lou Beets, a sixty-two-year old grandmother, had been battered and abused throughout her life. She never had a chance. She was executed. Capital punishment adds dehumanized military violence to social violence. It is a primitive solution unbefitting civilized intelligence.

To pardon is not quick absolution. Jesus did not overlook, excuse, or coddle adultery. With the adulteress, He confronted her guilt and gave her back her life for another chance at making it better. He demonstrated that there is more to authority than the duty to punish. He did not question the law, but the lawyers. The law focused on the crime more than the criminal, until Jesus helped the law enforcers shift their own self-image from accuser to accused.

Any visitor to a death row will come away surprised that the eyes being looked into are of a human being, not a monster. The thought begins to take root that if the sinner is more important than the sin, then the criminal is worth more than the crime. Reclamation needs to be the human concern, not destruction. The flotsam and jetsam of humanity are the usual candidates for aberrant behavior . . . when is the last time that a millionaire was executed?

This Gospel suggests that civilization has a long way to go for an enlightened solution to the problem of crime and punishment. History has confirmed that punishment is no guarantor of amendment. Insight is an interior experience that can do for reform what external pressure cannot. One responds to understanding more than to reproach. People do not change against their wills.

It is sad that the would-be stonethrowers in the Gospel did not stay around long enough to let the gentle words of Jesus to the accused woman be also applied to themselves, "Has no one condemned you? Neither do I condemn you." Look at the Crucifix! Maybe capital punishment should have been eliminated a long time ago.

5th Sunday of Lent
(John 8: 1-11)

Hard as Nails

The word *nail* has a wide variety of connotations. It can mean seize, snare, clobber, fasten, recognize, or victory. The criminal abhors being *nailed*. The athlete grooves on *nailing* a tough shot; or a student, a particularly troublesome exam. This unusual mixture of meanings says something about the ambiguous composite that human life can be. There is simply no existence without the inseparable twins, fortune and misfortune. Happiness and suffering are never far apart. It is significant, then, that the nail should play so prominent a part in the gruesome crucifixion. Nails must be cruelly hard if they are to penetrate and transfix, just as tragedy is meant to pierce the heart and to transform. What happened to Jesus on His Good Friday, sooner or later happens to everyone. Life eventually *nails* us. Goodness is overwhelmed by evil, but only temporarily.

She was a lively, witty, comely fifty-year old, enjoying her husband, her children, and grandchildren. A routine physical abruptly floored her with the diagnosis of cancer. She could not believe it. She wept for days and shook her fist at God, then suddenly decided she would thumb her nose at the malignancy, and live as though it did not exist. Finally, the cancer started to take its toll. Her strength and energy ebbed. She became depressed and withdrew. Desperation followed with grasping at every possible cure, mysterious herbs, and miraculous novenas.

It was Good Friday and she was idly listening to the radio, when the program presented a reading of the Passion of Jesus Christ. She did not turn it off. Something stirred within her—a new insight. Her ordeal began to make sense.

Courage took root—a fresh faith. She could accept what was happening to her and found a surprising relief in leaving it all in the hands of God. Everyone who dealt with her noticed a transformation. She was off of herself and showed a newfound interest in others. Gradually, she could do very little for herself. Around the clock, caregivers were moved by the consideration she gave them—gentle, polite, and graciously grateful for every effort. They marveled at the support and encouragement she gave to them. They went away lifted, cheered by her cheerfulness. She became a refreshing purpose in their lives. In her hours of pain, she longed for an ending. When it finally happened, her family reports that a nimbus of radiance and serenity surrounded her.

Today begins the week Christendom calls *holy*. The solemn threnody mounts to crescendo as Jesus dies on His upright deathbed. The world is invited to stand . . . and watch . . . and to try to make sense of His last sermon, namely that evil may flower, but never flourish.

One reality comes clear—goodness is no protection against pain. Even virtue gets punished. Life is not fair! But how does He handle this wrong He suffers? No outrage, no bitterness, no withdrawal, no self-pity; just alert, aware acceptance, strong surrender to a mysterious plan and an understanding prayer for His insensible executioners. "Father forgive them; they know not what they do."

What mortal life has not known a double-cross, the anguish of good-bye, the embarrassment of accusation, the sting of bodily hurt, the despair of abandonment? No life escapes its custom-built cross. Like Him, we dread our looming Good Fridays but do not flee. Like Him, we falter and fall beneath the weight, rise and stagger on. Still, Calvary's wood awaits our kiss—the pitiless nails, our reverent clutch. His story is our story. There is solidarity here. There seems to be no end to our spinning planet's pageant of pain!

Literary lights, Dickens, Dostoevsky, Hemingway, Faulkner, and O'Neill, to name a few, have related masterpiece versions of the intriguing human condition. Each human being has a bestseller story to tell that is usually stranger than fiction. But the story that comes nearest to the meaning of why people suffer is in the narrative of the Passion of Jesus Christ. This is reported in stark, undramatic, and telegrammatic simplicity. God makes good come out of evil. No suffering is, therefore, ever useless!

There is a subtle and profound mystery in the hard reality of travail. A person does not know who he or she is until an endured ordeal. The South African author, Alan Paton, expresses this discernment:

> *I cannot even conceive that life could have meaning without suffering. I suspect that the alternative . . . would be a universe of nothingness, where there would be neither good nor evil, no happiness, only an eternity of uninterrupted banality.*

Could the thief, Dismas, have stolen heaven in his last hour, had he not been on a cross beside Jesus? "This day you will be with me in Paradise."

Passion/Palm Sunday
(Luke 22: 14, 23-56)

Last Laugh

In Germany, a quaint tradition venerates the feast of the Resurrection. After church, worshippers gather in local parks and they picnic. They exchange jokes with one another for the whole afternoon. Uproarious laughter is their way of celebrating Easter, and what could be more appropriate! Easter Sunday is the trick God plays on Good Friday . . . evil had its hour and, now goodness has its day.

In his *Divine Comedy,* poet Dante, (whose surname was Durante), hears the paradisal music of the spheres as none other than *laughter,* nature's most jubilant expression of life. It's a pity that laughing is only accidental to church formality. A parish bulletin proposed this serious offer:

Why let worry drive you crazy—let the church help.

Easter laughs at evil, because evil can never win. Easter demonstrates that tragedy confronted is never the final curtain . . . that surrender to humiliation beyond one's control is not *giving up* . . . that *giving in* is not passive, impotent resignation, but the courageous willingness to participate in the mysterious plan of Providence.

Easter is a breakthrough to the mind of God; it's a peek into what God values. It is a dazzling contradiction to how the world thinks. To a puzzled humanity that recoils from death and pain, Easter announces that these natural adversaries are but incidents of history, accidents of time, temporary detours enroute to real living, for which humans were created—Eternal Life. We were never created just to die. Scientists verify the process that elements dissolve and merge afresh into a wider life in nature's endless cycle.

Easter proclaims that earthlings are only getting started. Planetary existence is only the preliminary to the main event. The human personality was created with an infinite capacity for growth, for intimacy, and for intense relating. *Terra firma* is just for openers. Humanity is still unfinished. Some never get a fair start. Children die; others are born paralyzed and mentally impaired. There is no justice here—there has to be a hereafter!

Easter does not abolish death; it absolves it from meaninglessness. What happened that first Easter is past understanding. The Gospel narrative is not a video replay; it is rather a message to all creation that the word *death* is not in the Creator's dictionary. What happened that first Easter is that favored son, Jesus, became alive more than He ever had been when He walked Palestine. No longer would geography or computed time confine Him. Bodily limitation would no longer restrict His impact to just a local audience. He was now set free to influence unnumbered souls, in every age, world without end.

Mark the history of Christianity. With all its tragic bungling, the presence of Christ has inspired myriads of heroic hearts to spend their lives in service to humanity. Hospitals, schools, shelters, and sanctuaries were invented in His name. A Francis rejuvenated a faltering Christendom with gladness and poverty. Abandoned lepers discovered hope in a Damian. Dying Calcuttans quickened to the touch of a Mother Teresa. Jesus is God's hallmark: "See how I love you—he knows the way. Join him and you can't lose."

So, Easter is an invitation to full living, which can never happen if one lives exclusively for self. Easter is a proposal to a partnership—to be His presence in a suffering world. What other hands but ours does He have?

Resurrections are not uncommon in the many, mini deaths we experience in everyday life–like recovery from a devastating illness, reconciliation after a long and painful alienation, or finding the way home after being lost. Most exhilarating is the awareness that we are His *Resurrection.* How else can He embrace humanity on the freeway, the shop, the office, or over the kitchen sink? It probably does not matter so much whether we literally believe in Jesus' Resurrection from the dead. What is important is that God believes in ours. *Alleluia!*

Easter Sunday
(John 20: 1-9)

More About Doubt

In his poem "In Memoriam," Alfred Lord Tennyson (1809-1892) injected the comment:

There lives more faith in honest doubt, believe me, than in half the creeds.

He was addressing a Victorian age disquieted by expanding Biblical criticism. The poet laureate, for more than four decades, was implying that the inflexible religious orthodoxy of the undoubters lacked the spiritual integrity of the sincerely dubious. He saw vigor in honest skepticism, as did the American poet, Louis Untermeyer (1885-1977) in his poem, "Prayer:"

Ever insurgent let me be,
Make me more daring than devout:
From sleek contentment keep me free,
And fill me with a buoyant doubt.

Dubiety is a theme in today's Gospel reading. The "doubting Thomas" again has center stage.

About the report of Jesus' Resurrection from the dead, Thomas chose to be an agnostic. In the company of his believing brethren, this was a lonely stand, but he held his ground and his certain *uncertainty* became a convinced certification: "My Lord and my God!" Honest doubt paid off for Thomas, as it often does for the probing researcher.

Questions are the first steps to answers. Education relies on both. Skepticism is as normal as inadequate information. The learner is willing to search.

Though doubting is normal to the human condition, some can make an unhealthy habit of it. Career doubters are afraid to take a stand, because they might be wrong, which feels like the pain of the abandoned. Perpetual perplexity seems safer than commitment; so ostrich behavior blinds them to any harsh light.

Then there is the opposite phenomenon—those who cannot stand doubt. These have no tolerance for ambiguity. They are uncomfortable with questions and are hooked on certitude. They often seek refuge in rigid, fundamentalist religions and are sitting ducks for hard-sell Elmer Gantrys. This devotion is doomed to collapse when scandal strikes the evangelist because the church has been substituted for God. The Apostles apparently had to give up on Jesus before they really discovered Him.

Both these extremes of doubt reflect a pathological mistrust of self, probably rooted in infant neglect. If an affectionate mother does not meet the infant's needs, fear and rage are seeded. As an adult, this victim cannot confidently attach or trust. Intimacy is hopeless. When the infant's needs are met by an attentive mother, fear subsides and the child learns to expect her presence even when she is not there, because her consistency has provided a predictable certainty. Trust and self-confidence are forged only when the child feels secure.

For the insecure, a benign relationship with an understanding other, who does not punish the seeming withdrawal, can be helpful. That is why Jesus was courteous to Thomas' stubbornness. He provided proof instead of reproof.

446

This Gospel demonstrates that doubt is a wholesome part of faith. They are as mutually supportive as strain is to strength. Over the centuries, the Church has defensively developed an apprehension that questions about articles of faith are dangerous and should be regarded as disobedience to ecclesiastical authority. The cruel reprisals that consequently ensued were directly counter to Jesus' behavior with doubting Thomas. It took four hundred years for a public papal apology for its treatment of Galileo.

It is quite rational to wonder about a loving Providence in the face of daily human agony caused by *acts of God,* like earthquakes, cyclones, and fatalities. Where is God in all this disaster? Faith responds, "on the cross with the rest of us." How does forsaking faith make any more sense of the mystery?

Like human beings, the church also learns. Its catechism has changed. It discovers that truth is secure enough to tolerate dissent; error forbids it. History is a long record of wild guesses about the universe. Whence, why, wherefore is the property of the inquisitive mind. Definitive conclusions end the search—a kind of mental rigor mortis. Now that DNA has been discovered, what fantastic changes lie in the future? Slowly but surely, the Creator continues to share His secrets with His creatures. Still, nothing will tell human beings how dearly they are loved, as well as the *word of God made flesh,* who said to Thomas and to us, "Have you come to believe because you have seen Me? Blessed are those who have not seen and have believed."

2nd Sunday of Easter
(John 20: 19-31)

"I" Contact

The most humanly identifiable of Christ's handpicked twelve . . . the Apostle of the hothead and cold feet . . . the impetuous and conscientious Simon Peter gets rehabilitated in this Gospel sequence. Tormented by his triple denial of his revered master, he is surprised by the Lord's third recorded Resurrection appearance. The second visitation involved the conversion of the agnostic apostle, Thomas. This time the concern of Jesus was the redemption of an apostate.

After a frustrating night of futile fishing, by dawn's early light, Jesus is spotted on the beach preparing a barbecue breakfast. Embarrassed, no doubt, by his defection, Peter, nonetheless, is no shrinking violet. He wants to be the first of his fishing partners to greet the Lord. But before diving in, he dons his tunic. This is like putting on a topcoat over swim trunks for a dip in the pool. Why this bizarre behavior? Jewish tradition regarded a greeting as a formal religious act, so a dress code was in order.

Jesus used this breakfast setting to interview Peter for a new job. Despite his disloyalty, Jesus does not disqualify Peter for the career He has in mind for him. In fact, now he may be better suited for it, if failing tends to make one wiser and humbler.

There was only one question to this audition, but it was momentous; important enough to be repeated three times . . . "Simon, son of John, do you love Me?" Simon Peter could now cancel his three denials with three avowals. But Jesus needed more than words from the big fisherman, who was good at these. He wanted action, so He linked devotion to

Himself with service to people: "Tend My sheep." Jesus took a chance; Simon Peter got the job—from fisherman to shepherd, the universal pastor of souls.

Love takes more than verbal protestations. *My Fair Lady*'s Eliza Doolittle chides one of her suitors in this lyric:

Words, words, words . . . Is that all you blighters can do?
Don't tell me of stars burning above, if you're in love,
show me!

If Peter was to be a spiritual leader, he had to get over being full of himself. His three denials helped him to realize that he was not as sure of himself as he once thought. Jesus gave him back to himself, flawed but salvaged . . . renewed. That is what love does. It helps the "love" come out from hiding to be the self that is totally surprised at being loved. The one thing that even an honest love cannot survive is unforgiveness. This is Pastor Peter's mission—to teach a forgiving heart to the world. This is the mission of the church—to be the presence of the compassionate Christ—*per omnia saecula saeculorum*—for all ages!

A pity that the Church's checkered history reflects the dark impulses of mankind for harshness and reprisal. Civilized human beings continue stone-age cruelty and are reluctant to be convinced that retribution does not work. Revenge never seems to get enough of what it lusts for— retaliation—that only locks the offender and the offended in a hopeless embrace of pain. Vengeance is simply an excuse for further violence, and violence is the mask that weakness wears. Vengeful violence is the last spasm of the impotent. Ruthlessness and overkill erupt when all defenses have failed and fear is in the driver's seat. Anger is the other face of fear. It is surface strength—a fast charge to a waning battery—a temporary surge—emergency energy to meet a threat. An unforgiving heart is a frightened heart. The forgiving heart values human life, even when it harms other lives. It trusts the capacity to change, to learn, to respond to understanding. The forgiving heart recognizes the virulence of evil, but seeks to stem the infection with caring. Patience defangs the viper, dilutes the poison. Was it Gandhi who said:

> *If an eye for an eye is the only justice, then the whole world will be blind.*

There is no reconciliation that is more important than a committed couple sundered by infidelity. They might well review together this breakfast encounter of Jesus and Simon Peter. After "How could you?" and "All we have meant to each other!" ... when everything has been said—all the hurt and recriminations exposed and expressed—the bottom line that matters most ... "Do you love me?"

No more questions!

3rd Sunday of Easter
(John 21: 1-19)

Who Cares?

Intimacy is one basic human need every bit as fundamental as food, shelter, and sleep. Infants deprived of it end up emotionally crippled adults, reluctant to trust long term commitments. Intimacy is an inherent longing for relatedness. No one is enough for oneself. As Dean Martin used to croon, "You're nobody 'til somebody loves you."

To become a mature grown-up takes being noticed. Redemption is a divine/human partnership that begins when the individual sees oneself as worthy of notice. Sadly, this does not happen to everyone. Some only get a partial notice for their outstanding beauty, brains, or brawn. But humans hunger for acceptance of their whole natures—the lightsome as well as the shadow sides. Marilyn Monroe needed more than adoration for her looks. Beauteous people, no doubt, resent being treated as ornaments. If women chose men on the basis of the same superficial aspects for which men choose women, most men would be outraged by the insult. Unless the child experiences connectedness, interhuman close encounters can be a fretful disappointment. Impersonal sex does not meet the standards of nurturing intimacy, and often, solace is sought in the safer sanctuary of religion. Maybe that is why Jesus styled Himself a *good shepherd*—Christendom's most appealing image through the centuries. He knew the isolation of the lost and the lonely. Though reputed a *carpenter, shepherd* better conveyed the message of caring, of rescue, of protection.

Hebrew history had typified sound leadership as shepherding. Moses was tending a flock when God caught his attention. So was young David, the most illustrious Jewish king. In the Lord's time, however, shepherds were not considered professional elitists. They were unskilled migrant workers and indifferently treated, though important to the economy, as today's are.

The sheep image can be an unflattering reference, since they are not notorious for their intelligence. Most animals are startled if a stone is thrown in their direction and scamper off. Sheep uncomprehendingly just stand still and await another stone to be aimed at them. Since sheep are such docile creatures, and since sheepishness does not equip them to survive a one-on-one with a wolf, shepherds have to be especially attentive and be prepared to risk life and limb in protecting their flocks. In contrast to the hireling, the good shepherd knows his sheep well enough to give each a name. In turn, the sheep learn to identify their guardian's voice and respond to his call. They unhesitatingly follow whither he leads to fresh pasture and running streams.

My sheep hear my voice and I know them and they follow Me. No one can take them out of My hand.

Does following this voice imply a sheep-like compliance that surrenders personal individuality, and the impulse to explore? Archibald MacLeish (1892-1982) acknowledged in his poem, "In Praise of Dissent":

The dissenter is every human being at those moments of his life when he resigns momentarily from the herd and thinks for himself.

In His parable, Jesus emphasizes how the non-conformist inspires the good shepherd to drop everything to recover the vagrant, then to rejoice. It is so easy to get lost in this whirring world. Over a half-century ago, the famous Canadian essayist, Marshal McCluhan (1911-1980) wrote:

Today the tyrant rules not by club or fist, but disguised as a market researcher; he shepherds his flocks in the ways of utility and comfort.

When Jesus refers to Himself as *shepherd,* He is asserting the mutual familiarity between Himself and His flock, who recognize His voice and spontaneously follow. Even young children hear and heed the sound . . . like the whole class of fifth-grade boys who each willingly had their heads shaved so that their classmate, who had all his hair fall out from cancer therapy, would not feel out of place.

One bitter cold winter day, driving on her way to work, she heard a news report—"The Salvation Army has run out of their store of food; emergency supplies are needed immediately." This busy businesswoman turned her car around, returned home, cleared her kitchen cupboards of all their contents, and delivered them to the Salvation Army with the comment, "I can shop again, but you need this stuff now!"

The symbol of the good shepherd is a gentle intrusion on a gothic, electronically controlled ecology. This image has the power of poetry, needing no analysis or interpretation. It speaks not of the exaggeration of might, but the calm understatement of a caring God—as clear to the sophisticated as to the naïve. Religions have identified Christ as moralist, preacher, teacher, but the good shepherd keeps shining through.

Who cares? The Good Shepherd does . . . but He needs us to do His shepherding.

4th Sunday of Easter
(John 10: 27-30)

Love Bout

The ever-pertinent Rabbi Harold Kushner relates a poignant instance in his book, *Who Needs God*. A grieving teenager at the bedside of her boyfriend dying of cancer is asked by the nurse, "Is there anything I can do for you?"

"Yeah," replied the desolate girl, "remind me never to love anybody this much again." Understandably, she had had enough of heartbreak!

The couple must have had happy times together. Precious memories of fun and laughs probably made the present tragedy all the more bitter, but there she was holding his hand. No drug could ease him like the comfort of her touch. Her aching heart would recall this tenderness in the years ahead, before she was ready to open it wider to an also hurting world. Mourning is not to be rushed, nor sedated. The tears, the resentment, and the "whys" take their slow motion pace.

The young woman no doubt never expected love and sorrow to be roommates. She never dreamed that her delights would fuel her weeping. It would not make sense for a while—perhaps never! But she had loved; she was a child no longer. Sooner or later, she could discover how good it was to have loved—to have been lost and found in another. What she loved most in him would grow clearer in his absence. Love can only love goodness. Letting go was unbearable!

Jesus was bidding farewell to His chosen. This time tomorrow He would be dead. Those He was leaving could make no sense of it either. They would most likely resent His failing them, but the best He had was His legacy—His love for them. And they were a motley mix not easy to love. Sharing close-up days together, Jesus was no stranger to their rashness, their arrogant ambition, their jealousies, their misinterpretations. Still He loved them for all their flaws, which could be why He called His a *new commandment*—loving the unlovable. "Love one another as I have loved you"—warts and all!

Love, therefore, is a decision, a choice, the will to give a darn about another, to hold still, to listen. Emerson gave this importance universally to human beings when he said, "Every man is divinity in disguise, God playing the fool." Thus, there is no reverencing God while any simp is not given respect. "I love mankind; it's people I can't stand" sounds like a riposte from someone even a mother might find hard to take. But today is her day. The nation honors the one person internationally acclaimed for fond attention to the most unwinsome child—a *mother!*

If we give ourselves passing grades for our caring-of-people competence, it is probably because *mother* showed us how. Most can boast of significant pockets of genuine love in our lives. We are polite to boors most of the time, respectful to the elderly, write checks for cancer research, and admire Mother Teresa. We are not muggers, child abusers or wife beaters, and we love humanity in bite-size proportions—one at a time. Generally, even strict moms are our instructors in humane behavior. The late Herb Caen, a popular *San Francisco Chronicle* scribe, wrote this in his 1990 Mothers' Day column:

> *She made me what I am today—a workaholic with a healthy sense of guilt and the desire to please. She made me practice the piano, do my homework, get good grades, and hang up my clothes in an orderly fashion—another lifelong*

habit. The strict mother, like mine, has an impossible task with today's restless and confused children. Once, there were rules, but drugs and the failure of education have changed all that.

It is appropriate here to raise the issue of induced, interrupted pregnancies. In December 1994, when John Salvi fired upon two Boston abortion clinics, killing two and wounding five, both Governor Weld of Massachusetts and Cardinal Law called for discussion between the two sides of the abortion debate, in the hope of deescalating the heated hostility. The woman director of the Public Conversation Project of Cambridge, Laura Chassin, emerged to conduct dialogue with six prominent female citizens—three pro-life and three pro-choice. Their meetings were confidential. On 28 January 2001, they went public with a jointly prepared article in the *Boston Globe*. The women disclosed that, "We have been able to listen openly and to speak candidly." By the time of the first anniversary of the shooting, "Each one of us had come to think differently about those on the other side." No one's position had altered. "We saw that our differences on abortion reflect two world views that are irreconcilable." One of the six said, "I'm more mindful now than I've ever been of speaking in love, speaking in peace, and speaking in respect to anyone, no matter how wide the differences are."

This must have been the attitude Jesus had in mind when He urged loving one another and loving the opposition. After all, no one can thoroughly understand a truth until he/she has contended against it. Jesus never commanded us to be right, or even to be holy, but to love.

Thanks, mothers, for the head start!

5th Sunday of Easter
(John 13: 11-35)

Shalom

A beautifully lyrical Hebrew word! *Salaam,* in Arabic, sounds every bit as lovely. In both languages, the word means more than *peace,* a sadly fickle climate for those fractious nations. As a greeting and a farewell, it conveys the gentle wish that the highest good may be the lot of the one addressed. It is a prayer for wholeness, salvation, oneness with God and His creation.

In bidding farewell to His disciples, Jesus imparted His love and His peace as a one-piece offering:

> *Peace I leave with you. My peace I give to you.*
> *Not as the world gives do I give it to you.*

What sort of peace does the world have to give? Distractions, enjoyments, and drugs, can offer temporary easement from life's burdens, but what is the peace of Jesus? Didn't He say once, "Do you suppose I came to establish peace on earth? No indeed, I have come to bring division!" (Luke 12: 51)

Is He contradicting Himself? Hardly had the infant Christian assembly gotten started when this stern prediction was verified. This day's first Scripture reading (Acts 15), relates a rousing argument about whether the new Christians were Jewish enough. Arguments persist today, twenty centuries later, over whether the church is Catholic enough . . . a stormy petrel then, so Jesus continues today!

Obviously the peace of Christ does not avoid turbulence. Disagreements have a way of clarifying issues, especially when courteously confronted. Jesus never seemed to be threatened by discord. He disputed freely with authorities as with friends. Where discussion is encouraged, learning can take place, hard feeling not withstanding. Jesus certainly did not please everyone.

The peace plan of Jesus, therefore, apparently was not conditioned upon a cessation of external hostilities, as much as the interior calm of a quiet mind. In any challenge, His approach invariably was not to vanquish, but to enlighten. He knew that dominance breeds resistance and that control sows conflict. Controversy occasioned exchange. He had His say and allowed others theirs. Truth is not a private preserve.

Interior tranquility needs a quiet mind. Years ago, a book was published, *Don't Sweat The the Small Stuff (And It's all Small Stuff)*. The title can imply that human life is no safer than the nest from which mother bird expels baby birds, reluctant, but ready to fly. Life is simply to be trusted. Sir (St.) Thomas More sought the security of the cloister as a teenager. After some years of contented monastic life, he began to feel that this was too safe a nest and opted for the more precarious path to salvation as a family man and lawyer. He was a realist. He confronted the actualities that he incurred. He had a quiet mind.

The quiet mind is no stranger to stress. It calls anxiety, anger, and affliction by its name because reality is its object, not wishful thinking. It does not fictionalize life's script for a happy ending. The quiet mind is, therefore, a brave mind. It does not search for risks, nor does it shrink from the unavoidable ones. It shudders at shock and is buoyed by beauty. It gives the bitter and the sweet equal attention. It can be stumped, and it pauses for lagging answers. It co-exists with doubt.

The quiet mind cannot be made quiet on command anymore than force can pacify an obstreperous child. With coercion, the cease-fire is only temporary. Embers smolder for the next eruption. The agitated child needs mindfulness and reassurance. Severity increases rebellion.

The quiet mind is zealous for the *now*. Each moment is seen as brand new—no matter how it may resemble yesterday—thus making problem solving always fresh. It is not complacent with denial, which only divides the mind. It deals with what hurts—chronic or terminal—and is cautious about cures.

People tend to associate peace with religion, but religion is nothing if not *awareness*—respect for facts that surround us—the fair as well as the ugly. Devotion to ritual may reduce tension, even guilt feelings, but ceremonials are symbolic—they point. Symbols are signs. The sign "5th Ave." is not Fifth Avenue. Belief in God is simply a step to find God; God gets the finder's fee.

The quiet mind is comfortable with prayer—another way to understanding. Its loftiest ascent to the stratosphere of contemplation is pragmatically described as the "lingering, loving look at reality." The quiet mind is most at home when it loves. That is why Jesus linked His love with His peace—they energize one another. Neither can be commanded, intended, or personally earned. They are gifts! Those who are convinced that they are unconditionally loved by God—whatever they may be—addict, agnostic, homosexual or streetwalker—they have heard God's greeting: *Shalom!*

6th Sunday of Easter
(John 14: 23-29)

463

Jesus Becomes "catholic"

Note the lowercase *c* in *catholic!* Webster defines catholic as universal; general; broad in sympathies, tastes and interests.

Catholic (capital *C*) designates the Church and its membership. St. Ignatius of Antioch first used this term when he wrote to the Christians of Smyrna in 110 A.D. "Even as where Jesus Christ is, there is the Catholic Church." St. Augustine in the fourth century used the same word as a synonym for the Church 240 times. It developed into a formal "mark" of the Church. Protestant controversialists who resented any monopolizing of the name catholic introduced the term "Roman Catholic."

The liturgy celebrates the Ascension on this seventh Sunday after Easter. In both readings, Luke metaphorically describes Christ's change of command ceremony with His Apostles.

But you will receive power when the Holy Spirit comes upon you, and you will be My witnesses in Jerusalem, throughout Judea and Samaria, and to the ends of the earth.

This is the commission to the Church and to its followers, not only to testify to the Good News of Jesus, but also to be the Good News. The term "Catholic" admittedly invokes less reverence than the label "Christian." The former has a definite denominational ring, but it does convey an important aspect of the Christian objective—brotherhood.

The initial syllable of the word "universal" signifies oneness. The unity that Jesus prayed for—that all may be one—could not have inferred homogeneity, or else why would the Creator have created nature with such vast, magnificent variety. Sameness implies monotony; variation suggests harmony, cooperation, and diversity. Lockstep uniformity never seemed to appeal to Jesus. Doctrinal orthodoxy was less His priority than basic human needs: nourishment, friendship, and inner peace. He assigned His Father's indiscriminate, unconditional love and forgiveness to the entire human family without exception. Everybody is invited to the banquet!

Religions have been notoriously distracted from humanity's indivisibility whenever preoccupied with sectarian governance and the exclusivity of creedal formulations. But "the times are a 'changin." The conciliar documents of Vatican II are steps in the direction of global fraternity. Such as The Decree on the Church's Missionary Activity, Declaration on the Church's Relation to Non-Christian Religion, and The Pastoral Constitution on the Church in the Modern World. These impressive instructions urge creative dialogue with other religions, and enter into a solidarity with the whole human race to make life more humane on this planet.

Christian churches met on a world level in Seoul in 1990 and issued this statement:

> We *have failed because we have not borne witness to God's caring love for each and every creature. We have failed because we have not overcome the division between the churches and have used our authority and power to strengthen false and limited solidarities, like racism, sexism, and nationalism. We have failed because we have*

caused wars and not exhausted all the possibilities for mediation and reconciliation. We have excused wars and often too easily justified them.

Imagine if the concerted power of the churches concentrated on these international crises!

• Every minute, the nations of the world spend 1/8 million dollars on military armaments.

• Every hour, 1,500 children die of hunger-related causes.

• Every day, a species becomes extinct.

• Every week in the 1980s, more people were detained, tortured, assassinated, and made refugees by repressive regimes than at any other time in history.

• Every month, the world's economic system adds over 7.5 billion dollars to the unbearable debt of 1.5 trillion dollars currently resting upon the backs of the Third World.

• Every year, an area of tropical forest, three-quarters the size of Korea, is destroyed and lost.

• Every decade, global warming threatens the sea coasts of the world.

His Royal Highness, the Duke of Edinburgh, expressed this concern, "The one world in which we live has a chance of survival only if there is no longer room in it for spheres of differing, contradictory, and even antagonistic ethics." We join the Duke in his fervent wish for "a more determined search for a shared belief in the beauty and value of this planet Earth as our common and unique home in the vastness of the universe."

We belong to only one race—the human one, because like it or not, we are all *catholic!*

7th Sunday of Easter/Ascension
(Luke 24: 43-56)

Man's Best Friend

Spell *dog* backwards! That's what Pentecost is about: God's ever-faithful collaboration with mankind. Pentecost proclaims that human beings can count on a powerful supplement to their flawed natures. Pentecost announces that Christianity is more than creed and code; it is vitality, stamina—it's bionic! Wind and fire are the elemental symbols that describe the Spirit of God merging with man. Quavering solitaries become stouthearted men. Forrest Gump is for real! The Holy Spirit happened! It's the Church's birthday!

This is a day for balloons and party hats—a day to remember the Church's origins and the phenomenal centerpiece of history it has been. The Church has seen the commencement of all the existing governments on this planet. It was there before the Saxon set foot in Britain, before the Frank crossed the Rhine, and before Grecian eloquence flourished in Antioch. No scandal has yet succumbed it; no betrayal by intimates has stilled its voice. In each generation, a needed Francis, a John XXIII, or a Mother Teresa emerge from its essence. The halls of the mighty acknowledge her presence. The Church survives because God's Spirit is alive and active in its history, initiating new insights and new understandings about human life. The exploding discoveries in science and medicine, in DNA and cybernetics,.all reveal the Creator's involvement in the human enterprise.

The twenty-first century Church is shifting its thinking, cautiously, but steadily, from the ethic of constraint and control to the direction of individual, responsible self-realization. Modern Pentecosts are at work in the human psyche enlightening it to trust the goodness inherent in it, and to recognize partnership with the Creator in the unfinished task of creation.

The human species has a way to go for the global humaneness it yearns for. Man is still a killing animal and shudders at its savagery. What twisted logic could protest the insensitive cruelty of the federal government to the Davidians of Waco, Texas, by destroying 168 innocent men, women, and children in the bombing of Oklahoma City? A slender membrane separates civility from barbarism. Only a moral conscience can domesticate the amoral monster raging in an outraged heart. Yet, in this unspeakable horror were instances of touching heroism.

Moments after the Oklahoma blast, medical and emergency professionals were on the scene. Hordes of volunteers raced to help rescue the injured buried beneath the rubble. Thousands of doctors, nurses, medical students, police, firefighters, clergy, blood donors, and structural engineers, rushed to provide whatever their expertise offered. Medical personnel and rescue teams from neighboring states poured into the stricken area. Within hours, church and social service agencies across the country mobilized their networks to provide donations of food, clothing, and equipment.

Rescue teams worked day and night, refusing relief when their shifts ended, clawing through debris with axes and crowbars, an inch at a time. Counselors were on hand to help rescuers cope with the sights that had stunned them; and right back inside they were eager to go, while there was any hope someone might be alive.

The structure's shell shook and tottered perilously while doctors, nurses, and firefighters risked life and limb, crawling into airless clefts to treat someone found still alive. One nurse, Rebecca Anderson, was killed by a piece of falling debris. Many nurses refused to abandon patients, even when ordered, because of a rash of bomb threats following the explosion. People stood in line for six hours to give blood at the Red Cross. A sporting goods store cleaned out its inventory of kneepads and sent every one to the rescuers scouring the wreckage. Local restaurants supplied food faster than it could be eaten.

This is the Spirit of God at work within the rank and file. A nobility is secreted in the human spirit that invariabley springs to life in the face of catastrophe. Pentecost is perpetual motion. The mystery of the Creator's efficiency with faulty mortal instruments is a continual *now* happening. And God's Spirit is non-elitist—anyone is fair game. The commonest wino catches God's breath when he shares his raggedy coat with a shivering buddy. Erin Brockovich, hardly a model Girl Scout—brazen, profane, minimally educated, twice divorced, mother of three—takes on a giant, billion dollar corporation, bringing it to its knees for lying to the people about poisoning their water supply.

A friend is a gift—an expander of awareness—a stimulant to surpass oneself. The restless, irrepressible impact of God's Spirit on the receptive human psyche is the instantaneous rapport of *best friends!*

Pentecost
(John 20: 19-23)

Soluble Mystery

Trinity appears less a mystery when the word is seen as metaphor. Metaphors are similes, which explain one thing by describing another, such as the memory of a computer, the current of electricity, the plowing of a ship at sea. Trinitarian theology was not intended to make divinity more remote or inscrutable to the human mind. Quite the opposite! The Church was interested in closer intimacy, indeed familiarity, of creature with Creator. A person is capable of being loved, not so is an extrinsic force, like gravity. Thus, both Testaments emphasize God as Person. But why three persons? That's where metaphor comes in!

Person is another way of expressing alive involvement. Human beings never outgrow the need for care, for relating, for energy. The Trinity proclaims that God is the source of these necessities, par excellence. Trinity announces that God is our begetter—Father; our brother—Son; our inspirer—Holy Spirit. All three functions personify a single providential design, "Someone to Watch Over Me." Trinity is a complex way to express God's participation in complex human existence. The accent is on a Father, the caring and loving family figure, not an exacting, avenging legislator.

It is said that human beings cannot really come to know themselves until they have had a child. As the child develops and its awareness grows, so does the parent's consciousness. The parent is continually surprised at what the child notices, and this turns out to be an unexpected education for the adult. Perceptivity expands in both, and the parent discovers that the child listens better to the parent when the parent listens to the child.

473

Suppose your teenager wants a total body tattoo, like basketball player Alan Iverson, along with rings through the tongue, ears, and nose, and for good measure, spiked purple hair. "Over my dead body," is a believable reaction! This crisis demands a conference—a willingness to take the time to explore why the youngster is so attracted to this rash fad. The ensuing exchange might reveal the adolescent's desperate hunger for attention. You could discover that your job is getting more of you than your child is.

Trinity is a theological way to say something about God's power-sharing with mankind. Because creatures exist, the Creator's existence becomes more complicated—just as parents when they beget children. The more they love their children, the more acute the pain when the child disappoints. But whatever the heartaches, no caring parent can ever disown flesh and blood.

An unusually insightful perception of creation surfaces from a surprising source, George Friedrich Hegel. Born in 1770 in Stuttgart, Germany, he was touted as Adolf Hitler's favorite philosopher because of his vindication of the totalitarian state. In his work *Philosophy of Religion,* Hegel proposes that creation is an "emanation" of the Creator. Simply stated, the creation process is an evolution from the *perfect*—to the *imperfect*—to the *perfect;* from the *infinite*—to the *finite*—and back to the *infinite.* This is a remarkable comprehension of the Christian belief that God created a deficient human nature only to find its completion in return to the perfection of the Godhead. This is the meaning of redemption—reclamation—mortals' bond with the Trinity's Second Person, *at the right hand of the Father.* For Hegel, the Creator becomes more conscious of Himself through His creation. By creating human consciousness, Divinity's consciousness expands—as does the parents' when they beget children.

The Trinitarian message is that human beings are intimately involved in God's life when they love, when they beget, when they relate, and when they care for and about another. It says that parents have a far better chance to know the mystery of God than the most erudite theologian. The Church reminds its faithful of the God-life that can be theirs as it begins and ends every prayer . . .

In the name of the Father,
and of the Son,
and of the Holy Spirit.
Amen.

Trinity
(John 16: 12-15)

Soul Food

The birth of the Eucharist at the Last Supper appears in the New Testament for the first time in Paul's first letter to the Corinthians. He is hopping mad at the discriminating way they were observing the Lord's Supper. Since there were no churches in those early days, worshippers gathered in private homes to celebrate the Agape. Naturally, the homes of the well-to-do provided for larger gatherings. Archeologists report that the spacious Roman houses of that era—Corinth being a Roman satellite—featured two separate dining areas. The *triclinium* (dining room) was furnished for privileged guests, with cushions for reclining. The broader *atrium* accommodated the commoner folk. This set up was much like today's airplanes with curtained first class separated from the coach section. Such partiality had no place for Paul in celebrating the Eucharist. *One bread, one body* for him meant *E Pluribus Unum*—(unity in plurality). All communicants were equally important and should be so treated.

The Church has recorded a variety of mood shifts in its zeal to safeguard this central focus of its worship. The days of the Latin Mass sternly forbade any handling of the consecrated wafers by anyone other than an ordained priest. To even touch altar vessels was considered a sacrilege. Then came Vatican II and again a wondrous shift. The emphasis on the sacredness of the Sacrament now moved to include the sacredness of the individual. Words of consecration over the bread and wine were meant for the assembly as well. Communicants became vessels of grace as prized as any precious chalice or ciborium (*Constitution on the Sacred*

Liturgy, paragraph 7). Consumers experience Holy Communion with a host of varied sentiments. Some are uneasy about getting too close to God. Some are embarrassed by the immorality in their lives and seek healing, reparation, and renewal. Others need a favor. The lonely are grateful to be welcome—to belong, somewhere! Eucharist reminds the soul of its longing for God. Echoing the insight of Augustine, Julian of Norwich declares:

> *For by nature our will wants God, and the good will of God wants us.*

The brilliant Blaise Pascal (1623-1662) was enormously fascinated by the ingenuity with which human beings evade entanglement with Divinity. He wrote in his sweeping tour de force *Pensees:*

> *It is the nature of self-esteem and of the human self to love only oneself and to consider oneself alone. That is to say, he concentrates all his efforts on concealing his faults from others and from himself and cannot stand being made to see them or their being seen by other people.*

Eucharist is the heaven-sent escape to the full-length mirror that reflects us as we are, without distortion, and with the total understanding with which only God is capable.

Eucharist was the Lord's way of intruding God's Presence wherever it seems to be least. Again, Thomas Merton captures the drift. The following appears in his *Raids on the Unspeakable:*

> *Into this world, this demented inn, in which there is absolutely no room for Him at all, Christ has come uninvited. But because He cannot be at*

*home in it, His place is with those others for whom
there is no room. His place is with those who do
not belong, who are rejected by power because
they are regarded as weak, those who are discred-
ited, who are denied the status of persons, who are
tortured, bombed, and exterminated. With those for
whom there is no room, Christ is present in the
world. He is mysteriously present in those for
whom it seems to be nothing but the world at its
worst. It is in these that He hides himself, for whom
there is no room.*

For many, faith is more a chore than a gift. Hardship
often brings faith into clearer focus. For seven years, Terry
Anderson languished as a hostage in Lebanon. He claims to
have found God in that ordeal. He credits Father Lawrence
Jenco, imprisoned with him, for helping him to rediscover
his faith. Terry remembers the times the priest celebrated
the Eucharist with the hostages in this poem:

*Five men huddled close against the night
and our oppressors,
around a bit of stale bread hoarded from
a scanty meal,
and a candle, lit not only as a symbol
but to read the text by.
The priest is as poorly clad,
as drawn with strain as any,
but his voice is calm, his face serene.
This is the core of his existence,
the reason he was born.
Behind him I can see his predecessors
back in the catacombs,
heads nodding in approval,*

The Now Testament

hands with his tracing out the stately ritual,
adding to the power of their suffering
and faith to his and ours.

The ancient words shake off their dust,
and come alive.
The voices of their authors echo
clearly from the damp, bare walls.
The familiar prayers come straight out of our hearts.
Once again Christ's promise is fulfilled:
His presence fills us. The miracle is real.

Thanks to *Connections*, June, 1995.

Corpus Christi
(I Corinthians 11: 23-26)

J.B. is Us

No event can match in importance the birth of a child. In ancient Jewish tradition, it was a neighborhood phenomenon. People gathered outside the birthing house, along with musicians, expectantly awaiting the announcement. If it was a boy, the crowd cheered and the musicians struck up the band. If a girl, the assembly silently dispersed and the musicians went home. . . . Good riddance to that discrepant custom!

Naming the child, however, continues to be an engrossing assignment. New Age appellations are becoming more and more the vogue today, like Misty, Cookie, Leilani. Dwight has been a popular male tag. All such would not be tolerated by any conscientious pre-Vatican II cleric at a christening ceremony. Saints names were *de rigueur.* Although it is conceivable that there could be a St. Misty some day, as there once was the first Agnes.

The Gospel narrative reports quite an argument about the naming of Zachary's and Elizabeth's extraordinary offspring. The convention entailed the perpetuation of the father's name. Elizabeth may have had an inkling that this lad would not follow his father's footsteps. "He will be called John," she insisted. Zachary knew better than to object. "John is his name," he agreed. That name would echo the length and breadth of Judea in the years to come.

Though entitled to the elite position of his father as priest, John eschewed the privilege for the rugged lot of a desert Bedouin and became the prophetic bridge between the Old and New Testaments. His fiery preaching earned him a huge following and, therefore, a cause of concern for the political powers of the day. In fact, John gained considerably greater historical notice than did his cousin, Jesus. Their contemporary Jewish historian, Josephus, includes John in a passage (Antiquities, Book 18) that is twice as long as his mention of Jesus and much more laudatory.

In his commentary on the defeat of Herod Antipas by King Aretas IV of Nabatea, Josephus wrote:

> But to some of the Jews, it seemed that the army of Herod was destroyed by God—indeed, quite justly punishing Herod to avenge what he had done to John, who was surnamed the Baptist (#116).

He further lauds John as:

> A good man who simply bade Jews to join in baptism provided that they were cultivating virtue, practicing justice toward one another, and piety toward God (#117) . . . When ordinary Jews gathered together around John, their excitement reached fever pitch as they listened to his words. Herod began to fear that John's powerful ability to persuade people might lead to some sort of revolt, for they seemed likely to do whatever he counseled. So Herod decided to do away with John by a preemptive strike, and so John was sent in chains to Machaerus, the mountain fortress (#118).

The historian represents John as far more formidable than Jesus, while the Gospels emphasize his subordination. Jesus Himself attests to John's singularity in Luke 7: 28, "In all humanity there is no one greater than John. And yet the least citizen of the kingdom of God is greater than he."

Most of us limit soap boxing to our living rooms. Then injustices flare up that inspire in us the lionheart of the

Baptizer. The "Bates Seven" for instance. *The New York Times* ran the story 4 May 2001. In 1940, seven NYU students vigorously protested the exclusion of their star fullback, Leonard Bates, from the University of Missouri game. Prestigious northern universities including Harvard, Rutgers, and Michigan observed a "gentlemen's agreement" to keep black athletes off their rosters if it embarrassed their southern opponents. The "Bates Seven" were suspended for circulating a petition without permission. One of the seven, Evelyn Maisel, a senior, was not allowed to graduate. It took sixty years for New York University to honor the expelled seven for their courageous action.

Twenty-six people have received federal sentences for participating in a peaceful protest at the Western Hemisphere Institute for Security Cooperation (WHISC), formerly known as SOA, The School for the Americas, Fort Benning, Georgia. It is a U.S. Army military program where various Central American government "death squads" are known to have been trained. On 19 November 2000, thousands marched to mark the anniversary of the slaying of six Jesuit priests, their housekeeper, and her daughter. Four of the defendants are nuns; one is age eighty-eight, Sister Dorothy Hennessey, and is sentenced to a federal prison for six months. "It won't kill me," she said, "but I hope they let me keep my hearing aids."

Another true story. For five years, Lauren had been tormented with an eating disorder. At age fifteen, she was hospitalized against her will to treat her obsession with gorging and disgorging food. The reluctant teenager found she had a roommate—who was drawn, haggard, and coughed uncontrollably. When she saw Lauren, a bright smile lightened her tired face. "Hi, I'm Julie and I'm ten years old. What's your name?"

"I'm Lauren. I'm fifteen."

"Wanna play Crazy Eights?" Julie cheerfully chirped.

As Lauren shuffled the cards, Julie chatted. "You know, Lauren, I'm going to die, but I'm not scared. I was born with a disease and they can't cure it. It's called leukemia. I've learned that I have to be happy every day that I wake up, and never take for granted what God gives me. I can see you are hurting yourself, and my mom says that people who hurt themselves are scared."

Two weeks later, Lauren left the hospital, her bingeing attitude toward food and weight under control—all because of a ten-year-old child who taught her more than any doctor or counselor. She began her new life. A week later, Julie died. (*Connections,* June 2001)

That we are the stuff of greatness may come as a surprise, but not so to Jesus, who could see that even the *least* of us is every bit as important as the great John.

Birth of John the Baptizer
(Luke 1: 51-66, 80)

Free for All

The nation celebrates Independence Day this week. A quantum leap from the historic Magna Carta, 561 years before Jefferson's extraordinary Declaration resonated throughout the world. For the first time, the primacy of the individual was boldly proposed as a self-evident reality: a right inherent by nature, and not the whim of a sovereign. Fittingly, this day's Gospel ratifies a blueprint for the freedom that every living existence dearly cherishes. The impact of the Good News is to liberate the human spirit. Luke has Jesus respond to four separate situations designed for releasing people to more fully functioning humanhood. But freedom is not cost-free. This Gospel features again Jesus' brand of tough love.

The first circumstance deals with the resentment that rejection can usually generate. Like all ruthless intolerance, prejudice is taught along with mother's milk. For eight centuries, an outworn antipathy seethed between heretic Samaritans and zealous Jews. Religious hostilities were meaningless to Jesus. He extended the hand of friendship to the traditional enemy and was rebuffed. Infuriated, the "Sons of Thunder," James and John, demand punishing redress:

Lord, do you want us to call down fire from
Heaven to consume them?

They seem almost to relish the snub that could justify such harsh retaliation. "Jesus turned and rebuked them and they journeyed to another village."

Most persons have a built-in need to be somebody—to be admired. To be overlooked, put down, and repudiated, smarts! There is a story about Buddha, the Enlightened One, who lived six centuries before Christ, and who some believe, influenced the Good News message. Accosted one day by a detractor shouting insults at him and challenging a response, the Buddha finally answered:

When someone makes you an offering, and you do not receive it, who owns the offering?

Jesus refused to allow the Samaritans to make Him a victim. Resentment chains the offended to the offender. Refusing to get even sets one free to move on, as Jesus did, to other fresh encounters. The free person decides his/her own worth and does not abdicate it to others.

The second situation is a puzzler. "As they were proceeding on their journey, someone said to Him, 'I will follow you wherever you go.'" This obviously enthusiastic devotee gets what sounds like a brush-off. "Foxes have dens and birds of the sky have nests, but the son of man has nowhere to rest his head." What did Jesus see in this willing adherent to prompt His admonishing reply? Did He see impulsiveness? "You haven't a clue what you could be letting yourself in for," He might have thought. Was the man a security seeker, a celebrity hound, a people-pleaser, and an unrealistic idealist? Or was he a Type A personality, aggressively striving to achieve more and more in less and less time; one who substitutes urgent activity for creative stillness, so important for objective self-appraisal? Perhaps Jesus was suggesting that the man needed more insights into himself, which he might be avoiding by excessive religiosity. What was needed was not freedom *from*, but freedom *to!* Freedom honestly to feel His feelings—the sharp edges of life's hurts and His own self doubts—to plumb the vulnerability of being human, but without self-judgment.

The third involvement is another poser. "And to another He said, 'Follow Me.' But he replied, 'Lord, let me go first and bury my father.' But He answered him, 'Let the dead bury their dead.'" Is this cryptic counsel of Jesus satire—tongue-in-cheek irony? One meaning is clear—postponing is not to be tolerated! Actually, He seems to be recommending a veiled foil for the stalling ploy. Behavioral specialists indicate that the habit of procrastination is the fruit of a coerced childhood. Parents who relentlessly correct, redirect, nag, and press a child to constant peak performance set up the resistance defense for dawdling and delaying. Possibly Jesus spotted this problem and was urging the man to some independent thinking, in the hope of releasing him from the bondage of infantile shame and impotence.

Everyone is guilty of something, but guilt differs from shame. Guilt says, "I lied." Shame says, "I'm a liar." If perfection is the standard, the perfectionist is under perpetual indictment. If innocence is hopeless, then a sense of unspecified shame persists. It is a feeling of being dominated by some blind power of an old authority. Such a one cringes from any disapproval and lacks the courage to challenge the putative accusing judge and jury. Acknowledging one's guilt is at least a more advanced stage of individuation than living in the encircling gloom of shame. Maybe Jesus had this in mind when He advised "the dead to bury the dead."

Memory can be our jail and our liberation. It can bind us to an outworn past, or be a file rich with research, experience, and information. It is the prime instrument of our education, and sometimes what has been learned needs to be unlearned. If one is to achieve autonomous maturity, one must take responsibility for being the parent of one's own values. Maybe that is what Jesus meant when He spoke of "being born again." It is a lonely enterprise to grow up. There are so many crises unverified by previous experience. It is natural to hesitate, to tremble . . . "Do it," says the Lord, "and don't look back!"

Living is a tangle of ideas, beliefs, and opinions that fight it out in our minds, until the surviving choice chooses us. Everything until then has been only practice! Choose to be who you are, and you are who you have been, but you are saying yes to it now. Let yesterday confirm today, not contaminate it. Failure gives one the chance to start over. Our dignity lies not in our innocence, but in our power to forgive our guilts, as God does.

Be free—God and country agree!

13th Sunday of Ordinary Time
(Luke 9: 51-62)

488

God: Mother

A lady hospital chaplain I have known was so indignant at male dominance in the Church, that in her feminist fervor she refused to recite "Our Father" with patients. The gender of God has undoubtedly taken a masculine tilt in past centuries, but pro-feminism factions are having their justified say of late. Still, theology is confined by the frustrating feebleness of language. The Bible rejects capitulation and pours forth its plethora of figures to describe the nature of the divine mystery.

Metaphors for God abound: The Proprietor of a Garden, Creator of its caretakers, Legislator, exacting Enforcer, Monarch, Warrior, forgiving Father. Eight centuries before Christ, in depicting Jerusalem, Isaiah personifies God as a nurturing, consoling Mother (today's first reading selection, Isaiah, Chapter 66). In chapter 42, God is woman "in labor, crying out, gasping and panting, until the child, Israel, is reborn unto freedom." Chapter 49 features a touching divine maternity, "Can a mother forget her nursing child, or show no compassion for the child of her womb? Yet, even if the love of a human mother should wane, I will not forget you. I have your name written on the palms of my hands."

What image could more movingly characterize the Creator's affection for creatures? The Bible is intent on indicating that man's struggle for survival on this planet is never remote from the Maker's care and concern–He knows to be human is no walk in the park. In fact, it is downright dangerous. Bacteria and microbes outnumber us. Delicate nervous systems wear out—dementia, Alzheimer's. Disasters descend without warning—floods, fires, earthquakes, and hurricanes. Most tragic of all, we are raised to believe that killing one another is natural and right—warfare, conquest, capital punishment. Churches and schools have been around for centuries and have failed to teach us how to get along together.

This perilous world was even more so when the prophet Isaiah preached. Eight hundred years later, Jesus sent His *seventy-two*—emblematic of the then known nations of the world—with His Good News for a harassed mankind. Twenty centuries since, mortal beings continue to twitch in a sea of troubles and wonder if a sympathetic Providence is still on the job. And through it all, paragons of compassion appear to remind the world that God still loves it like a mother.

There was Martin Luther King and the intrepid multitude that peaceably followed him into the promised land of expanded racial justice. Though a doctoral degree from Boston University qualified him for the tenured security of academia, he chose to pastor. Accepting leadership in the Montgomery bus protest, threats on his life and family became a daily curse. Violence raged. The clammy grip of fear alienated sleep. "I am at the end of my powers. I have nothing left. I have come to the point where I can't face it alone," he prayed aloud at the kitchen table in the middle of a sleepless night. "At that moment, I experienced the presence of the Divine as I had never before experienced Him. I know now that God is able to give us the interior resources to face the storms and problems of life."

Some agents of the Good News are totally helpless invalids. The late best selling author of illuminating spirituality, Father Henri Nouwen, was invited to spend some time at Toronto's Daybreak community—a family of six mentally handicapped individuals and the four adults that lived with them. There he met Adam, who made a profound impact on the priest. Father Nouwen wrote:

Adam is a twenty-five-year-old man who cannot speak, cannot dress or undress himself, cannot walk alone, and cannot eat without help. He does not cry or laugh. He suffers from severe epilepsy and, despite heavy medication, sees few days without grand mal seizures.

A virtual vegetable to many, he was not so to Father Nouwen.

As my fears gradually lessened, a love emerged in me so full of tender affection that most of my other tasks seemed boring and superficial compared with the hours spent with Adam. Out of his broken body and broken mind emerged a most beautiful human being offering me a greater gift than I would ever offer him.

My career was so marked by rivalry and competition, so pervaded with compulsion and obsession, so spotted with moments of suspicion, jealousy, resentment, and revenge. Adam's peace, while rooted more in being than in doing and more in the heart than in the mind, is a peace that calls for community. Adam, in his total vulnerability, calls us together as a family.

(Courtesy *Connections*, July 2001).

God's best-unkept secret is that we humans *are* His Providence. Whenever we are useful to another, we are His Good News, and that is genderless.

14th Sunday of Ordinary Time
(Luke 10: 1-12, 17-20)

High Neighbor

The road from Jerusalem to Jericho is all down hill. Jerusalem stands 2,300 feet above, and Jericho, near the north shore of the Dead Sea, is 1,300 feet below sea level. Craggy, narrow, twisty, and infested with bandits, the setting is made to order for Jesus' unforgettable parable of the Good Samaritan. Tourists today generally stop at the wayside Good Samaritan Chapel, which the guide points out to be the reputed location for the merciful rescue. There is no such historic event since the story is fiction.

The immense impact of the parable has been immortalized by so naming benevolent institutions and benefactors throughout the centuries. When Robert Kennedy was fatally gunned down in 1968, he was taken to Good Samaritan Hospital in Los Angeles.

Jesus used parables, thirty-seven of them, to illustrate His teaching of what God values in human behavior. Many of them were shockers to His hearers. Open-ended, no happy endings, hero and villain were often indistinguishable. He seemed to want His audience to see themselves in each of the characters in His stories. In order of appearance, the principals in today's narrative are the *victim, priest and Levite,* and the *Good Samaritan.* We have played them all at one time or other.

We have even played the lawyer, asking the wrong question: Who is my neighbor?; the correct one being: Am I the neighbor? Everyone has been a victim! Perhaps not cruelly mugged, we have been painfully wounded by indifferent people, often family, by heartless putdowns that have robbed us of dreams, initiative, and optimism. Priest and

Levite we have been when we kept going past that stranded motorist, too busy or too afraid to stop. And we've been the Good Samaritan whenever we paused to risk it.

Consistent with the parable theme of theft, this chapter liberally helps itself to the fresh, street savvy style of fellow accomplice, Father Bill O'Donnell, reflecting on this Gospel in his St. Joseph the Worker, Berkeley, parish bulletin for 15 July 2001:

> *The gospel story Jesus lays on us is of the robbers, the robbed, the helper and the avoiders. The storyline, you remember, how the Good Samaritan aids a victim of a severe mugging as two religious types steer clear of getting involved.*
>
> *Hey! Everybody's a winner . . . the mugged is rescued and cared for. The do-gooder gets a Boy Scout medal. The muggers get what they mugged the guy for. And the two religious types walk around the mess, thus keeping their hands clean. Everybody wins! I seriously doubt that this hermeneutic take would win an Oscar at the Hermeneutic Academy.*
>
> *Try this one on. Rather than winners, everyone is a victim . . . the robbers were victims. I can't imagine waking up some morning and thinking, "I know what I'll do today. I'll get my gang together and we'll go out looking for some sucker to loot." The law of the street when I was a teenage hood was that any time the odds were less than four-to-one, you never, never engaged. If you did you were crazy.*
>
> *The priest and the Levite, and the religious types, were victims, too . . . of fear. They pretended that they even saw one of their own in critical con-*

dition, so paralyzed were they in terror of the marauders returning for them; or how getting involved would effect their status; would people blame them as the robbers? Denial was the best course of action—'I won't tell, if you don't.'

It is difficult to see how the Samaritan is victim unless he lamented the loss of the silver that the good deed cost him. Maybe the innkeeper stood to make the only profit— he got a room rented.

We may never be in a position to risk life and limb for heroically helping the helpless, but our lives are surrounded by the lonely whose lives could be better for our active interest. In a 1986 *Newsweek,* columnist George Will reports on a group of Chicago laymen who call themselves "Little Brothers of the Poor":

They shop for the poor, deliver meals, drive ailing to clinics, find housing, fill out interminable forms for people too shaky to write, or eyes too blurry to see. They bring friendship and joy. They escort elderly to dinners at fine restaurants—not Jack in the Box or Taco Bell. They throw dinner parties for birthdays and anniversaries and never use paper plates.

A group of college girls have adopted a nursing home. From beauty operators, they have learned hair styling, and they regularly fuss over the oldsters like any first class hair salon. They have noted the birth dates of all the residents and see to it they are remembered. They managed to gather a class of elementary school children to play bingo each week with the old folks.

Want the most out of life? Try good neighboring—it's the stuff of eternal life! And that makes God our best neighbor.

15th Sunday of Ordinary Time
(Luke 10: 25-37)

Nervous Service

Eastern cultures are notorious for the uncommon courtesies they accord guests. A scene in David Lean's film, *Lawrence of Arabia,* shows "Arabophile" Lawrence being honored with a singular, local culinary delicacy by his desert Shaykh host: a sheep's eyeball. Table sharing signifies friendship bonding. In that part of the world, hospitality enjoys a profoundly religious meaning. Jewish custom esteems the same tradition. "Do not neglect to show hospitality," admonishes the author of Hebrews 13: 2, "for by that means some have entertained angels without knowing it."

Frenzied fuss, however, is not the way to make a guest feel more at home. In this day's Gospel reading, harried hostess Martha is offered some apt advice about cordial congeniality. Apparently, Jesus values discussion more than menu. But surely His gentle chiding is no disparagement of kitchen calisthenics. He is simply stating that it deserves no priority compared to intercommunication. After all, were it not for Martha's industry, her sister, Mary, could not have been an audience, or the guest at dinner. Making the soup, tossing the salad, mixing the drinks, of course, is important, but then so is exchanging ideas.

Like a good Jewish housekeeper, Martha focused on what she knew was expected of her—*woman's work*—serving the menfolk. Mary was more revolutionary; she wanted to learn. She seems more laid back—self-assured—open to finding out, and willing to take the time it takes. *Doing* probably defined her less than *being.* The behavior of both sisters exemplifies contrast appropriate in the process of human equilibrium. There are times for action and there are

497

times for holding still. Both belong, and it takes wisdom to know when. The maturely functioning believer needs Martha's hands and Mary's heart.

The Marthas of the world tend to miss out on the unplanned, spontaneous joys of life. Mary wanted to savor every moment, every syllable, of her fascinating guest. She reflects a modern feminine mystique and Jesus complimented her for it. At a Democrat Convention this past decade, an enlightened male speaker emphasized, "Women have a right to go at whatever men have failed at." According to Charlotte Whitten, "Whatever women do, they must do twice as well as men to be thought half as good."

Busy bees are usually control freaks. The queen bee needs worker bees and this situation often generates dependency and rage. Offspring of over-conscientious parents know about this! Busy-ness can also be a cop-out for a frustrating relationship. Frantic activity distracts from the inner ache. Often as not, such unhappy acting out can be traced to a childhood where parental affection was doled out only as a reward for "command performance." Task-oriented types naturally feel a sense of self-righteousness for fulfilling their duty. They even may feel that this gives them the right to coerce others. An unconscious self-doubt lurks beneath this need to dominate—a fertile breeding for burnout! They resent not being taken seriously, and they are not easy to live with.

The cartoon *Peanuts* has an angle on this situation. Chronically ill-tempered Lucy is ranting on and on. Her ever calm and pensive little brother, Linus, finally has had enough. To Lucy he snaps, "You're not the only one . . . I can be crabby too, you know!"

Lucy challenges him, "Okay, go ahead."

Linus is silent, clearly daunted by the challenge. Lucy finally speaks up, "See, it isn't that easy, is it?"

At complaining, Martha had practice. She had no trouble telling off the Lord for not hastening to her brother Lazarus' deathbed (John 11: 20). But she is not to be criticized for being annoyed at Mary's indifference to her share of the serving chores. Martha is guilty for laying a guilt-trip on her guest, however, instead of confronting her sister directly with her gripe. "Lord, do you not care that my sister has left me by myself to do the serving? Tell her to help me." Jesus was too polite to tell Martha, "Tell her yourself." Instead, He tactfully tuned-in on her officiousness. "Martha, Martha, you are anxious and worried about many things. There is need of only one thing." What did He mean by *only one thing?* Was a single course enough for dinner? He probably was referring to something more important—like hospitality is what matters, not hostility!

In case this chapter is coming down too hard on Martha, Cecily W. Hallack offers an empathic understanding in her poem, "The Divine Office of the Kitchen:"

Lord of all pots and pans and things,
since I've no time to be a saint by
doing lovely things,
or watching late with Thee,
or dreaming in the dawn's light,
or storming Heaven's gates,
make me a saint by getting meals
and washing up the plates.

16th Sunday of Ordinary Time
(Luke 10: 38-42)

To Pray is to Pry

No, not to prod, snoop, or meddle, but to go deep—deeply inside of ourselves, where God lives! Whatever moves, touches, and excites is good to talk with God about. Whatever makes us laugh, weep, and fear is God tugging at us for attention. It could be the unaffected glee of children at play, or the silent companionship of the elderly hand-holders who have weathered a lifetime together. It could be the brave promises of the young couple standing before the altar, or the raucous airport reunion of well loved people separated by too many miles and years, or the heart-wrenching farewell as a daddy has to leave.

Prayer springs from the stuff of life. It brims from the heart that is allowed to be penetrated by what it sees. An English Jesuit, Michael Campbell-Johnston, wrote this realistic comment on prayer in a Lenten series:

> *It is not so much raising the mind and heart to a God up or out there or even hidden within, but rather discovering Him/Her present all the time in the essence of things, in others, in encounters, places, events, situations, even the most unlikely. These include, of course, suffering, pain, tears and anguish, for the God of surprises is lurking there too, if only we will peel away the layers to uncover Him/Her.*

One cannot enter deeply into a human experience and not automatically think God.

Scripture selections for this day supply some surprising advice about addressing Divinity. Abraham politely, but boldly, bargains with Yahweh about the fate of Sodom and Gomorrah (Genesis 18: 20-32). No doubt that doomed neighborhood would be a tourist attraction today if it existed. Alas, it lies beneath the bottom of the Dead Sea. Centuries ago, the valley floor sank and the salt water engulfed it. It was long gone by the time of Jesus.

Luke has Jesus teaching His disciples to pray and emphasizes by parable that God does not mind being badgered. Noteworthy in this narrative is the implication that the sleep-disturbed friend comes through, not because of the merit of the midnight nuisance, but because of his need. A recitation of Christendom's most venerated vocal prayer, the "Our Father," prefaces the story. It is meant to be a sketching, more like a negative to the undeveloped print. Genuine prayer needs no words—sighs and attentive waiting can be enough.

The Lord's Prayer is the essence of courtesy: "You first, God, then me!" Children do not resist this deference. In a Religious Education class, the teacher explained how praying was like writing a letter home. Their homework was to write a letter to God. Next class the letters were read:

Dear God,

Is it okay to pray even if you don't want anything?

Love,

Ernie

Dear God,

Does saying thanks over spinach constitute an endorsement?

The most discriminating comment: "Sometimes I say my prayers and sometimes I pray." This youngster understood that the heart has its own language.

Prayers taught by rote can have the impact on children that the following hilarious variations reveal:

> *Our Father who art in Heaven, Halloween be Thy name* . . .
> *Give us this day our day-old bread* . . .
> *Forgive us our deaths as we forgive those who are dead set against us* . . .
> *Lead us not into Penn Station* . . .
> *And deliver us from all eagles* . . .

It would seem that if youngsters were first instructed about the wonders of the universe, the luxury of literature, the magic of music, their curiosity concerning the divinity behind such creations might be better stirred.

Why pray, if God knows our needs, and is immutable besides? Kierkegaard maintained that prayer does not change God, it changes us. What we pray for, we become more of. To pray for healing makes us more conscious of health issues. To pray for peace involves us with personal peace-making and justice. To pray for employment turns our attention to training and improving competence. St. Thomas More prayed, "Lord, give us the grace to work for what we pray for."

French priest-author, Louis Evely, tells this moving story. A mother's child is ill; she doesn't want him to die, but the doctor has told her, "I've tried absolutely everything. All we can do now is resign ourselves to the inevitable." She neither believed the doctor nor listened to her husband as he tried to reason with her. Instead she told them what she thought, "You're giving up too easily; but I won't abandon my son like you, because I am sure he can still be saved."

So here she is in church. She has come to tell God that her boy mustn't die, that he simply can't, that she doesn't want him to, that God couldn't permit such a thing. Then, by dint of praying—if she does it sincerely and long enough—she enters into a deeper prayer. Slowly the detachment she rules out begins to permeate her, and when she gets up, she is amazed to hear herself say, "Lord, I entrust him to You. From this moment on, he's Your child much more than mine. I know he's better off in Your hands. You're responsible for him now, and You'll take better care of him than I ever could. May Your will be done."*

So praying is prying—deeply below our surfaces where the Kingdom of God lives in each of us. Poet Ted Loder understood this when he wrote the inspired "Pry Me Off Dead Center:"

O persistent God,
deliver me from assuming your mercy is gentle.
Pressure me that I may grow more human,
not through the lessening of my struggles,
but through an expansion of them
that will undam me
and unbury my gifts.
Deepen my hurt
until I learn to share it
and myself
openly,
and my needs honestly.
Sharpen my fears
until I name them
and release the power I have locked in them
and they in me.
Accentuate my confusion
until I shed those grandiose expectations

*that divert me from the small, glad gifts of the now and the
here and the me.*

*Expose my shame where it shivers
crouched behind the curtains of propriety,
until I can laugh at last
through my common frailties and failures, laugh my way
toward becoming whole.
Deliver me from just going through the motions and wasting everything
I have which is today, a chance,
a choice,
my creativity,
your call.
O persistent God,
let how much it all matters
pry me off dead center
so if I am moved inside to tears
or sighs
or screams
or smiles
or dreams,
they will be real.
I will be in touch with who I am
and who you are
and who my sisters and brothers.*

– Ted Loder, *Guerrillas of Grace* **

* Thanks to Fr. Joe Nolan for his 27 July 1986 edition
of the *Good News*.
** If this appears elsewhere in this trilogy, it is well
worth repeating.

*17th Sunday of Ordinary Time
(Luke 11: 1-13)*

505

Who Wants to be a Millionaire?

Most likely those who aren't! The lottery is providing more of them each week, but there are still those rare, unencumbered free souls who could care less about being financially rich. This Gospel deals with the fatuous surety that wealth seductively promises.

In August 1492, Christopher Columbus was at sea with three small ships manned by 120 men. He did not go where he thought he was going, so when he got there, he thought he was someplace else; and he did it all on borrowed money. What Columbus happened upon has become the world's richest nation. Which is a cause for concern, especially whenever this fabulous opulence is unwisely misapplied. Six hundred billion dollars of it went for the ten thousand-day war that we lost in Vietnam. Not to mention the loss of infinitely more precious treasure: over fifty thousand American lives.

The U.S.A. boasts of its generosity to needy nations. Yet of the seventeen-member nations of the OED, Organization for Economic Development, designed to aid Third World countries, this republic stands in last place—contributing just one one-fifth of one percent of its Gross National Product (GNP). Television commercials during the Super Bowl game went for three-hundred thousand dollars per minute. With all our reckless spending, we are not a contented people, leading the world in crime, violence, and addictions.

Like Columbus, many of us have chartered our life course, and have ended up in some quite different place. Extravagant fortune has eluded most of us. The majority of families have both parents working in order to manage the mortgage, the car payments, and the children's staggering college tuition. We are fascinated with money, perhaps due to the lack of it, even though we know it is not real wealth. Money is simply a convention that is more convenient than bartering. During the Sicily invasion of World War II, the GI's were surprised that the impoverished natives preferred things—rations, clothing—to cash. Money could not be worn or eaten. It can buy many things—prestige, power, people—but not an expired life term. J. Paul Getty, Aristotle Onassis, and the Shah of Iran could not escape. Pulitzer Prize winner Earnest Becker believes that "All power is in essence the power to deny mortality."

In the parable about the "rich farmer," Jesus does not criticize his wealth, but his foolishness. It can be assumed that he came by his fortune honestly and by dint of hard work. Nor is there any complaint about an earned, relaxing retirement. From the words Jesus uses to describe the retiree, *my* and *mine* stand out. Therefore, one aspect of the fool is self-absorption—thinking only of oneself. To out-grow this inborn, infantile self-centeredness, one needs to experience the empty frustration of living for oneself alone. If one has only oneself to please, then too much is never enough. Such an existence is as valid as the eye intent on looking at itself, or the ear to hear itself, or one's lips to kiss one's own. Narcissism is an aborted development. Growing old is mandatory; growing up is optional.

A more subtle insight inherent in this parable is its reference to foolishness. It is certainly not foolish to be industrious, to want a pleasant life and to plan for it. What *fooled* the rich farmer? Was it that he felt more secure because he was rich? Isn't that why most people want to be rich? To be more protected from life's grim uncertainties? But, to be protected from the flux of life is to be separated from life. Wealth can make it all much easier, but it is a false fortification from the inevitable. The parable suggests that it is foolish to bet on a phantom horse. Security is a fake! There is no such thing this side of eternity. As Douglas MacArthur once said, "There is no security, only opportunity." Human species have only intimations of security. Life's journey is a perilous adventure, and the final chapter is a matter of faith. A faith that does not cling, but lets go. A faith that does not need to know and goes with the punches.

The Judo technique understands the power of allowing the flow. "Ju" means gentle; "do" means way. The Judo master uses the opposing force by going with it. To the wise person, insecurity is no enemy because every human being can be seen as insecurity itself, and thus changing it into opportunity. Vulnerability makes one more sensitively conscious of existence and to the rhythmical balance of pleasure and pain. There is no escape. The fly struggling in the honey only gets more entrapped. One does not keep one's breath by holding it.

Interesting people are interested people—people fascinated by the pure miracle of the moment. Goethe (1749-1832) felt that "The highest to which man can attain is wonder." John of the Cross (1542-1591) contended that by faith the soul could "See so distinctly and to feel so profoundly that it cannot comprehend God at all." Eddington (1881-1944), the brilliant English physicist, concluded simply, "Something unknown is doing we don't know what." Rudyard Kipling (1865-1936), addressing the graduates of McGill University, Montreal, said, "Don't pay too much attention to fame, power, money. Some day you will meet a man who cares for none of these. Then you will know how truly poor you are."

Still want to be a millionaire? If you don't care to be . . . you are already!

18th Sunday of Ordinary Time
(Luke 12: 13-21)

Got it Made!

"Do not be afraid any longer, little flock, for the Father is pleased to give you the kingdom."

There is no Sunday Gospel opener with more reassuring lines! Jesus was addressing people who were intrigued by Him and pretty much concurred with His values. Their faith was blossoming. The *Kingdom* was happening to them. So, "Don't worry," He urged endearingly, "you've got it made!"

A faith is something not everybody has. Money can't buy it. It's a gift. Those who have it feel blessed. For almost half a century, the Gallup organization has been assaying current religious beliefs and practices in America. Recently, pollster George H. Gallup has probed more deeply into this issue and has reported his findings of the impact of faith in the lives of believers. "The evidence overwhelmingly points to their being better and happier," he stated in an interview. The Gallup study is more fully reproduced in book form as *The Saints Among Us.* Faith people are shown to be more honest in their personal dealings, more tolerant and respectful of differing ethnicities and economic backgrounds, and quicker to perform charitable service. That a strong faith benefits health and longevity inspires no argument even among non-believers.

Inscribed on the wall of a pub in the town of Bray, near London, is the oft quoted: "Fear knocked at the door, faith answered, and there was no one there." Running from fear and denying it, only makes it worse. There is no escaping the clammy grip of it when it strikes; sweating the biopsy report, the child's surgery outcome, or the teenager's first night with the family car. Being afraid is natural. Jesus sweat blood in dread in Gethsemane that night before He died. Facing His terror with faith apparently imparted a remarkable composure throughout His ordeal. When fear clutches the human spirit, it seems more useful to look it in the eye. Fear is not something one has, like the flu; fear is something one *is*—from head to toe. When afraid, admitting that, *I am fear* can change it from an enemy to be exterminated to a frightened child that needs support and understanding.

A strong faith helps, but faith in what? Most people believe in God. What is important is the kind of God they believe in. For Jesus, He was a festive Father, obviously partial to partying. His Kingdom was described as a wedding feast to which everyone was invited. In this Kingdom, there were no barriers, no discrimination. Even the "Upstairs" Lord of the Manor dons an apron to serve the "Downstairs" help—as this day's parable recounts. A belief in this zestful Divinity minimizes fret and even gives it meaning.

The faith Jesus proposed was an elixir to life, not an anesthetic, nor an antiseptic. Life's tensions were meant to be faced with it: to help see one through traumas, not around them. He disapproved of religion that burdened believers with useless guilt. He sought to release sincere consciences from the imposing tyranny of grandiose religious bureaucracies. He opted for His flock to become their own responsible authority, with love their standard, not law.

Jesus apparently seconded the Boy Scout motto "Be prepared." Being *ready* for Him might be interpreted as being alert—in touch with what's happening. He saw faith as a visual aid to reality—the ability to perceive beneath the appearance of things into the heart of them, as the brave non-violent protester can see the panicky fright behind the mask of swaggering violence. Jesus must have been convinced that faith is nothing if it is not attention to awareness.

Jazz great, musician and composer Duke Ellington, was asked if he could explain his extraordinary professional success. He answered:

If you are lucky enough to have opportunity knock, it is useless if you are not ready. I was always ready in case I got a break.

Another winner among jazz greats was trumpeter Roy Eldridge. In the segregated '30s and '40s, Roy was the only African-American in Gene Krupa's band. Hotels would not accept him with the rest of the musicians. Tired of being routinely separated, he happened upon a clever and benign solution. Roy got himself a porter cap. When the band was checking into their hotel, "Porter" Roy approached the desk with his luggage. "Where shall I take Mr. Eldridge's bags?" he innocently inquired. He was handed a room key and enjoyed a pleasant rest. In the morning, he approached the desk. "I am Mr. Eldridge. I am here to pay my bill, and would you please give these two tickets to the night clerk."

Courage is another word for faith. It sometimes takes more courage to adapt than to attack. So, don't be afraid, little flock, trust God, trust life, trust yourself, trust your bliss . . . that's the *Kingdom!*

19th Sunday of Ordinary Time
(Luke 12: 32-48)

Trouble Maker?

"Do you think I have come to establish peace on earth? No, I tell you, but rather division."

Sounds more like *Mein Kampf* than the Good News! Is this the Prince of Peace talking? Did Jesus really say these words, or did a later generation say He said them, in order to explain the epidemic of violent persecution? Luke wrote his Gospel some fifty years after the execution of Jesus. No instant replay . . . oral tradition was all the Evangelists had to go on.

A group of New Testament experts have collected to study the recorded statements of Jesus for authenticity. Their project is known as the Jesus Seminar. These scholars submit the reported sayings of Jesus to the exacting scrutiny of linguistic evidence, historical data, and textual critique. Their findings are tallied and the majority concluded that the actual and exact words of Jesus are few and far between.

Though controversial, the Jesus Seminar arouses intriguing curiosity. How would the reader vote on the harsh opener to this chapter? Did Jesus actually make that statement, or were these words put into His mouth by a subsequent generation? Yea or nay? This writer votes yea! Why? Because Jesus was a realist. He could readily predict that those who would take Him seriously could expect His fate. As have politically incorrect disciples right on down to the present: Archbishop Romero of El Salvador, the four American missionary women, and the six Jesuit priests murdered by Contra death squads. He knew that sincere religion had dangerous side effects, ever since Cain killed his brother, Abel, because Yahweh preferred Abel's sacrifice to Cain's. Jesus Himself died an outlaw, as did the Coliseum martyrs who were called "atheists" for not worshipping the Roman emperors.

Was Jesus divisive? Was the *father* in the parable, when he threw a party for his errant prodigal, which made the elder dutiful son mad at him? Jesus was uncompromising and aware of the trouble people could get into for having that divisive trait. If one cannot look the other way, one better not work for a crooked boss or a munitions plant.

Human existence abounds in discord since human nature itself is dissonant—off pitch. A lifetime is too short to get mind and body in workable agreement. The head is calorie conscious; the body says "So what!" The brain says, "Exercise is good for you"; the flesh says, "So is the easy chair." Ideals battle instincts. Mankind is still a partial product. It is still in process.

Civilized people persist in fighting over religion. In the Persian Gulf War, during the prosperous '90s, modern oil-rich countries that the U.S. forces were defending, forbade uniformed chaplains to wear their cross insignia when off their military base. Fidel Castro once called Christians "social scum" but shook hands with the Pope anyway.

Divisions in our technicolor world are inevitable, but they need not be terminal. In fact, difference can be unifying when respectfully confronted. Opposites attract as well as separate. There is education in communicating with contrasts. Diversity is no threat to the celebrant of life. "Fight or flight" has another option: "Stay and relate." "Returning violence for violence," Martin Luther King maintained, "multiplies violence, adding a deeper darkness to a night already devoid of stars." Retaliation only perpetuates a senseless, endless chain reaction.

That is why Jesus urged loving the enemy—the safest, sanest technique for bomb diffusion! There is no enemy trickier than the enemy within; that demonic shadow-side that bedevils every mortal. When that adversary is considerately confronted, no external antagonist can prevail. To accept this aggravating reality as a rooted participant of the personality is to step in the direction of wholeness—integrity.

Here is the statement of a man who made this peace with himself and his Creator. He is about to die because he is a Jew. He wrote his words on a soiled scrap of paper and squeezed it into a small bottle. He is Yossel Rakover, whom the Nazis exterminated in the infamous Warsaw ghetto of Poland.

God, you have done everything to make me stop believing in you, now, lest it seems to you that you will succeed by these tribulations. In driving me from the right path I notify you, God, and God of my fathers, that it will not avail you in the least. You may insult me. You may castigate me. You may take from me all that I cherish and hold dear in the world. You may torture me to death, but I will always love you and these are my last words to you.*

*Reverend Joseph Nolan, Good News, "A Short Homily," 17 August. 1986.

20th Sunday of Ordinary Time
(Luke 12: 49-53)

No Reserved Seats

This hard-line Gospel is apparently addressed to a clannish audience who felt that membership in the Jewish religious community guaranteed a privileged place in the Kingdom. Jesus emphasized that there were no seats reserved even for practicing temple/churchgoers. According to Him, everyone is offered a free pass. Even the moral riffraff is welcome.

Whenever Jesus mentioned the Kingdom, He was referring to a condition where God is in charge—where goodness holds sway—when creatures great and small care about each other. This Kingdom exists here as well as the hereafter, wherever love, the other name for God, happens.

In his book, *The Individual and His Religion,* contemporary sociologist Gordon Allport contends that churchgoers tend to be more prejudiced than the average non-attendee. He theorizes that adherents of religion are motivated by either *extrinsic* or *intrinsic* religion. The extrinsic variety needs rules to guide, and authoritarian assurance to comfort them. Ritual is important and they resist challenge or change. Intrinsic types appear to understand what Jesus means about leaven, salt, and light. They are open to newness, to the adventure of creative spirituality—to the mystery of life, of themselves, of God. It is unlikely for them to ask the question Jesus did not answer: "Lord, will only a few people be saved?" They would understand what He meant when He said, "Strive to enter through the narrow gate." They would most likely sympathize with the remainder of His reply. "For many, I tell you, will attempt to enter, but will not be strong enough." There is no condemnation in this statement—possibly a trace of pity—or a sadness for the "try-outs" unable to make the "varsity." The query is comparable to the law school students anxiously supplicating their professor, "How many will pass the Bar?" His answer, "Just study, take the exam; you will learn something."

The narrow gate? Could it involve making the most of the cards life deals? The recently deceased popular Archbishop of Recife, Brazil, the sprightly minded Dom Helder Camara, senses the spirit of the successful narrow gate crashers. "Accept surprises that upset your plans, shatter your dreams, give a completely different turn to your day, and—who knows—to your life. It is not chance. Leave the Father free to weave the pattern of your days." Tolerance for the unexpected lends spice to life. Dante described Hell at its depth as blue ice, utterly frozen—no change—no life. Cardinal Newman believed, "To live is to change, and to be perfect is to change often."

Human nature being what it is, not that many make it through the confined straits of emotional and spiritual maturity. Thus chronic angst is the common denominator for most human existence. When "copability" is diminished, some will retreat into religion, much as the diffident resort to alcohol for ersatz confidence. Which is why Marx and Freud regarded religion as an "opiate." But substituting piety for courage never elicited the hallmark of approval from Jesus. "I do not know where you are from," He repeated. "But, we ate and drank in your company and you taught in our streets!" The withering rejection of Jesus for presumptuous believers is particularly disquieting. "For behold, some are last who will be first and some are first who will be last." Whatever will be, we are in for a surprise! Worship is simply not enough unless human beings are cared about and cared for. Mother Teresa had to leave the safety of the cloister to find richer days among the starving and dying of Calcutta. The narrow gate was no obstacle course for the anonymous composer of this creed:

In some way, however small and secret, each of us is a little mad. Everyone is lonely at bottom and cries to be understood; but we can never entirely understand someone else, and each of us remains part stranger even to those who love us. It is the weak who are cruel; gentleness is to be expected only from the strong. Those who do not fear are not really brave, for courage is the capacity to confront what frightens us. You can understand people better if you look at them—no matter how old or impressive they may be—as if they are children. For most of us never mature, we simply grow taller. Happiness comes only when we push our brains and hearts to the farthest reaches of which we are capable. The purpose of life is to matter—to count—to stand for something, to have it make some difference that we lived at all.

21st Sunday of Ordinary Time
(Luke 13: 22-30)

Trivial Pursuit

In his play *The Cocktail Party*, T. S. Eliot attests that, "Half the harm that is done in this world is due to people who want to feel important." Human nature tends to exaggerate what it does not have. When a sense of self-worth is wanting, the appeal of position and prominence can become a quick-fix addiction. The powerless lust for power; the overlooked long to be looked over. What you run from, you run into. Jesus points out the hazards of social climbing in this day's Gospel:

> *On the Sabbath, Jesus went to dine at the home of one of the leading Pharisees, and the people were observing him carefully.*
>
> *He told a parable to those who had been invited, noticing how they were choosing the places of honor at the table. "When you are invited by someone to a wedding banquet, do not recline at table in the place of honor. A more distinguished guest than you may have been invited by him, and the host that invited both of you may approach you and say, give your place to this man, and then you would proceed with embarrassment to take the lowest place . . . for everyone who exalts himself will be humbled, but the one who humbles himself will be exalted."*

Star status has an extremely transient mortality. Chagrin is ever lurking in the wings. The Scot creator of Peter Pan, Sir James Barrie, observed, "Life is one long lesson in humility." By His parable, Jesus is neither urging heroic virtue, nor severe abstinence from the impulse to be a somebody. He is simply recommending a common-sensed etiquette to avert the painful blush of looking foolish.

Embarrassing moments are the common side effect of our flawed humanity. Every adult has a personal file of them that sometimes draws a smile to recall. Cardinal Spellman (1889-1967), this writer's ordaining prelate, liked to tell this story on himself. Of the many honorary doctorates he was awarded in his lifetime, he was proudest of the bachelors degree he earned at Fordham University prior to World War I. Returning home to Boston to savor his achievement, after work as a streetcar motorman, his Irish father greeted the young graduate. "You must feel very important with that new college degree of yours, but I have one bit of advice for you. If you really want to be a success, surround yourself with people smarter than you are. And do you know something, Frank? For you that will not be hard."

Someone once said, "The woods would be silent if only birds with trained voices did the singing." A church had a man in the choir who couldn't sing. Several members hinted to him that he might better serve elsewhere, but he continued fidelity to the choir. The choir director desperately sought the help of the pastor. "You've got to get that man out of the choir," he pleaded. "If you don't, I'm going to resign. The choir members are going to quit, too. Please do something." So the pastor went to the man and suggested, "Perhaps you should leave the choir."

"Why should I get out of the choir?" the man asked.

"Well, five or six people have told me you can't sing."

"That's nothing," the man snorted, "fifty people have told me that you can't preach!"

Modern mores tout the glory of being number one. For Jesus, the value of every human being was a gift from the

Creator, not an achievement by the creature. Power and prestige have been more man's amusement than God's. No external notoriety alters human worth with the Deity. The wonder is that worshippers continue to assume that Divinity is better pleased by outsized extravagant praise than the wordless sigh of a humble heart. The lyrics from a *Camelot* song testify that, "Humility means to be hurt. It is not the earth the meek inherit, it's the dirt." Cynical, perhaps, but accurate!

Humus is the Latin word for topsoil, and the root word for *humility*. This loam is one with its environment: wind, rain, sun, frost, and drought. It takes what it gets and from it emerges fertile life. Open to the atmosphere's uncertainties, it forthrightly yields its fruit silently, compliantly. The humble person takes life much like this: bad breaks are not penalty, they are opportunity.

From the outset, the life of Jesus embraced insecurity. "The Son of Man has not where to lay his head" (Matthew 9: 20). His death became a source of life even in its destruction. "Unless the grain of wheat falls into the ground and dies, it remains alone" (John 12: 24). The lowly have no need to be top dog. That position presents a whole new set of insecurities, more defenses, and added worries. They can confront insecurity calmly because they *are* insecurity! This implies no inferiority, but rather awareness. The humble person has no notion of being humble, but understands the transitoriness of existence. Each moment is born only to die in the next. The present is instantly becoming the past. Still, the humble one can sense an inner permanence that survives the shifts and twists of finite life. Humility is a sanity—a wholeness. It sees no separation—no difference—from a human feeling and the human being feeling it. This is twenty-twenty interior vision. "When your eye is sound, your whole body, too, is filled with light" (Luke 11: 24).

"Humility," according to Thomas Merton, "is recovering our original unity, what we have to be we already are." Though life is bigger than we are, we are the big part of it. Getting God's attention involves no special feat—just being what God made—*ourselves*—and that's special!

22nd Sunday of Ordinary Time
(Luke 14: 7-14)

Family Value-Less?

Among the rare times that this writer relished the Church's rule of clerical celibacy, one of them was upon reading this day's Gospel. At least there were no wife and children to hate, in order to prove affection for Jesus:

> *If anyone comes to me without hating his father and mother, wife and children, brothers and sisters, and even his own life, he cannot be my disciple.*

An utterance impossible to be taken literally!

The narrative reports, "Great crowds were traveling with Jesus," when He dropped that blockbuster. All were enroute to Jerusalem. He knew it was His finale. They thought He was on His way to empire; such was His impact on them. They were eating out of His hand. Why would He make so outlandish a statement when He consistently urged loving enemies? Why would He create the narcissistic impression that competition for His fellowship was forbidden? Was there only so much cordiality to go around that it had to be rationed? Must we love Him more than ice cream and television? Did He really resent the modest comforts humans enjoy?

Any response in the affirmative would totally negate the Good News. Once again, the Scripture is exploiting the exaggerated style of that day in order to emphasize a salient point. Something like the extravagant expressions in current usage that accompany intense reactions: "One more time and I'll throw you through the window."

So, what point is Jesus making? It is unthinkable that He intended to add to life's sorrows. In fact, precisely the opposite! He could have been referring to attachments that bog down life, like a demanding family or imprisoning possessions. He could be saying that the things you feel you cannot live without are sometimes the very things that can kill you. Ask recovering alcoholics if they want to go back to drinking, or if cleaned up addicts want to do drugs again. Yet, they once felt that their habits were irreplaceable. Insensitive family members can be an anchor to impede creative progress. To move toward the fullness of one's potential, Jesus advised turning one's back on the authorities and influences that prevent fulfillment. He recognized forces within us and surrounding us that wither the spirit when love is missing.

Jiddu Krishnamurti, the renowned sage of Madras, since 1922 had addressed thousands from his Ojai, California retreat. His small, quiet voice was heard in the august halls of the United Nations in 1984 when he was almost ninety. He claimed no faith, no religious affiliation, but his thoughts share a remarkable resemblance to the logic of the gospel. In his book, *The First and Last Freedom,* he writes:

> *If there is love you will understand the unknown, you will know what God is and nobody need tell you—and that is the beauty of love. Therefore, we should not invest our happiness in things, in family, in ideals. They are secondary*
> *The truth is what liberates, not striving to be free.*
> *You really love when you do not possess.*

In this startling Gospel, Jesus is inviting followers to the freedom of common sense. "Don't begin a building that you can't complete or a war that you can't win," He advises. Take stock first, then leap, right into the arms of God, into what is happening, into reality—another metaphor for God—*the Ground of Being*. He taught that faith was *letting go*—it does not need to control—it lets God! This leap may involve leaving home, the familiar, the comfortable, the secure, for the uncertainty of newness, the freshness of experience, openness to learn.

For Jesus, religion was much more than creed and code. It was more than belief in belief, which can harden into dogma. It was trusting in an outrageous God who apparently holds still for earthquakes, fires, floods, and tragic accidents. Who heard His Son sob "My God, My God, why have you forsaken me?" The hyperbole of this Gospel is asking, not for half-hearted, but whole-hearted commitment to His cause—to love, to freedom. Freedom to doubt, to question, to wonder. Freedom to spontaneity, to aloneness, to innocence. The freedom to feel, not what *should* be felt, but what *is* felt—fear, anger, hate, love. They all have their turn. That is why He promised to stick with us through it all. "Behold, I will be with you always, even to the end of time."

23rd Sunday of Ordinary Time
(Luke 14: 15-33)

9.11.01

"Terror Tuesday"—*a horror tale of two cities*—an historic end to an era! The rubble of New York's Twin Towers and Washington's Pentagon is literally dust compared to the immeasurable wealth of talent and brain trust of which the future has now been deprived. Suddenly, a nation's fixation with trivia has come to a crashing finale. Monday Night Football lost its excitement; the faltering economy was paltry news. Nothing would ever be quite as before. Travel would be different. Safety became a phantom; precautions, a hassle; aliens, a suspicion. Moments of clarity made vivid what matters to human life. People important to us instantly became precious fortunes and we blessed a routine reality—the gift of time. It was good to care, to be able to touch, to hold, to feel enough to mourn.

The massive sorrow of that tragic day aroused a national hunger for the soul's more solid food: courage, selfless generosity, and sensitivity to suffering, compassion, and prayer. Small school children, with their own hands, prepared lunches for exhausted rescue workers. Citizens stood in line for hours, anxious to give blood. "Take it from both arms," they urged. As disaster tends to elicit the best in human beings, so does it expose the worst.

After the shock and alarm, follows the fury. "Nuke the SOBs" becomes the blind instinct! A reckless rashness takes the place of the impotence of fear. Hatred for the conqueror is the one illusion of power available to the vanquished. Which can explain the fanatical contempt of Middle East extremists for America. Some Arabic societies are a turmoil of frustrations from their own autocratic leadership. The immense extremes between imbalanced wealth and poverty are handily attributed to intrusive American policy and its preoccupation with petroleum. Western materialism is seen as a satanic invasion on their way of life. Like most racial repugnance, it is taught along with mother's milk. As a Buddhist priest prayed at a memorial service in New York, "Hatred has never been a successful tool in combating hatred."

To the fundamentalist mind, modernity is a corruption to be fought and exterminated. It is the mentality that burned heretics of the medieval church and witches by Puritans in Salem. It is a regression of civilization to zealotry theology. Religion, even the rabid variety, enjoys political protection and insulation in free societies, until human rights are traduced. Terrorists, however convinced of their just cause, are still killers.

What makes human beings do the inhuman things they do to one another, and in the name of God? Can it be that whoever is defined as enemy ceases to have a human face? Americans are raised on good guy versus bad guy fiction. Even biblical logic separated good sheep from bad sheep when most are a combination of both. It is virtually impossible to think of the suicidal hijackers as anything but savage. Helpless anger fueled by self-pity demands retaliation and violence accelerates. One "righteous cause" refuses dialogue with another "righteous cause."

Mankind has yet to evolve to tolerance for the cause of universal brotherhood. As long as excessive nationalism is touted as patriotism, as long as nations insist on sovereignty and borders pre-empt human exchange, there will be wars.

Yet our diverse natures present an astounding oneness. Like the universe, which is a network of likes and opposites, in perpetual motion, this mass of energy is an astonishing harmony. Each human being is a mini-cosmos, comprising all the elements of the universe. Human beings are stardust! Can we imitate their teamwork? Fanatics will see this as capitulation, and thus terrorism thrives. Four centuries before Christ, the philosopher Plato understood that it was better to suffer injustice than to perpetrate it. The following lines of verse appeared in a local daily "Letters to the Editor" for 16 Sept. 2001:

> *Choreographers in the destruction*
> *of our world*
> *taking pleasure in this foolish*
> *game of tit-for-tat*
> *between nations.*
> *The hate is deep.*
> *We must set an example for*
> *humanity is watching.*
> *How will we respond?*

The Gospel reading for this same day suggested a response. It featured three parables about how the heart of God deals with the wayward:

The Lost Sheep: no one is a lost cause to God; no one is written off.

The Lost Coin: the least of us has value and is worth turning everything upside down to get to it, as the housekeeper did.

The Prodigal Son: more so the Prodigal Father, who did not mind looking foolish to restore a relationship.

Love is the bottom line secret underlying creation. The Creator certainly did not make it to lose it. People are divided from one another because individuals are divided within themselves. I am separated from me when I deny my feelings. I cannot make peace with you if I am not at peace with me. The demons I despise in you are the demons asleep in .my consciousness. I cannot befriend you until I've made friends with the shadowy stranger in me. It was Meister Eckhart who said, "When you are thwarted, it is your attitude that is out of order." I can only get to the love in me when I work through the layers of accumulated resentments of my lifetime. The immense tragedy of that "Terrible Tuesday" shall have been wasted unless it has made us more caring, more forgiving, more loving. The once soaring World Trade Towers and the imposing Pentagon are not symbols of America's real might. America's power, or any nation's, for that matter, is in its will to rescue, which includes attention to why a people are seen as the "bad guys." New York firefighters and police have scrambled tirelessly in search for fallen brothers—a far fitter strategy than killing fellow beings, even when they are the enemy.

24th Sunday of Ordinary Time
(Luke 15: 1-32)

BOOK COOK

Another odd parable!

This one commends a crook. Last week, a Prodigal Son gets feted. This week, a Prodigal Steward gets pink-slipped and praised. "I'm not strong enough to dig and I'm ashamed to beg," so, in one last ditch wily move, he cooks the books by making false entries.

The story is reminiscent of a real one that happened years ago in Maryland. An accountant in his mid-thirties, after an annual medical check-up, was shocked to learn that he had a terminal disease and had no more than two months to live. He decided to make them memorable. He would live it up for the time he had left, and embezzled twenty-nine thousand dollars from his boss. By the time the theft was discovered, the employee reasoned that he would be long gone. A month later, he was informed that his medical report was a misdiagnosis. He is still in jail.

The mismanaging manager of the parable escapes that fate and even gets praised for his ingenuity. "And the master commended that dishonest steward for acting prudently." What could Jesus have been thinking when He stunned His audience with that puzzling illustration? It can only be guessed! Which may well be what He intended by using this parabolic pedagogy.

His outrageous tales have a lampoon quality. They are like verbal cartoons that poke fun at grim-faced life, but are meant to tweak the mind to think for itself. His startling stories have no endings, so as to leave the hearer to discover his/her own meaning. His parables are as fresh today as they were then. In the words of Tagore, Gandhi's teacher,

"Where the clear stream of reason has not lost its way into the dreary sand of dead habit." Jesus apparently wished to jar His hearers from the stale numbness of repetitious authoritarian teaching. "Think for yourself," He seemed to accentuate, "but not by yourself." So, He invited dialogue.

One clear inference from this fraud yarn is that believers seem to be more naïve than are non-believers. "For the children of this world are more prudent in dealing with their own generation than are the children of light." Jesus consistently exhibited admiration for alert, enterprising, resourceful personalities. He appreciated self-starters; the inner directed who could esteem and not envy, follow and not copy, motivate without artifice. Though His focus was on a *hereafter,* making a go of *here* received His common-sensed accent. He knew it took the brazenness of a burglar to survive, so He implicated that there was more to religion than going to temple. Avoiding the temptation to make a fix or a fast buck, does not qualify for the medal of honorable virtue. Care for the needy always rated higher marks.

The parable also intimates that had the clever embezzler worked as hard at this job as at feathering his nest, he probably would still have the job. What a different world if the savvy it takes to be a smart criminal were applied to humanity's welfare!

There are wholesome entrepreneurists who have left mankind in a better place. Mimi Silbart, for one. Dr. Mimi founded the Delancey Street Foundation, which is an organization of skilled volunteers and teachers who instruct convicts willing to further their education. Thousands have earned high school diplomas and taken advanced courses to equip them for meaningful employment. It is the most successful rehabilitative program in the annals of correctional history.

The famed Mayo Clinic, created by brothers, Charles and William, has been supplying a superb health care delivery system for decades because the brothers have plowed back the majority of its income into further expansion. As Dr. William explains, "That holy money, as we call it, must go back into the service of that humanity which paid it to us. If we can train five hundred pairs of hands, we have helped to hand on the torch."

Then there is Dorothy Day, renowned founder of the *Catholic Worker* and sanctuary for thousands of needy over the years. A communist, a promiscuous Greenwich Village swinger in her earlier days, she eventually became a convert. She embraced a life of personal poverty, fostered her private spirituality, and openly differed with the hierarchy on the "just war" issue. She never deplored her ill adventured past, but felt that the experience led her to her subsequent commitment to sanctity. Her cause for canonization has been begun.

A final nuance from the parable . . . both the Prodigal Son and the Unjust Steward may have been surprised that they were spared punishment for their wayward ways. Can it mean that even the errant can expect the same break from God?

25th Sunday of Ordinary Time
(Luke 16: 1-13)

Never Noticed

A man known throughout the town for his great wealth—and tight-fistedness— never contributed anything to charity or supported any effort to alleviate the suffering of the poor and needy. The chairman of one of the community's worthy charitable organizations decided to approach the rich man at his office.

"Sir," the fundraiser said, "our records show that despite your great wealth, you have never given to our drive."

"Oh, really," the rich man fumed. "Well, do your records show that I have an elderly mother who was left penniless when my father died? Do your records show that I have a sick brother who is unable to work? Do your records show that I have a widowed sister with three small children who can barely make ends meet? Do your *records* show any of that information?" the miser railed.

"No, sir," replied the embarrassed volunteer. "We did not know any of that."

"Well, if I don't give anything to them, why should I give anything to *you*?"

This story offers a hint of *Dives* in this day's Gospel parable. The narrative had been around for centuries. Ancient Egyptian folklore used it to console unfortunates, with Osiris in charge of their netherworld. Rabbis borrowed the tale to encourage attention to Moses and the Prophets. They assigned Abraham to the Osiris job. Lazarus is the only character given a name among all the Gospel parables. It is the Latin form of the Hebrew Eleazar (meaning *God my help*), the faithful, gentile servant of Abraham. *Dives* is the Latin word for *wealthy*.

The Now Testament

It is a natural inclination to look away from unpleasant-
ness. Selective vision is often a protective maneuver, and
like many defenses, it can hinder more than help. Sometimes
substance abusers who wish to avert a view of their flaws
only succeed in escaping from the ugly to the uglier. To look
takes an instant; to see takes longer. The sight of affliction is
invariably a heartache. It is meant to be. Suffering is meant
to be an agency for human change.

Albert Schweitzer (1875-1965) was so moved by the
Lazarus/Dives parable that he allowed it to alter his entire
life. A sought-after university lecturer, a heralded preacher,
he was also a world-renowned Bach virtuoso and a celebrated concert organist. In 1905, he abandoned his star-studded
career to enter medical school at the age of thirty. He wrote,
"I want to be a doctor so that I might be able to work without having to talk. For years, I have been giving myself out
in words. This new form of activity I could not represent to
myself as talking about the religion of love, but only as an
actual putting it into practice." In 1913, Schweitzer founded
his famous Lambarene Hospital, in the depths of impoverished equatorial Africa, where he served for more than half
a century. He explained that the impact of the Gospel led him
to visualize Europe as Dives—prosperous, comfortable—
and Lazarus as Africa—desolate, poor.

Grizzly bears are the most solitary of large animals.
They abhor packs. When they gather at streams to fish, they
seem to get along by not looking directly at one another.
Shy humans employ the same strategy. The tendency is to
look away from what is felt cannot be fixed. "It's none of
my business" is the rationalization. "I can't be bothered." To
be bothered is uncomfortable, but an indispensable stimulant to often surprising useful action. It is irritation that produces the pearl.

540

The popular *Seinfeld* television series' much-publicized final episode deals with the apathy theme. The featured characters plan a trip to Paris. They have a layover in a town called Latham, Massachusetts, where they are unexpectedly arrested. They happen to witness a carjacking. They watch a man being pulled from his car and the thief drives off with it. They stand by and do nothing. They are shocked to be arrested and to learn that the town is enforcing a "Good Samaritan" law obliging witnesses of a crime to make some effort to assist the victim. Instead of Paris, the four end up in jail.

The beloved *padre* of the trenches, G. A. Studdert Kennedy, was known all along the Western Front of World War I, and also for being an extraordinary poet. In his volume of poems entitled *The Unutterable Beauty*, he calls this one "Indifference:"

*When Jesus came to Golgotha they hanged
him on a tree,
they drove great nails through hands and feet and
made a Calvary:
they crowned him with a crown of thorns,
red were his wounds and deep,
for those were crude and cruel days,
and human flesh was cheap.*

*When Jesus came to Birmingham they simply
passed him by,
they never hurt a hair of him, they only
let him die:
for men had grown more tender, and they
would not give him pain,*

they only just passed down the street
and left him in the rain.

Still Jesus cried, "Forgive them, they
know not what they do,"
and still it rained the wintry rain that
drenched him through and through:
the crowds went home and left the streets
without a soul to see,
and Jesus crouched against a wall
and cried for Calvary.**

*Hodder Stoughton, Great Britain, 15th edition, Feb. 1959, pp. 34-35.

26th Sunday of Ordinary Time
(Luke 16: 19-31)

Supra-Vision

How long, oh Lord?
I cry for help but you do not listen!
I cry out to you, "violence"!
But you do not intervene.
Why do you let me see ruin,
Why must I look at misery?

This plaintive plea of the prophet Habakkuk (1: 2-3), six hundred years before Christ, has the ring of the world's reaction to the unspeakable terrorist destruction of 11 September 2001. By a baleful coincidence, as his ancient words were recited for the first reading of this day's liturgy, retaliatory bombs were exploding in the very Middle East where the prophet preached. Little has changed over the long centuries of that tormented land. Violence and ruin persist. Where is God in all this, we protest with the prophet? The Scripture offers a cryptic response: look beyond to a "vision that will not disappoint."

What vision?

Darkness is still dark and hatred is still as cruel today as it ever was. Floods, and famine, atrocities, and war remain unabated disasters on our planet. Is there a vision that can see past catastrophe to some kind of meaning? *Webster's New Collegiate Dictionary* provides a variety of meanings for the word *vision:* "something seen in a dream; a supernatural appearance that conveys a revelation; the act or power of seeing." The definitions all denote a suggestion of discovery. Those who have been to ground zero, where near three thousand in the bloom of their days were abruptly snatched from the lives they loved, and from the lives that loved them, have come away changed. Some can face only despair and shake their fists at heaven, but surely they are touched by the preciousness of life. In their honest anger, in the agony of their heartache, there is God . . . watching, brooding, waiting. Toiling rescuers sensed the mystery of God as they strained to pick up the faintest whisper of a trapped victim. Bystanders knelt in the rubble to plead a merciful salvation for the fallen. God was as near to ground zero as He had been on Golgotha!

Vision then, is the ability to see. Faith is another word for it. What people believe in is as diversified as are cultures, races, nationalities, climates, and environments. Universally, however, most of mankind agrees that the cosmos is attributable to a Supreme Being. But what kind of Supreme Being? The Bible presents a plurality of impressions. The Hebrews saw their God to be a companion, a liberator, a legislator, a chastiser, a warrior, a monarch, and even a jealous husband. Most of all, their pushy Jewish God was an involved God who participated intimately in their history.

It wasn't until the coming of Jesus that the world heard about a God who was a lavish party-giver. He told about His Father, so immensely and intensely in love with an errant son, He forgives him before the boy asks for it. Who can't wait to celebrate with the neighborhood for recovering a "lost sheep" or "lost coin?" Who stuns creditors by throwing away the account ledgers, and rewards late-come laborers the same as the early birders? No one gets thrown away, or left out of His Father's Kingdom. Rabbi Jesus shocks the right-wing moral majority by His liberality with the local riff-raff. Among His handpicked disciples are a terrorist, a crook, a denier, a doubter, and a betrayer. They would hardly pass seminary inspection today.

The vision of a wildly extravagant God of love is not something one eases into like learning to ride a bike with training wheels. Nor does it improve with practice. It is more like a bungee-jump—a letting go, a decisive leap into the void—trusting the tether. The thrill of the flight is like the first time, each time. This viewpoint then, sees all reality seeded in love. The wonder is, this kind of Creator is almost too good to be true.

Religious extremists and fundamentalists cannot understand this vision. They are too angry to let people be. They have to save them. Jesus never compelled people to be anything but what they were. He resisted categories of behavior that would qualify for His Father's Kingdom. Specific regulations were too limiting to His unconstrained welcome. Theological formulations only hint at divine largesse, but belief in it can miraculously transform the spirit.

In this day's Gospel narrative, "The apostles said to the Lord, 'Increase our faith.'" Jesus responds that if they have even a smidgeon—the size of a "mustard seed"— it will develop with the inevitable certainty of yeast leavening dough. In this opening to human wholeness, human goodness blossoms. With eyes wide open, the heart opens to the amazing world of rare treasures as never before seen. Like the lover to the beloved, one cannot do enough. There is no thought of a return, just the joy of giving. This is the faith that brings the communicant to the altar as to one's nuptials:

I do take You to be my God,
for better, for worse,
for richer, for poorer,
in sickness and in health,
through death, never to part.

The Now Testament

I therefore pledge my troth
To keep Your commandments—
not to be saved,
but because I am saved.

And that's the Good News!

27th Sunday of Ordinary Time
(Luke 17: 5-10)

Gratitude Attitude

In the Navy, authority's routine complaint is that ten per-cent never "get the word." The gospel typically inverts this count. In today's narrative, of the lepers for whom Jesus occasions cleansing, it is the ten percent who "get the word." "Ten were cleansed, were they not? Where are the other nine?" Jesus chides. It could be conjectured that they were busy with ceremonial rites. After all, they were following orders. "He said, 'go show yourselves to the priests.'" The scant medical knowledge of that time superstitiously attrib-uted disease to demon possession rather than to bacteria or microbes. Consequently, the clergy assumed responsibility for public health. Their certification was required before any cured individual could return to normal society.

This episode suggests a subtle sidelight; namely, the hazard of exalting formal ceremony to the level of sponta-neous worship. Both have their place; both nourish the reli-gious spirit. Belief systems depend on community unity as well as extemporaneous spontaneity. The former tends to be sectarian and regulation-bound. The latter is more open to flexibility and familiarity. The florists' luxurious bouquet from the office staff is probably not nearly as memorable as your four-year-old's clutch of dandelions on your birthday.

Solemn is not necessarily sacred. Prior to the Vatican II Council, the Roman Church reflected the mien of its pontiff, Pius XII, patrician, remote, imposing. Then in 1958, Angelo Roncalli was elected—rotund, smiling, enjoying company with his pasta and vino. Thus, church demeanor changed. *The Unbloody Sacrifice of the Mass* focus gave way to the Lord's Supper. A touch of light-heartedness was introduced to the liturgy: guitars, mariachis, even polite jazz. Women and youth were invited to the sanctuary. But like any change, there would be resistance and resentment to encroaching improvisations. Still, the world would take John XXIII to its heart. The sacred seemed more accessible, more commonplace once again!

This Gospel's major message, however, is *eucharistia,* the Greek word for *thankfulness.* "Gratitude is the memory of the heart," wrote J. B. Massieu in a *Letter to Abbe' Sicard.* A grateful heart is a heart fully grown. Dag Hammerskjold, the admired United Nations Secretary from 1953 to 1961, when he died in a plane crash, disclosed his well-developed heart, "For all that has been, thanks. For all that will be, yes!" Dag wasted no time at life's complaint counter.

A grateful heart is an aware heart. It is in touch with its surroundings. It pauses as the rose grows, watches rain, and hearkens to spoken words. It is inquisitive to know and alert to a human sigh. It is at home with fragile flesh.

The grateful heart is a courteous heart. Politeness is more than a social armistice in a competitive society. It is a chance to break free from confining self-absorption into the broader range of other viewpoints. It is impossible to top the lines of Hilary Belloc (1870-1953):

> *Of courtesy—it is much less*
> *than courage of heart or holiness;*
> *yet in my walks it seems to me*
> *that the grace of God is courtesy.**

Like gratitude, courtesy needs to be taught. No one is born with them. "Did you say 'thank you?'" recurrently prompts the parent to the child. The youngster who wrote this note to God apparently learned well:

Joseph M. Wadowicz

Dear God,
We are going on vacation for two weeks Friday,
so we won't be in church Sunday. I hope You will be
there when we get back. When do You take Your vaca-
tion?
Donny

In Jonathan Swift's *Gulliver's Travels,* for the ideal society of Lilliput, ingratitude is a capital crime. The church calls Mass *Eucharist* because it is the faithful's opportunity to offer "thanks" to God in a public, vocal, ordered fashion. Can a grieving nation say "thanks" in the wake of the devastation of 11 September 2001? It can say thanks that every week is not like that week. There are countless blessings, often taken for granted, that deserve a nod of appreciation: aspirin, anesthetic, mechanics who can fix a car, stylists who do hair, comics who make us laugh. The grateful heart takes life in stride—the bitter with the sweet—and with a grin. As says the prayer in verse found centuries ago in the Chester Cathedral:

Give me a mind that is not bored
that does no whimper, whine or sigh.
Don't let me worry over much
about this fussy thing called I.
Give me a sense of humor, Lord;
give me the grace to see a joke,
to get some happiness from life
and pass it on to other folk.
Amen.

28th Sunday of Ordinary Time
(Luke 17: 11-19)

True Grit Never Quits

A memorable commencement address by Winston Churchill consisted entirely of one sentence and only three words: "Don't give up!" America's thirtieth president, the low-keyed Calvin Coolidge, may have exposed the inconspicuous secret of his success, when he once said:

> *Nothing in the world can take the place of persistence. Talent will not; nothing is more common than unsuccessful people with talent. Genius will not; unrewarded genius is almost a proverb. Education will not; the world is full of educated derelicts. Persistence and determination alone are omnipotent.*

Luke agrees with this evaluation in the Gospel for today.

Maybe Jesus wished to quicken the flagging spirits of His disciples with a bit of whimsy. "Did you hear the one about the crooked judge and the pesty widow? Well, this judge boasted, 'While it is true that I neither fear God nor respect any human, because this widow keeps bothering me, I shall deliver a just decision for her lest she finally comes and strike me.'" In Jerome's *Latin Vulgate,* the word used for *strike* is *sigillo,* meaning, *beat black and blue.*

The defenseless but feisty widow of this Gospel's parable calls to mind the contemporary Rosa Parks. On 1 December 1955, this forty-five-year-old African-American boarded a bus in racially segregated Montgomery, Alabama. Strict segregation laws reserved the front seats exclusively for Caucasian passengers. Even if no Caucasians were aboard, African-Americans were forbidden the forward seats. If Caucasians occupied all these seats, African-American riders, who paid the same bus fare, were obliged to surrender their seats or be arrested and fined.

That December night, Parks was asked to yield her seat to a Caucasian passenger. She refused. She was arrested. This galvanized the African-American community to action. For 380 days they boycotted Montgomery busses, and segregation was headed for dissolution in the United States. Unpretentious, undefended Rosa Parks probably never suspected that her lone, immovable, persevering resistance to injustice would create this pre-eminent chapter in national history.

The point of this Gospel story is to encourage perseverance in prayer. "Jesus told His disciples a parable about the necessity for them to pray always without becoming weary." To pray is to cast a vote for tomorrow. C. S. Lewis observed that to pray is not as much to change God as to change oneself. It is a way of seeing it through—of not giving up! Of his Nazi concentration camp experience, Viennese psychiatrist, Victor Frankl, writes:

> *The prisoner who had lost faith in the future—his future—was doomed. With his loss of belief in the future, he also lost his spiritual hold: he let himself decline and became subject to mental and physical decay. Usually this happened quite suddenly, in the form of a crisis. Usually it began with the prisoner refusing one morning to get dressed and wash or to go out on the parade grounds. No entreaties, no blows, no threats had any effect . . . he simply gave up. There he remained, and nothing bothered him anymore.**

The pertinacity urged in this parable uncovers the notion that God is not averse to being dunned. Jesus explains to His disciple, "Pay attention to what the dishonest judge says. Will not God, then, secure the rights of His chosen ones who call out to Him day and night?" Persistence in prayer, therefore, tells God that we mean business about what we want. Maybe God wants to be convinced of that. Like a caring parent who sees virtue in expecting a child to save his ' own earnings in order to buy his own bike, God seems to be no more indulgent toward His creatures. Providence is surely aware of how roughly fragile creatures are tossed about on life's stormy sea. But if they are to weather the tempest, rescue needs to be delayed. It is the struggle that toughens and the Creator appears unwilling to impede that process.

True grit cannot quit; it has heart. It is not the cold, unshrinking spunk of the stoic. Nor is it utopian or sensational. It just makes up its mind to do what needs doing: ferrying the children, doing the wash, making that phone call! Nor does it have to win; failure, discouragement, and disappointment are not allowed to reduce resolve. Despair is a luxury true grit cannot afford, for it knows there is more to any good deed than the doer of it. It refuses to feel abandoned; it collaborates with the *Unknown*. If the physician's focus is the patient, he modestly joins his knowledge and competence to the healing process—a mystery quite beyond his gifts. True grit has faith, a valid synonym for courage. It knows love does not fail. It dares to believe a Providence that tolerates calamity for its Own purposes. One thing is for sure, life is unfair, but without God, it's unbearable!

Man's Search for Meaning, Pocket Books, New York, 1963, pp. 117-118.

29th Sunday of Ordinary Time
(Luke 18: 1-8)

The Odd Couple

. . . is today's Gospel feature!

The *Pharisee* fits Mark Twain's description of "a good man in the worst sense of the term." Most prefer to identify with the *Publican*. Parables have been the attempt of Jesus to get His hearers to think about themselves in terms of the characters in His stories—all the characters. In this narrative, both personalities reveal their feelings about their respective selves, and neither has a clue about God's reaction to their self-evaluation.

We most resemble the Pharisee when we stoutly deny that we are one; or when we congratulate ourselves for not being as evil as terrorists; or when we litany our good behavior: never miss Sunday church, always drop twenty dollars in the collection, never go to X-rated movies, always coach Little League, never cheat on the spouse or on income tax.

We are most like the Publican when we see little likeable in ourselves, as when we are saddened by our deviance from the straight and narrow. When we have the least to recommend us, the parable reminds us that that is when God is closest. We alternate from Pharisee to Publican in our self-assessments, depending on how closely we meet our own standards.

The Pharisee is not disparaged for hymning his virtues. They were considerable. Good deeds deserve applause, even when oneself is the applauder. His flaw is his sense of superiority over the disreputable rabble—"greedy, dishonest, adulterous—or even like this tax collector." He lacked the sympathy that could feel "there, but for the grace of God, go I." He was good in a frosty way, but not good enough—he did not love.

This parable exposes a subtle menace for all conscientious custodians of a moral code, namely, the tendency to be preoccupied about sin. Unless pity seasons one's devotion to rectitude, one's ethic antenna can work overtime to detect impropriety. Clinically, this condition can assume pathological proportions that old abnormal psychology texts call "reaction formation." This is defined as a personality defense mechanism that struggles to control unwanted feelings by performing exactly opposite behavior. The classic Sadie Thompson story and the rebuking but beguiled clergyman, vividly dramatize this plight.

The Pharisee registers the more common projection syndrome that transfers blame to the Publican, thus distracting the former for having to deal with personal guilt. He sounds typically like the "nice boy" who always did what he was told. Complying for approval, however, keeps the center of gravity on the self and the rest of the world takes on an adversarial cast. People are thus polarized; they become competitors. The search is on for miscreants so as to look good by comparison. The Pharisee's prayer confirms that he thinks he is okay and he wants to make sure that God thinks so, too!

To the Publican, public enemy number one is his very self. There is no plea-bargaining in his case. He is guilty. He concludes: admit it, and throw yourself completely on the mercy of the court! "Oh God, be merciful to me, a sinner." His admission sounds liberating. No more running, no more defense, just accept! "I tell you," Jesus affirms, "the latter went home justified, not the former." This inner recognition by the Publican could not have taken place had he played the Pharisee's blame game.

The contrite heart speaks to God more appealingly than does the upright, uptight heart. Clearly, sin does not get in God's way. In fact, it qualifies the sinner for reconciliation with Him. Perhaps his sins helped the Publican to see reality more clearly than did the Pharisee. Humility sees things as they are. As they ought to be is the province of the idealist. Humor blends them both. There is a story about Mohammad Ali, world famous boxing champ, who prides himself on saying it like it is about himself. "I am the greatest," he would chortle (presumably tongue in cheek). Aboard a plane preparing for take-off, the flight attendant instructed the fighter to please put on his seat belt. "Superman don't need no seat belt," Ali retorted. "Superman don't need no airplane, either," snapped the stewardess. Ali must have grinned as he buckled his seat belt. Humility is simply good mental health. It is vigorously realistic.

This parable also suggests that grace is not reliant on a good conduct medal. Relationship with God is not conditioned on moral excellence. It thrives on abandonment to Him. The Pharisee's security was in his personal probity and he missed the point. The Publican trusted that mercy would coordinate with misery. He had no exemplary deportment with which to bribe the Deity—only his surrender. But this is not to trivialize the importance of good works. High morals are merely a blueprint, a preliminary to life's supreme achievement—a loving heart. Goodness for Jesus was not an ethical issue. Love, compassion, and forgiveness were the worship that mattered. There is one unfailing seat belt for life's flight to eternity, that is the faith that not only believes in God, but that God believes in us . . . *passionately!*

30th Sunday of Ordinary Time
(Luke 18: 9-14)

Friendly Persuasion

Trivia pursuers will recognize 5 November as Guy Fawkes Day. It is a British national holiday and commemorates the foiled Gunpowder Plot of 1605 when a young Catholic radical attempted to blow up the English king and Parliament for oppression of Catholics. Pages of history teem with the wild and crazy things extremists do in behalf of even worthy causes. Our nation continues to quiver from such a disaster, the 9.11.01 terrorist frenzy. After a week's cancellation, popular television's late night hit, *The Tonight Show,* resumed programming and its host, Jay Leno, had this to say in his opening monologue: "In a world where people fly airplanes into buildings for the sole purpose of killing innocent people, a job like mine seems incredibly irrelevant."

Gripped in anger and anguish, national leadership, supported by the majority of its citizens, retaliates with its own brand of "controlled" terrorism. Bombs rain on an impoverished country and innocent collateral fatalities are accepted as an unavoidable evil. The contagion of violence continues to breed itself. Such a personal comment as this is admittedly controversial, like most political opinions. The gospel, however, is incontrovertibly clear in the matter of dealing with enemies. They are to be made friends of! No easy strategy, unless one is self-assured enough to regard all human beings as equally deserving the same courtesy and respect as oneself.

Today's narrative setting is the prosperous ancient trading center, Jericho, in the fertile Jordan valley, about fifteen miles east of Jerusalem. Jesus is passing through and He encounters a much-despised public enemy, the local tax commissioner, Zachaeus. Interestingly, the Hebrew *Zachae* is the word for innocent, for which the conniving collaborator was not notorious among the locals. The pressing crowd prevents his catching a glimpse of the celebrated Nazarene, but like diminutive people often are, Zachaeus is wily and spry. He winds up in the "best seat in the house" by climbing a tree along Jesus' path. Looking up, He spots Zachaeus bracketed in the branches. Possibly amused, Jesus might have thought to Himself, "Anyone going to that trouble to get a look at me deserves more than a passing glance." Jesus said, "Zachaeus, come down quickly, for today I must stay at your house." Scrambling from his perch joyfully, the surprised host may have mused, "He even knows my name!" The bystanders were thoroughly scandalized. "He has gone to stay at the house of a sinner," they grumble. The scene is as jarring as Queen Elizabeth inviting Heidi Fleiss for tea. Jesus is rehabilitating!

Courtesy works better than contempt. No badgering, no scolding, no reproof, just the relaxed, "Let's have dinner together!" *Jesus* is the Greek version of the Hebrew *Yeshua* (Joshua) and is translated as *savior.* The name comes from the Hebrew word *Yesha* meaning roomy or wide. Jesus is making space for a loathed misfit. He asks nothing of him, no pressure, and it awakens new depths of generosity in the corrupt official.

The episode highlights the awesome influence of ordinary friendliness and its power to alter an adversary's attitude. An example: the international Student Exchange program has done more to generate understanding among disparate nations then formal state diplomacy has ever achieved. Strangers enjoy being called by name and being addressed in their own language. Maybe Americans need to learn "Taliban" if the Taliban are to learn English. There is room at the top for other *number ones*! Imagination staggers at what could have been done for the hungry with the billions spent on armament during the fruitless Cold War years. Narrow minds regard punishment as reparative and amnesty as cop-out, until resolute Nelson Mandela regenerated South Africa by his reprieving spirit. Nearly thirty years of imprisonment and generations of cruelty to his black race would not inspire retaliation, after the collapse of apartheid. Christ-like benevolence glows in his presidential inaugural of 1994:

And, as we let our light shine, we unconsciously give other people permission to do the same. As we are liberated from our own fear, our presence automatically liberates others.

Somewhere in the Scripture is this reassuring rescue: "Whoever falls from God's right hand is caught by his left." Human beings are God's left hand. Years ago, a movie entitled *The Left Hand of God* starred Humphrey Bogart posing as a missionary priest in order to escape life-threatening Chinese bandits. The story reveals that even an imposter can accomplish the good he is imitating. All mankind longs for completion—another way of thinking of *salvation*. Yet, there is no wholeness in isolation from each other. Mankind is still up a tree while hatred pre-empts love. Jesus invites us, "Come on down and take me home with you!"

31st Sunday of Ordinary Time
(Luke 19: 1-10)

The Marry Widow

A lively musical of years past was entitled *Seven Brides for Seven Brothers*. This day's Gospel narrative features a much less balanced ratio: seven brothers for one bride. Attempting to stump Jesus, the aristocratic Sadducees use a frivolous tale of seven frail males and a seven-veiled (all-in-black) widow, to make fun of a new-fangled theological theory, Resurrection. The notion of an afterlife began to take root in Jewish thinking only about two centuries before Christ. For the well-to-do priestly Sadducee class, this life was enough. Only the first five books of the Bible, known as the Pentateuch, were also enough for them. Since these volumes contained no allusions to another world, for them Resurrection after death was nonsense. Their oblong reach for a laugh was not funny to Jesus because dying was no joke. In His belief, a caring Father would not allow the wrenching heartache of losing loved ones unless there was something better beyond.

But what?

Whatever it is, Jesus points out that *hereafter* is not more of the same that *here* affords. For Him, eternity with Divinity is not an earthly replay. The human mind, however, can only imagine what it humanly experiences, so it constructs a heaven from the joys of earth. Jesus is saying that it is nothing like that. The implication being that it's much more!

The suicide terrorists believed that they were headed for a sensual paradise. Ancient Greeks were confident that the worthy would delight in the Elysian Fields. Brave Vikings looked forward to the drinking bouts of Valhalla. American natives envisioned Happy Hunting Grounds. For Eskimos, the abundance of Caribou spelled bliss. For desert Bedouins, a palmy oasis was enough. Hindus entertained a more numinous everlasting future, Nirvana, absorption into the Godhead. The instinct for immortality has intrigued mankind through the ages. The mind of man simply refuses to comprehend extinction. Science reinforces that persuasion. The classical Greeks saw matter as indestructible. Their word *atom* means indivisible. Though the past century has divided the atom, matter maintains its imperturbability; quantity transforms into energy. But living things all die! Why?

A child's solution addresses this mystery:

Dear God,
Instead of letting people die and having to make
new ones, why not just keep the ones you got now?
Janie

A dandy idea, Janie, if a guarantee of non-wear or tear goes with the deal! Maybe death is not the final sentence? A child psychologist, Robert Coles, has worked for decades at Children's Hospital in Boston. "I spent a lot of time with children who were never going to be grown-ups—and they knew it." He tells of eleven-year-old Madeleine, who handed him a note about herself, "I had a nice time here most of the time. I'll be going soon. Good-bye." They could not look at each other for their tear-brimmed eyes.

To leave the familiar for the uncharted, takes the nerve of an explorer. The human psyche is constitutionally equipped for this enterprise. Risking the unknown is happening all the time. Human nature has a built-in curiosity for wanting to know what is around the corner. Can this inquisitiveness be evidence that there are other horizons out of this world awaiting discovery? Could the common compulsion to survive be a hint that there is an existence beyond the one that is ending? Still, Shakespeare's "the great world of light that lies beyond all human destinies" is not to everyone's taste. W. C. Fields' tombstone (1946) reads: "I'd rather be in Philadelphia."

Mankind's hankering for completion suggests resurrection. The human capacity for love is never fulfilled within the boundaries of time. Its appetite for the infinite leaves it content with nothing less. The human hunger for permanence is another pointer to an everlasting Presence. Why would the Creator create if not to extend Divinity—to share—to expand Its consciousness to Its creatures? Parents imitate the Creator when they generate children. Birth initiates a new consciousness. This tiny consciousness expands the parents' consciousness. As the child's awareness grows, so does the parents'. The maturing child helps parents to discover who they really are as adults. In procreating, parents produce an equal nature to themselves. In creating creatures, the Creator produces other particles of Himself. "Let us make man in our image, in our likeness" (Genesis. 1: 26). As a child is separate from the parent, so is the creature from the Creator, but each is eternally related in a deathless bond.

The strongest testimony on behalf of resurrection lies inherent in the very nature of man and his infinite capacity for growth. Becoming is never finished. Every day is a coming attraction for the forthcoming premier feature. Recurring daily renewals, like recovered health, a reconciliation, falling in love, are previews of the Producer's masterwork—*eternal life*. Miniature Resurrections yield a refreshing sense of a new self when a past trauma is revisited and given burial; when guilt is confronted and forgiven; when fear is faced and welcomed as a tutor. Everyday crises are merely rehearsals for the command performance.

Is resurrection illusory? Is the child's trust an illusion at mom's reassurance that there is nothing to fear from the dark? "I'm here, dear" and the child discovers that there really is nothing to fear? Is the buoyancy of life an illusion for the tope who refuses to sink under drink? Is youth an illusion for the eighty-year-old mind that stays young as the body wears out? All of earth's formidable challenges are indices of the durability of the human spirit.

"Is that all there is?" sighed the widow. "Only seven honeymoons? Oh well, they are all just practice!"

32nd Sunday of Ordinary Time
(Luke 20: 27-38)

God in the Dock

. . . is an original 1948 C. S. Lewis essay imaging the Deity on trial by a Peoples' Court for atrocities known as "Acts of God." In this day's first reading, the prophet Malachi (3: 19) adds further grim evidence of a terrorist God:

> *Lo, the day is coming, blazing alike an oven, when all the proud and all evil-doers will be stubble, and the day that is coming will set them on fire, leaving them neither root nor branch, says the Lord of hosts.*

Malachi's distress signal reflected the typical formula of firebrand Old Testament prophets' intent on alarming the wayward. Isaiah (13: 6) tried this attention-getter:

> *Scream in terror, for the Lord's time has come and the time of the Almighty to crush you . . . For see the day of the Lord is coming, the terrible day of his wrath and fierce anger.*

Why much of their audience turned away can come as no surprise!

As the days of the liturgical year dwindle down, the Church feels that it is necessary to remind its faithful that all the things of time will also end. This is a fact, but the way things end is why Divinity is on the "witness stand." Why the tragic loss of innocent lives, earthquakes, floods, fires, famine, accidents, and senseless killings? Is it arrogant to want to bring God to account? What do humans know about the God business? Who are we to presume a job description for God?

In a television interview, the actor, Robert De Niro, was asked what his first words might be when he came to face God? De Niro replied, "You have a lot of explaining to do!" When another testy soul demanded to know what God intended to do about all of earth's tragedies and injustices . . . His answer, "I made you."

What we want God to be is what we need to be. It's possible!

Doug Harrington, Ph.D., is a practicing neuro-psychologist in Orange County, California, and he caught this conviction in his volunteered invocation at a charity affair for SOS, Share Our Selves, a Costa Mesa, California philanthropy, as he substituted for this writer, soon after the 9.11.01 attack:

The horrific events of two weeks ago have challenged the foundation of our faith; yes, maybe even challenged our belief in a Higher Power. We have asked, "How could God let this happen? Where was God?"

Let's not forget . . .

God was in the voices of the businessmen and women as they called their loved ones from the planes and the towers one last time.

God was in the strength and perseverance of the passengers who were able to overpower the terrorists in the flight over Pennsylvania.

God was with those passengers in the three other flights as they huddled in the back of the planes not knowing their fate.

God was in our guts as a nation witnessed over and over again the most abominable act ever taken against our country.

God was in the hearts of the firefighters and peace officers as they rushed into the burning Twin Towers not knowing their fate.

God was with the heroes that helped protect, console, and even shield their fellow workers as the walls of the buildings came crashing down.

God was in the sweat of the rescue workers digging through the rubble looking for survivors.

God was in the leadership of those who skillfully took command of the situation in New York City and our nation as a whole in response to the crisis.

God was in the charity of our nation as we lined up at blood banks, contributed to emergency fund-raising efforts, and volunteered by giving time, energy, and resources to the healing process.

God was in the spirit of our community, maybe never before pulling together in such grand fashion, through a united effort of patriotism, flag waving, and defiance of evil.

And God is with us tonight as we try to move forward with our lives, accepting this horrific reality, yet not letting it paralyze us from our daily activities and commitments such as helping the poor and downtrodden of Orange County. Our mission has grown from this disaster.

Catastrophe leaves us bitter or better. Most of the time, it takes the former to get to the latter. History is blessed with great souls who have defied disaster to make a better world. Gandhi, a Hindu, valued the impact of Christ:

*Jesus was the most active practitioner of personal non-violence in the history of the world, and the only people who don't know it are Christians."
The Mahatma advises his disciples, "Let your life speak to us, even as the rose needs no speech, but simply spreads its perfume. Even the blind who do not see the rose perceive its fragrance. That is the secret of the gospel of the rose. But the gospel that Jesus preached is much more subtle and fragrant than the gospel of the rose. If the rose needs no agent, much less does the gospel of Christ need an agent.*

If agents are not necessary, delegates are; delegates of love, who have "power of attorney" with the Lord for healing a fractured society. Thomas Merton wrote:

*As long as we are on earth, the love that unites us will bring us suffering by our very contact with one another, because this love is the resetting of a body of broken bones.**

In her book *Choices*, actress Liv Ulmann discusses the new meaning brought to her existence after visiting a Cambodian refugee camp:

Now I want to know more. I want to find out what life is to all of us, and how we use it, and whether there is joy in having it, and what we are for, and why there are lonely people. I want to discover the feeling of life as it begins. I want to discover the feeling of life as it approaches its inevitable end.

This is the thinking that made sense of what Jesus meant when He said, "When you hear of wars and insurrections, do not be terrified. Nation will rise against nation, kingdom against kingdom. There will be powerful earthquakes, famines, and plagues from place to place. You will be hated by all because of My name, but not a hair on your head will be destroyed!"

Not to worry!

The television series *Hill Street Blues* repeatedly ended on that note. After fifty minutes of gang war, rape, violence, screaming sirens, flashing dome lights, and squealing tires, the screen dims, music fades, and the female counselor comforts the heartsick cop. She explains nothing away, nor coddles. She reaches for the unspoiled little boy in the dispirited policeman and talks of a finer world beyond Hill Street. Hidden under humanity's lust and larceny, she speaks of the tarnished dignity subsisting in all human beings and the gracious mercy that envelopes them, as she reassures, "Everything's going to be okay, pizza man."

Martin Luther King understood this when he concluded:

The choice is no longer violence or non-violence. It is non-violence or non-existence.

*"New Seeds of Contemplation," *New Directions,* 1972, pg. 72.

33rd Sunday of Ordinary Time
(Luke 21: 5-19)

Mission Accomplished

Kings are not important these days, except in the realm of entertainment: king of rock, of swat, of comedy, of late-night television, and big-screen televisions. Pilate thought it a good joke to confer royalty on a capital criminal—a crucified Galilean carpenter.

"And above him was the inscription that read: 'This is the king of the Jews.'"

Pilate counted on this jest to infuriate the Sanhedrin, Jewish religious rulers. Wouldn't he be surprised that two millennia later, in 1925, a Roman pontiff would take his joke seriously and expand the realm of Jesus of Nazareth to include the entire universe?

Why would the Church insist on this title when Jesus steadfastly refused it throughout His lifetime? One justification could be an attempt to counter the acclaim that national dictators were demanding of their subjects in the twentieth century. The kingly bearing of Pilate's bruised defendant apparently made the judge feel suddenly on trial. Finding no crime in Him, Pilate sought His release, but that was politically incorrect. So, history records this governor's unjust sentence with its own never-to-be-forgotten sentence through all the ages: "And He suffered under Pontius Pilate."

Jesus deserves better company than emperors, whose historical reputations were rarely notorious for virtue. But Jesus talked a lot about the Kingdom. To Him, His Father's Kingdom was a wedding party, to which everyone was invited—good and bad alike. It was a figure to emphasize the universality and inclusivity of God's unconditional love

for all mankind. And this means *everyone*—terrorists, eth-
nicists, atheists, addicts, the Mafia, gays, and lesbians!
Organized religions that claim affiliation to the Christian
Good News and refuse ministry to any of the above, need to
review the Good Shepherd's approach to wayward sheep.
Since those days, however, the Kingdom has weathered
many interpretations. Sectarianism has succeeded in
restricting access to it. To Jesus, the Kingdom did not dissolve polarities. It synthesized them. Creation colorfully
vindicates the Creator's affection for variety.
Fundamentalism, another warped spin, is not comfortable
with diversity. It aggressively forbids deviation based on the
illusion that sameness spells equilibrium. The fundamentalist is frightened by a society that does not control events,
and so, opposes surrender to what is classified as the perils
of modernity. Thus, for them the Kingdom assumes the air
of tribunal rather than a festival.

While the Kingdom's banquet features open, unlimited
seating with no one denied, Jesus indicates that some qualify for admission more than others. He names "little children," for instance, whom He wished adults were more like.
Youngsters have no problem associating with black, brown,
red, or yellow playmates. They hunger to learn. They are
spontaneous. They do not mask feelings.

Then there are "the bold who bear heaven away," another classification of favorites. Jesus obviously admired personalities who could march to their own drummer—tread
paths less traveled. He Himself asserted His own self-hood
without equivocation, evasion, or compromise. He ignored
useless, outworn religious traditions and was condemned as
an outlaw for it.

In his 1961 bestseller, *Franny and Zooey,* J. D. Salinger
has Zooey arguing with his sister Franny, who is wavering
on the brink of a nervous breakdown, for her superficial
recitation of the "Jesus Prayer:"

Joseph M. Wadowicz

I'd like to be convinced—I'd love to be convinced that you are not using it as a substitute for doing whatever the hell your duty is in life, or your daily duty. Keep Him in mind if you say it, and Him only, and Him as He was and not as you'd like Him to have been. My God! He's only the most intelligent man in the Bible, that's all! Who else, for example, would have kept His mouth shut when Pilate asked for an explanation? Who in the Bible besides Jesus knew—knew—that we're carrying the Kingdom of Heaven around with us, inside. You have to be the Son of God to know that kind of stuff.*

This chapter is a wrap. Our trilogy is ended, but the melody lingers on whenever the chord of God's unmeasured, intemperate love for His every human creature is struck. As a life theme, this score can be dangerous. It was for Jesus. But nowhere did the extreme counterpoints of evil and love come to blend more clearly than on that Golgotha hill. No ruthless crucifixion could deter benevolence for His butchers or for the criminals dying beside Him. More painful than the nails must have been the mocking crowd: "He saved others, let him save himself if he is the chosen one, the Christ of God."

The origin of the following insight into unconditional love is unknown to this writer. The poem is probably titled "Judas:"

Let's see him come down from that cross
and then we will believe in him.
He didn't tho.

575

The Now Testament

The poet dreamed he did.
To save himself? No.
To save Judas? Listen:
On swift strong feet still dripping red
he would have sped
to where a "friend" lay dead (friend, would you)
'neath April skies,
unloosed the halter, kissed the face
to wipe all trace
of suicide disgrace.
Judas, arise.
Christ would have come down for that.

As He does in every Mass to give Himself and His royalty to each one of us. Arise, your majesties, and proclaim your charter:

We believe in one God,
the Father, the Almighty,
maker of heaven and earth,
and all that is seen and unseen.

* Bantam Books, Little, Brown & Co., Inc.; Boston, MA, pp. 169-171.

Christ the King
(Luke 23: 35-43)

576

Index E
LITURGICAL CALENDAR
(Cycle C)

The Now Testament

Index F
SCRIPTURAL INDEX
(Cycle C)

Index G